Samuel Beckett and Arnold

Historicizing Modernism

Series Editors

Matthew Feldman, Senior Lecturer in Twentieth Century History, University of Northampton, UK; and Erik Tonning, Director, Modernism and Christianity Project, University of Bergen, UK

Assistant Editor: Paul Jackson, Senior Lecturer in History, University of Northampton, UK

Editorial Board

Professor Chris Ackerley, Department of English, University of Otago, New Zealand; Professor Ron Bush, St. John's College, University of Oxford, UK; Dr Finn Fordham, Department of English, Royal Holloway, UK; Professor Steven Matthews, Department of English, Oxford Brookes University, UK; Dr Mark Nixon, Department of English, University of Reading, UK; Professor Shane Weller, Reader in Comparative Literature, The University of Kent, UK; and Professor Janet Wilson, University of Northampton, UK.

Historicizing Modernism challenges traditional literary interpretations by taking an empirical approach to modernist writing: a direct response to new documentary sources made available over the last decade.

Informed by archival research, and working beyond the usual European/American avant-garde 1900–45 parameters the series reassesses established images of modernist writers by developing fresh views of intellectual backgrounds and working methods.

Series Titles:

The Autobiographies of Mina Loy
    Sandeep Parmar

Katherine Mansfield and Literary Modernism
    Edited by Janet Wilson, Gerri Kimber and Susan Reid

Reframing Yeats
    Charles Ivan Armstrong

Samuel Beckett and Science
    Chris Ackerley

Samuel Beckett's 'More Pricks Than Kicks'
    John Pilling

Samuel Beckett's German Diaries 1936–1937
    Mark Nixon

Samuel Beckett and Arnold Geulincx

Tracing 'a literary fantasia'

David Tucker

BLOOMSBURY
LONDON • NEW DELHI • NEW YORK • SYDNEY

Bloomsbury Academic
An imprint of Bloomsbury Publishing Plc

50 Bedford Square	1385 Broadway
London	New York
WC1B 3DP	NY 10018
UK	USA

www.bloomsbury.com

Bloomsbury is a registered trade mark of Bloomsbury Publishing Plc

First published 2012
Paperback edition first published 2013

© David Tucker, 2012

David Tucker has asserted his right under the Copyright, Designs and Patents Act, 1988, to be identified as Author of this work.

All rights reserved. No part of this publication may be reproduced or transmitted in any form or by any means, electronic or mechanical, including photocopying, recording, or any information storage or retrieval system, without prior permission in writing from the publishers.

No responsibility for loss caused to any individual or organization acting on or refraining from action as a result of the material in this publication can be accepted by Bloomsbury or the author.

British Library Cataloguing-in-Publication Data
A catalogue record for this book is available from the British Library.

ISBN: HB: 978-1-4411-3935-1
       PB: 978-1-4725-2407-2
       ePDF: 978-1-4411-0817-3
       ePUB: 978-1-4411-0656-8

Library of Congress Cataloging-in-Publication Data
Tucker, David, 1978–
Samuel Beckett and Arnold Geulincx: tracing a literary fantasia/David Tucker.
p. cm. – (Historicizing modernism)
Includes bibliographical references and index.
ISBN 978-1-4411-3935-1 (hardcover)
1. Beckett, Samuel, 1906–1989 – Criticism and interpretation. 2. Geulincx, Arnold, 1624–1669 – Criticism and interpretation. I. Title.
PR6003.E282Z858 2012
848'.91409–dc23
                                                            2011051217

Typeset by Newgen Imaging Systems Pvt Ltd, Chennai, India
Printed and bound by CPI Group (UK) Ltd, Croydon, CR0 4YY

For my family and Tatiana

Ubi nihil vales, ibi nihil velis.
[Wherein you have no power, therein you should not will]

Arnold Geulincx (*Ethica*)

He had manipulated that sentence for years now, emending its terms, as joy for grief, to answer his occasions, even calling upon it to bear the strain of certain applications for which he feared it had not been intended, and still it held good through it all. He walked with it now in his mind, as though it had been there all the time he slept, holding that fragile place against dreams.

Samuel Beckett ('Yellow')

Contents

Historicizing Modernism	viii
Acknowledgements	ix
List of Abbreviations	xi
Notes to the Text	xiii
A Chronology of Samuel Beckett and Arnold Geulincx	xiv
Introduction	1
1 Beckett and Geulincx	6
2 *Murphy* and 'Mechanical Writing'	42
3 *Watt*: Ineffable Forces	71
4 *Suite/La Fin/The End*: Continuations and Conclusions	97
5 The Trilogy: Imagery and Axioms	118
6 Late Works	144
Conclusion	177
Notes	183
Bibliography	199
Index	211

Historicizing Modernism

This book series is devoted to the analysis of late-nineteenth to twentieth century literary Modernism within its historical context. *Historicizing Modernism* thus stresses empirical accuracy and the value of primary sources (such as letters, diaries, notes, drafts, marginalia or other archival deposits) in developing monographs, scholarly editions and edited collections on Modernist authors and their texts. This may take a number of forms, such as manuscript study and annotated volumes; archival editions and genetic criticism; as well as mappings of interrelated historical milieus or ideas. To date, no book series has laid claim to this interdisciplinary, source-based territory for modern literature. Correspondingly, one burgeoning sub-discipline of Modernism, Beckett Studies, features heavily here as a metonymy for the opportunities presented by manuscript research more widely. While an additional range of 'canonical' authors will be covered here, this series also highlights the centrality of supposedly 'minor' or occluded figures, not least in helping to establish broader intellectual genealogies of Modernist writing. Furthermore, while the series will be weighted towards the English-speaking world, studies of non-Anglophone Modernists whose writings are ripe for archivally-based exploration shall also be included here.

A key aim of such historicizing is to reach beyond the familiar rhetoric of intellectual and artistic 'autonomy' employed by many Modernists and their critical commentators. Such rhetorical moves can and should themselves be historically situated and reintegrated into the complex continuum of individual literary practices. This emphasis upon the contested self-definitions of Modernist writers, thinkers and critics may, in turn, prompt various reconsiderations of the boundaries delimiting the concept 'Modernism' itself. Similarly, the very notion of 'historicizing' Modernism remains debatable, and this series by no means discourages more theoretically-informed approaches. On the contrary, the editors believe that the historical specificity encouraged by *Historicizing Modernism* may inspire a range of fundamental critiques along the way.

Matthew Feldman
Erik Tonning

Acknowledgements

I have been fortunate during the course of researching and writing this book to benefit from many different kinds of support from a number of people. Without the support of my family I would have been unable to complete the doctorate from which this book draws, and it is to them that I owe a debt of gratitude and dedicate this book. To friends who voiced their support when I embarked upon the project, I thank them for encouraging me.

I am very grateful to those who have been generous with their time and have read and commented on work that has gone towards this book over the past few years. These include David Addyman, Sara Crangle, Laura Salisbury and Shane Weller. Particular thanks go to my doctoral supervisors, Peter Boxall and Keston Sutherland. Peter's patient, enthralling readings of Beckett and Keston's brilliant and incisive criticism are a context in which I have been very lucky to work. Chris Ackerley has offered invaluable comments at various stages of this book's composition, for which I am also extremely grateful.

I have benefited from discussions with a number of Beckett specialists that have directly and indirectly informed this book, as well as my thinking about Beckett more broadly. Thanks are therefore gladly due to Iain Bailey, Julie Campbell, Daniela Caselli, Peter Fifield, Dirk Van Hulle, Kumiko Kiuchi, Emilie Morin and Adam Winstanley, as well as to the now sadly missed Seán Lawlor and Barney Rosset. Both Matthew Feldman and Erik Tonning, editors of Continuum's 'Historicizing Modernism' series, have helped me greatly with this book.

A very special thank you goes to those affiliated with the Beckett International Foundation at the University of Reading. The enthusiasm, expertise and generosity of James Knowlson, Mark Nixon and John Pilling are a credit to Beckett's multifaceted legacies and to humanities scholarship in general, and I have been lucky to benefit from this friendly support.

Many other friends and colleagues, including Christoforos Diakoulakis, Philip Newman and Alex Pestell, have been of valuable support during my research and the writing of this book.

I would like to thank the kind staff at the University of Sussex and at Special Collections at the University of Reading, and, for going beyond the call of duty, Justine Hyland at the Burns Library Boston College and Elizabeth Garver at the Harry Ransom Humanities Research Center at Austin.

Acknowledgements

Versions of some parts of this book have been published in the past few years. Parts of Chapters 1 and 2 appeared as '*Murphy*, Geulincx and an Occasional(ist) game of Chess' in Daniela Guardamagna and Rossana Sebellin's *The Tragic Comedy of Samuel Beckett: 'Beckett in Rome' 17–19 April 2008* (2009), part of Chapter 3 appeared as 'Towards an Analysis of Geulincx and the Ur-*Watt*' in *Samuel Beckett Today/Aujourd'hui* Volume 22 (2010) and part of Chapter 6 appeared as 'Beckett's Guignol Worlds: Arnold Geulincx and Heinrich von Kleist' in *Sofia Philosophical Review* (2011). I have also presented this work in progress at a number of conferences and seminars, and I gratefully acknowledge all those with whom I have had discussions about it.

Lastly, my gratitude to Tatiana Kontou is for many things. This book is dedicated to her generosity and affection.

Extracts from *The Letters of Samuel Beckett* reproduced by kind permission of the Estate of Samuel Beckett c/o Rosica Colin Limited, London, and Cambridge University Press, © The Estate of Samuel Beckett.

Extracts from Samuel Beckett's 'Philosophy Notes' reproduced by kind permission of the Estate of Samuel Beckett c/o Rosica Colin Limited, London, and Trinity College Dublin, © The Estate of Samuel Beckett.

Extracts from Samuel Beckett's 'Geulincx Notes' reproduced by kind permission of the Estate of Samuel Beckett c/o Rosica Colin Limited, London, and Trinity College Dublin, © The Estate of Samuel Beckett.

Extracts from Samuel Beckett's correspondence with Barbara Bray reproduced by kind permission of the Estate of Samuel Beckett c/o Rosica Colin Limited, London, and Trinity College Dublin, © The Estate of Samuel Beckett.

Extracts from Samuel Beckett's 'Whoroscope' notebook reproduced by kind permission of the Estate of Samuel Beckett c/o Rosica Colin Limited, London, and The University of Reading, © The Estate of Samuel Beckett.

Extracts from Samuel Beckett's manuscript and typescript of *Watt* reproduced by kind permission of the Estate of Samuel Beckett c/o Rosica Colin Limited, London, and The Harry Ransom Humanities Research Center, Austin, Texas, © The Estate of Samuel Beckett.

Extracts from Samuel Beckett's 'Suite' notebook reproduced by kind permission of the Estate of Samuel Beckett c/o Rosica Colin Limited, London, and Boston College, © The Estate of Samuel Beckett.

Extracts from Samuel Beckett's correspondence with Richard Seaver reproduced by kind permission of the Estate of Samuel Beckett c/o Rosica Colin Limited, London, and The Harry Ransom Humanities Research Center, Austin, Texas, © The Estate of Samuel Beckett.

List of Abbreviations

Works by Beckett

CDW	*Complete Dramatic Works*. London: Faber & Faber, 1990.
Co	*Company, Ill Seen Ill Said, Worstward Ho, Stirrings Still*. London: Faber & Faber, 2009.
CSP	*The Complete Short Prose*. New York: Grove Press, 1995.
Dis	*Disjecta*. London: Calder, 1983.
Dr	*Dream of Fair to Middling Women*. New York: Arcade Publishing, 1993.
E	*The Expelled, The Calmative, The End with First Love*. London: Faber & Faber, 2009.
HII	*How It Is*. London: Faber & Faber, 2009.
L1	*The Letters of Samuel Beckett, Volume 1*. Martha Dow Fehsenfeld and Lois More Overbeck (eds). Cambridge: Cambridge University Press, 2009.
L2	*The Letters of Samuel Beckett, Volume 2*. George Craig, Martha Dow Fehsenfeld, Dan Gunn and Lois More Overbeck (eds). Cambridge: Cambridge University Press, 2011.
Mu	*Murphy*. London: Faber & Faber, 2009.
Mo	*Molloy*. London: Faber & Faber, 2009.
MD	*Malone Dies*. London: Faber & Faber, 2010.
MPTK	*More Pricks Than Kicks*. London: Faber & Faber, 2010.
Pr	*Proust and Three Dialogues with Georges Duthuit*. London: Calder, 1999.
SP	*Selected Poems 1930–1989*. London: Faber & Faber, 2009.
TN	*Texts for Nothing and other Short Prose*. London: Faber & Faber, 2010.
U	*The Unnamable*. London: Faber & Faber, 2010.
W	*Watt*. London: Faber & Faber, 2009.

Works by Geulincx

Et	*Ethics: with Samuel Beckett's Notes*. Han van Ruler and Anthony Uhlmann (eds). Martin Wilson (trans.). Leiden & Boston: Brill, 2006.
Met	*Metaphysics*. Martin Wilson (trans.). Wisbech: Christoffel Press, 1999.
Op	*Arnoldi Geulincx Opera Philosophica*, Volumes I–III. Jan Pieter Nicolaas Land (ed.). Hagae Comitum: Apud Nijhoff, 1891–3.

List of Abbreviations

Library Archives

HRHRC   Harry Ransom Humanities Research Center, The University of Texas at Austin.
TCD   Trinity College Dublin Library, Department of Manuscripts.
UoR   Beckett International Foundation Archives, University of Reading.

People as Correspondents

Alexander Trocchi (AT)
Arland Ussher (AU)
Barbara Bray (BB)
Erich Franzen (EF)
George Reavey (GR)
Georges Duthuit (GD)
Mary Hutchinson (MH)
Richard Seaver (RS)
Samuel Beckett (SB)
Sighle Kennedy (SK)
Thomas MacGreevy (TM)

Notes to the Text

Manuscript citation is by recto/verso.

Translations are mine unless otherwise indicated.

Quotations from pp. 311–53 of Geulincx's *Ethics* are of Beckett's transcriptions.

Italics and capitalizations are quoted exactly as they appear unless otherwise indicated.

Ellipses are quoted exactly as they appear unless with the use of square brackets, in which case they are mine unless otherwise indicated.

A Chronology of Samuel Beckett and Arnold Geulincx

1930s

Beckett produces the 'Philosophy Notes', 267 folio pages summarizing the history of Western philosophy, a compendium that was itself cribbed from summarizing sources. Primarily, these sources are John Burnet's *Greek Philosophy, Part 1: Thales to Plato* (1914), Archibald Alexander's *A Short History of Philosophy* (1908) and Wilhelm Windelband's *A History of Philosophy* (1901). According to Deirdre Bair, Beckett produced these notes 'Because he had not taken a philosophy course at Trinity College, which he felt was a serious defect in his education' (Bair 1978, p. 91). On the 189th and 190th folios, in a section titled 'Philosophy of Renaissance' (TCD MS 10967/172r), and sub-headed 'Natural Science Period' (TCD MS 10967/179r), Beckett wrote three sides of notes about Geulincx and his place in the history of philosophy.[1]

In the 'Whoroscope' notebook of the 1930s Beckett noted the following: '21. Murphy: I am not of the big world, I am of the little world: ubi nihil valeo, ibi nihil velo (I quote from memory) & inversely' (UoR MS 3000).[2]

1936

9 January	Letter from Beckett to Thomas MacGreevy (then McGreevy). Beckett describes his return to Trinity College Dublin (hereafter TCD) library to research Geulincx after discovering that the National Library did not hold an edition.
9 January	Letter from Beckett to George Reavey, in which Beckett writes that 'my Geulincx could only be a literary fantasia' (SB to GR, 9 January 1936: *L1*, p. 295).
16 January	Letter from Beckett to MacGreevy. Beckett tells MacGreevy he 'suddenly' sees *Murphy*, the novel he was working on at the time, as a 'break down' (SB to TM, 16 January 1936: *L1*, p. 299) between Geulincx's ethical axiom *ubi nihil vales, ibi nihil velis* and Malraux's '*Il est difficile à celui qui vit hors du monde de ne pas rechercher les siens*' ['it is difficult for one who lives isolated from the everyday world not to seek others like himself'[3]]. The French original of the latter became the epigraph for *Murphy*'s Chapter 9.
29 January	Letter from Beckett to MacGreevy. Beckett tells MacGreevy that Brian Coffey had 'promised me Geulincx & Eluard informations' (SB to TM, 29 January 1936: *L1*, p. 305), which were not forthcoming.
6 February	Letter from Beckett to MacGreevy. Beckett reveals of *Murphy*'s progress that 'There only remain three chapters of mechanical writing' (SB to TM, 6 February 1936: *L1*, p. 312). In Chapter 9 of the 13-chapter *Murphy* Beckett quotes Geulincx's axiom, describing it as 'the beautiful Belgo-Latin of Arnold Geulincx' (*Mu*, p. 101). He then goes on to make allusions to Geulincx in later chapters.

A Chronology of Samuel Beckett and Arnold Geulincx

5 March	Letter from Beckett to MacGreevy in which Beckett expresses his enthusiasm for the TCD Geulincx research. He compares Geulincx's philosophy variously to Berkeley, Balzac, Rimbaud, Heraclitus and Greek mythology via contrasting imagery of seeing and looking away, and describes Geulincx's calm 'vision' as 'the only excuse for remaining alive' (SB to TM, 5 March 1936: *L1*, p. 319).
25 March	Letter from Beckett to MacGreevy in which Beckett describes how he is bored and listless at home in Dublin, his reading Geulincx at TCD one of only a couple of things that get him out of the house.
25 March	Letter from Beckett to Arland Ussher. Beckett recommends Geulincx to Ussher 'most heartily' (SB to AU, 25 March 1936: *L1*, p. 329) and describes his favourite part of *Ethica* as the long section (Treatise I, Chapter II, Section II, § 1–3) on humility.
9 April	Letter from Beckett to MacGreevy. Beckett has stopped reading Geulincx, and he jokes about his own inability and incapacity, specifically his being unable to read any more of Geulincx's ethical lessons about abstinence 'even in Lent' (SB to TM, 9 April 1936).[4]
9 June	Finishes a first draft of *Murphy*.[5]

1938

Writes 'Les Deux Besoins', which uses Geulincx's term 'autology'.

1941–5

Works on *Watt*, during which time specific words and broader themes traceable to Geulincx are written into, before being predominantly written out of, drafts of sections of the novel in notebooks and typescript.

1946

13 March	The date in the 'Suite' notebook where Beckett composes a passage, first in English then in French, in which the narrator recalls being gifted Geulincx's *Ethics* by a now dead tutor. The short passage directly marks Beckett's turn from English to French prose. *Suite* was later altered and published as *La Fin/The End*.
5 July	Begins *Mercier et Camier*, which will be completed on 15 October. Towards the end of the novel a greatly altered version of Watt appears. The newly extroverted and prophetic Watt announces his author's future aesthetic horizons with a drunken outburst in which he proclaims the possibility of 'one' to be born from the ashes of previous protagonists, and uses Geulincx's ethical axiom to describe this 'one', who 'having nothing will wish for nothing, except to be left the nothing he hath' (*MC*, p. 93).

1947

2 May	Begins *Molloy*, which will be completed by 1 November. In the novel Molloy claims he 'loved the image' (*Mo*, p. 50) from *Ethica* of a man on board a ship who attempts to travel in the opposite direction to that in which his ship is moving.

xvi *A Chronology of Samuel Beckett and Arnold Geulincx*

27 November — Begins *Malone meurt*, which will be completed by 30 May 1948, towards the end of which the narrator references, in a partial quotation, Geulincx's axiom. This fragment becomes transformed again in the translation into *Malone Dies*.

1948

29 March — Begins *L'Innommable*, a first draft of which will be completed by January 1950, to be revised later that same year. Beckett returns to the imagery of Geulincx's ship a number of times in this novel.

1949

9 March — Letter from Beckett to Georges Duthuit, which uses the term 'autology' to describe the artistic process.

On or after 30 April, before 26 May — Letter from Beckett to Duthuit. In this undated letter Beckett tells Duthuit that Geulincx's axiom says everything ('*Tout est dit*'). The axiom's correctness should be taken for granted, according to Beckett, and assessing its importance solely a matter of agreeing on the domain ('*s'entendre sur ce domaine*') implied by Geulincx's conception of incapacity.

1953

2 December — Letter from Beckett to Niall Montgomery, in which Beckett gives the now familiar *ubi nihil vales, ibi nihil velis* axiom.

1954

17 February — Letter from Beckett to Erich Franzen, the German translator of *Molloy*, in which Beckett discusses how the image of the traveller on a ship taken from Geulincx also incorporates allusions to Dante.

1956

7 November — Letter from Beckett to Mary Hutchinson in which Beckett, who himself 'cannot bear' the prospect of looking back at his previous work, proposes that Geulincx and Democritus are in some 'queer' way the focus of this work (SB to MH, 7 November 1956).

28 November — In a reply to questions raised by Hutchinson about Geulincx, Beckett describes his search 20 years earlier for an edition of the philosopher's works. He writes that Geulincx presents, in a phrase that complicates the description in *Murphy* of Geulincx's 'beautiful' language, a 'Frightful kitchen Latin but fascinating guignol world' (SB to MH, 28 November 1956).

1958

17 December — Beckett begins composing *Comment c'est*, which was not completed until late 1960, before it was slowly translated into *How It Is* over a further 3 years. The novel makes no mention of Geulincx but does name the more famous Occasionalist Nicolas Malebranche, and retains surprising residues of earlier Geulingian imagery and phrases.

1962

Lawrence Harvey (publishing in 1970) dates an interview in which Beckett talked about Geulincx as taking place in this year. According to Harvey, Beckett repeated the substance of letters sent to Hutchinson in 1956 and to Sighle Kennedy in 1967, to the effect that were he a critic analysing his work 'he would start out with' (Harvey 1970, p. 267) Democritus and Geulincx.

1967

14 June   Letter from Beckett to Kennedy in reply to Kennedy's promptings about Proust, Joyce and notions of Greenwich Mean Time as pertaining to the structure of *Murphy*. Beckett quotes Geulincx's axiom along with Democritus's as possible 'points of departure' for those in the 'unenviable position' (SB to SK, 14 June 1967: *Dis*, p. 113) of studying his work.

1969

2 September   Letter from Beckett to Barbara Bray. Beckett appears to have encountered Heinrich von Kleist's influential essay on the marionette theatre around this time, and the encounter reinvigorates Beckett's ideas of puppetry, expressed in relation to Geulincx in 1956 (as the 'fascinating guignol world'). A new sense of the possibilities of puppetry then contributed towards the prose piece 'Still' (1972), as well as certain of the late plays for television such as *Ghost Trio* (1975) and *Nacht und Träume* (1982).

1972

17–26 June   Beckett begins 'Still' (completed the following month), described by C. J. Ackerley and S. E. Gontarski as 'a return to the concerns of Geulincx and the Occasionalists' (Ackerley and Gontarski 2006, p. 543).

Undated

Beckett added marginalia to his copy of Berkeley's *A New Theory of Vision, and Other Writings*, which reads 'Against Geulincx?'. The annotated edition is in the library of Beckett's Paris flat, where it has been since his death in 1989.

Introduction

With a few chapters left to write of *Murphy* in January 1936, Samuel Beckett ventured within what he called 'the abhorred gates' (SB to TM, 9 January 1936)[1] of Trinity College, Dublin (hereafter TCD) library for the first time since resigning from a teaching post at his old University 4 years earlier. He returned repeatedly to the library over the following 3 months to transcribe extensive notes from the works of the little-known post-Cartesian philosopher of 'Occasionalism' Arnold Geulincx (1624–69). It was not a small undertaking, and it was also not the first time Beckett had encountered Geulincx. Earlier in the 1930s he had taken notes on the obscure thinker as part of the 267 pages of 'Philosophy Notes', where he wrote a brief section on Occasionalism as part of a genealogy derived from one of his compendium source books for philosophical history, Wilhelm Windelband's *A History of Philosophy* (1901). Following these two research projects, Beckett went on to name Geulincx in *Murphy* and *Molloy*, as well as in personal correspondence. As a consequence of all this, Geulincx has long been recognized as a name of some importance for Beckett. From the very first collection of articles on Beckett in 1959[2] and the first single-author monograph in 1961,[3] to C. J. Ackerley's work in 1998, which shed new light on Beckett's uses of philosophy in *Murphy*, and publication in 2006 of the first ever English translation of Geulincx's *Ethica* as *Ethics* in an edition that includes translations of Beckett's 1936 transcriptions from that work, as well as further publications since 2006 that make use of the new *Ethics*, there are numerous studies devoting sections to Geulincx's importance for Beckett.[4] Nevertheless, and a little surprisingly, no full-length study has explored the relationship. Is there any real need for one now, given how much information is already in the public domain?

The extent to which Beckett mentions Geulincx by name or deploys terminology derived from the philosopher, not only in his fiction and drama and drafts of these but in personal correspondence as well, is in fact yet to be fully recognized. Consequently, the possibility of Beckett's long-term thinking about Geulincx has been proposed only rarely, and explored with precision even less. Beckett names Geulincx or mentions Geulingian terms such as 'autology' in at least 17 separate instances of correspondence. This correspondence spans three decades and itself powerfully counters a hypothesis that Geulincx for Beckett was merely an early, throwaway reference, one easily exhausted of limited potential before being forgotten.

A further constraint on prior Anglophone scholarship involves translation. Until 2006 there had been no authoritative English translation from the original 'beautiful Belgo-Latin' (*Mu*, 112) as it is recalled in *Murphy* of Geulincx's masterpiece *Ethica* (from which the majority of Beckett's transcriptions derive). Even the Latin had been out of print for 185 years before resurrection in Jan Pieter Nicolaas Land's complete collected edition of 1891–3, the three-volume *Opera Philosophica* that Beckett consulted.[5] Land's edition is itself quite rare, as it was in 1936 when Beckett discovered that Ireland's National Library did not possess a copy. While other translations survive in Mainland European libraries, these have thus far failed to pique much curiosity among Beckett scholars writing in languages other than English, though as of 2012 this is changing.[6]

Also, Beckett's transcriptions from Geulincx have only recently been made available at TCD for scholarly consultation. Prior to this any close textual comparative work on the topic was severely hampered. Consequently, it is only since 2006 that a full-length study with recourse to an authoritative translation could be properly founded. Geulincx, then, simultaneously occupies a revivified and established older area of Beckett studies, and despite his recurring presence in this scholarship, the precise nature of this presence is in fact far from fixed. Scholars are not even agreed on how to pronounce Geulincx's name.[7]

Studies that address themselves to Geulincx's presence in specific works by Beckett are discussed in detail in the following chapters. Nevertheless, it is worth highlighting here certain of the broader claims made about Geulincx's importance for Beckett. Deirdre Bair, for example, asserts that 'Geulincx's philosophy had the most lasting effect on Beckett of anything he had read to date. So impressive was it that he made it the key of his novel *Murphy*, written in 1935' (Bair 1978, p. 92).[8] More recently Ackerley and S. E. Gontarski have claimed that Geulincx's 'ethical axiom became for SB the foundation of doubt and humility, the bêtise that underpins his life's work' (Ackerley and Gontarski 2006, p. 224). Ackerley has also asserted that, luminous among the wide-ranging contexts of Beckett's literary and philosophical backgrounds, 'Beckett's gospel is Geulincx's *Ethica*' (Ackerley 2004a, p. 20). Pascale Casanova argues, moderately at first, that 'Geulincx became one of Beckett's major intellectual references' (Casanova 2006, p. 59). But overly reliant on Bair's biography, Casanova does not date Beckett's Geulincx research to 1936, so is able to justify finding Geulincx's very direct presence in works earlier than *Murphy*:

> Beckett would seek to illustrate Geulincx's system of mutual externality very precisely, by conveying it in literary form with the introduction of the indolent, nonchalant character from Dante's Purgatorio, Belacqua.

Casanova goes on to assert the almost unlimited scope of Geulincx's importance: 'Beckett discovered in Geulincx's system a formulation of his own intellectual, national, literary, social and psychological confinement and a tool for understanding it' (Casanova 2006, p. 61).

In stark contrast to such grand claims, arguments that Geulincx's place within Beckett's range of reference is minor and fleeting are only slightly less prevalent. J. D. O'Hara insisted in 1981 that 'Geulincx appears in his [Beckett's] works in a single repeated sentence' (O'Hara 1981, p. 249), while P. J. Murphy has argued that if Beckett's philosophical reading was an influence upon *Murphy* then it derived rather from his 'very close reading of Spinoza, which underlies all the other more superficial philosophical references in the novel (Geulincx, Descartes and Democritus included)' (Murphy 1994, p. 229).

Tracing 'a literary fantasia' follows a route through Beckett's oeuvre that finds a mutable, protean Geulincx whose importance lies variously between the poles of the above claims. It argues that Geulincx's importance can most clearly and persuasively be identified in discrete moments of text, and yet also that these moments speak of broader shifts in Beckett's aesthetics. 'Moments' in Beckett's works, be they of fragmentary recollection, as a sudden slippage of one realm of existence into another, as a pause in the otherwise seemingly perpetual stream of unlovable experience in the world, even as an amalgam of all three, are vital. To disregard them can be to fail to take note of an important minor key in Beckett's work that finds a realm of tangible experience opposable, albeit at times with futility, to a void of forgetting and, paradoxically, to impermanence. When, for example, Krapp recalls old 'moments' via his self-made recordings, they are fragmentary little pieces of time as 'hard' and distinct from the surrounding flux, and as ironically 'never to be forgotten', as the 'small, old, hard, solid rubber ball' that Krapp holds back a moment from a dog as 'the blind went down' on a conversation he attempted with a woman whose eyes of 'chrysolite' rather stunned him: 'I sat on for a few moments with the ball in my hand and the dog pawing and yelping at me. [*Pause.*] Moments. Her moments, my moments. [*Pause.*] The dog's moments'. Naïvely, at the crest of this little wave Krapp records of the ball 'I shall feel it, in my hand, until my dying day' (*CDW*, p. 220).

This brief look at a specific type of 'moment', however, is not to intimate that when Geulincx comes to the fore of a text his presence thereby consistently manifests a moment of pause or opposition to impermanence, even though this might sometimes be the case. Rather, it is merely to assert the less controversial primacy in Beckett's oeuvre of the fragmentary, the momentary and the half-forgotten. As will be seen, it is frequently in the context of these important foci that Beckett brings Geulincx to bear.

In 1936 Beckett tantalizingly referred to 'my Geulincx' as 'a literary fantasia' (SB to GR, 9 January 1936: *L1*, p. 295). By writing 'my Geulincx' Beckett pointed to the existence of a version of the philosopher that existed privately, for himself. At the same time, Geulincx as 'a literary fantasia' implies that this individual version is unfixed, open to change, to spontaneity in the somewhat non-Beckettian notion of fantasy. The chapters of this book argue that for Beckett, Geulincx was indeed changeable, and was thus not simply a fixed paradigm of interiority or solipsism, even with due notice taken of the philosopher's emphasis on what he calls *inspectio sui* (inspection of the self). Nor is 'my Geulincx' a monomaniacal rationalist, whose spring might be wound while Beckett and the reader laugh together at the follies of 'philosophy', 'language' or even hubristic 'worldliness'. Primarily, Geulincx's ethics as derived from his metaphysics have implications for Beckett's altering conceptions of freedom, incapacity and impossibility, and these conceptions morph and re-morph in interrelated realignments with Beckett's altering aesthetic focus. I argue that multifaceted attentiveness to the various ways in which Geulincx is implicitly invoked, explicitly cited and even avoided entirely in different published works as well as in the grey canon, is required if the extent of his importance across the changeable impetuses of Beckett's oeuvre is to be properly understood.

To these ends *Tracing 'a literary fantasia'* proceeds with an empirical impetus, staying close to textual evidence in final published or staged form as well as in correspondence, manuscripts, notes, transcriptions and typescripts. In these terms a 'Geulingian reading' of a Beckett text is one that seeks to first establish specific identifiable appearances of Geulincx before proceeding to questions about what these appearances might do in, or to, a text. Such empirical procedures, however, need not necessarily rush too fast to dismiss claims such as those made by Casanova that might lack a well-argued empirical basis. As will be seen, if something called 'influence' is at stake in Beckett's relationship with Geulincx, such influence is not categorical, and nor does it necessarily imply a radical break with the past. 'Tracing', then, involves a doubled procedure: first an archaeological tracing to origins and beginnings in draft versions of works and the grey canon, prior to a close textual analysis, a 'tracing' over the contours of moments of text where Geulincx operates.

Chapter 1 introduces Beckett's interest in Geulincx and his transcriptions from the philosopher's works, and discusses a lineage of correspondence dating from 1936 to 1967 in which Beckett cites or alludes to Geulincx. Chapter 2 builds on this groundwork by proposing a chronology of *Murphy*'s composition that reveals Geulincx's importance to that novel to be as a frame of reference located predominantly in *Murphy*'s later stages, but with important caveats. Chapter 3 investigates Geulincx's presence in drafts of *Watt*, and argues that this presence is predominantly refined out of the novel's final stages at the same time as it becomes variously hidden and subsumed. Chapter 4 focuses in on a specific paragraph that names Geulincx in the short prose text *Suite*, a text that became *La Fin/The End*. The different versions of this paragraph stage a number of textual manoeuvres in translation and revisions that are revealing about Beckett's attitude towards Geulincx specifically as a source, and more broadly about philosophy as a synecdoche for what the short poem 'Gnome' (1934) calls 'the loutishness of learning' (*SP*, 9) more broadly. Chapter 5 traces the consequences of an aesthetic attitude that sought to rid itself of overt learning through imagery derived from Geulincx in *Molloy*, *Malone meurt/Malone Dies* and *L'Innommable/The Unnamable*, this last as a novel that also enacts certain of Geulincx's ethical principles in the performativity of narrative voice. The final chapter argues that there are highly refined and abstracted reengagements with Geulincx that can be located in *Comment c'est/How It Is*, *Act Without Words 1*, 'Still' and in certain of the later television plays read as a reinvigorated fascination with puppetry that is also owed to Beckett's reading Heinrich von Kleist.

This full-length study finds that Geulincx's altering and recurring presences across Beckett's oeuvre bear new, and close, scrutiny; they are more thoroughly embedded within this body of work than previously noted by scholars, and in this they frequently reflect broader changing concerns, as what Beckett called his 'series' of works develops. Much as he had been in 1936, Geulincx and his singular philosophy remained for Beckett a lens though which a number of curious matters might continue to be observed.

Chapter 1

Beckett and Geulincx

Reviving Occasionalism

Geulincx is most frequently named as occupying a minor niche within Early Modern post-Cartesian philosophy. Along with Nicolas Malebranche (1638–1715), the physician Louis de la Forge (1632–66) and Parisian lawyer Géraud de Cordemoy (1626–84), he has what Han van Ruler calls 'the dubious honour of being classed among those whom history has labelled "occasionalists"' (*Et*, p. xxiii).[1] These thinkers, who melded together diverse and sometimes seemingly contradictory influences into a multifaceted system of metaphysics, now reside predominantly in historical footnotes. Yet certain of Occasionalism's underlying assumptions, particularly those regarding scepticism towards the knowability of natural causality, have much in common with other thinkers, ranging from Nicholas of Autrecourt in the fourteenth century to David Hume 400 years later. Occasionalism itself, however, along with a group of eleventh-century Muslims theologians,[2] is distinguished among this historical company in its extremism in outright rejection of the possibility of causal relations in nature.

Unfortunately for Occasionalism's advocates, the philosophy's very proximity to other more prominent systems of thought has frequently worked against it. At one time such proximity even formed part of a highly successful and concerted effort specifically to marginalize Geulincx, whose association with one particular name – his compatriot and contemporary, Spinoza – saw so determined an effort to damage his reputation that his work would go out of print for nearly 200 years. After which time, and with no little irony, Land was only able to bring Geulincx back into print with money from 'what remains of the Spinoza-fund' (Land 1891, p. 224).[3]

As van Ruler and Anthony Uhlmann point out of more recent scholarship, thinkers as diverse as Slavoj Žižek, Martha Nussbaum and John Cottingham have all, in very different works, argued that the ultrarational transcendent impetus, that which certainly motivated Geulincx's ethical project, testifies less to the reality of a revelatory logic than to a particular, though variable, brand of psychological insidiousness. Such an impetus might take root in, for example, the secretively legislative 'Superego [. . .] on the side of knowledge' (Žižek 2004, p. 41) in Spinoza, or the childishly permissive drives inherent in ultrahigh moral standards as Nussbaum argues (again targeting Spinoza).[4] Similarly, Cottingham claims that rationalism can exhibit self-delusive forces that take little account of extenuating circumstances of psychology.[5] As the editors of the *Ethics* of 2006 point out, while these arguments all explicitly target Spinoza, due to certain confluences in their thought, 'Where Spinoza is targeted, Geulincx is often implied'[6] (*Et*, p. xxxiii). As a consequence of such influential criticism, 'Reviving a philosophy from the past has therefore become a dangerous business' (p. xxxiv).

However, an exploration of Beckett's fascination with Geulincx must necessarily set itself against any straightforward revival of Occasionalism. While this study is intended as a contribution to scholarship on Geulincx's legacies in the intertwined histories of philosophy and literature, and more directly to that on Beckett, the contribution it makes to scholarship on Geulincx is primarily a literary one, and must be put in terms of Beckett's specific uses and understandings of him. Therefore, complicities inherent in reviving such a philosophy from the past can, at least for the most part, be sidestepped and left to scholars focusing on republication of the *Ethics* itself. This caveat is important because even though the chapters that follow deal with Beckett's own refracted versions of Geulincx, nevertheless a laying out of Geulincx's thought is necessary; without an understanding of his metaphysical, epistemological and ethical Occasionalism established at the outset, it would be much harder to understand how Beckett's uses of it might deviate from simple appropriations of Geulingian thought, as unproblematic allegory or symbol, for example. To this limited extent an ultrarationalist philosophical impetus must be revived, that is in order to see just how it might appear to Beckett as being amenable to the more flexible boundaries of literature. Beckett was a master of cohering disparate connexions into what *Watt* calls, in regard to the marvellous 'poss' of medicine, food and drink, 'quite a new good thing' (*W*, p. 72); music hall meeting the Old Testament in *Waiting for Godot*, or ancient philosophy combined with something akin to ballet in *Quad*, and of course such a list could go on. That the two lonely figures of Beckett and Geulincx would be drawn into each other's unstable orbits might, at first sight, appear very anomalous. Perhaps it seems an example of some abstract intellectual curiosity, according to which the haughty and brilliant, young and frustrated Beckett was merely flexing his intellectual muscles in TCD's Long Room, sending his friends Latin quotations and writing of obscure, aesthetic redemptions. But just as Beckett wrote to MacGreevy of the lure of Geulincx's obscurity, he also sensed an instinct for the thinker; Beckett realized that he had more in common with Geulincx than a liking for axiomatic 'phrase-bombs' (SB to TM, 3 February 1931: *L1*, p. 64), as he had admitted to admiring in T. S. Eliot, for example. Beckett recognized a kindred figure in Geulincx, whose ultrarationalist philosophy also speaks of friendship, the persistence of failure and a kind of doomed quest the object of which is singularly intangible. One author then languishing in netherworld obscurity reading another likely to always remain so: to imagine Beckett patiently reading and rereading Geulincx brings to mind Reader and Listener in *Ohio Impromptu*. From January's hope of resting where 'shade will comfort you', to a final 'No need to go to him again' (*CDW*, p. 446–7) in April, Beckett's few months of 1936 provided vital lessons in how rational needs for knowing, resolution and conclusion might find more productive trajectories in irresolution, non-ending, and not reaching.

Arnold Geulincx

Beckett probably knew little of Geulincx's life. The biographical chronology that appears in the front matter of *Opera*'s volume 1 is necessarily brief. Yet, the circumstances of Geulincx's life are not only fascinating in their own right, but they also bear on his philosophy. So while a summary biography must stray from material that was of undisputed direct relevance to Beckett, nevertheless it is a suitable place from which to begin an introduction to Geulincx's thought.

Geulincx was baptized on 31 January 1624 in St James' Church, Antwerp. According to Wiep van Bunge et al., Geulincx 'probably had a sister and three younger brothers' (van Bunge et al. (eds) 2003, p. 322), and benefitted from his parents' keenness to provide their children with a good education, matriculating at age 16 at Leuven University. Geulincx continued to do well academically at Jansenist Leuven over the next few years, where he obtained his licentiate. He went on to study theology and was appointed junior professor of philosophy in December 1646. By 1652, as Land details, he 'was entrusted with the treatment of the so-called *Quaestiones quodlibeticae*' following a promotion to the grade of *primarius*. These *Quaestiones* took the form of propositions posed publicly by a single *magister* on subjects of general interest. The *magister* had to propose, 'with intelligence and in agreeable form' (Land 1891, p. 225), reasons for and against a given proposition. Certain of Geulincx's *Quaestiones* are included in the first volume of *Opera*. Beckett's transcriptions of these public and frequently playful debates are scant; he noted only five of the 28 *Quaestiones*, leaving out the lengthy discussions for and against that are also recorded by Land. The transcriptions include fire-themed propositions such as the following:

> 25. Atrocior est noster quam Jovis ignis.
> 26. Mitior est naturalis quam artificiosus ignis. (TCD MS 10971/6/1)
> 25. Atrocities belong to humanity like fires belong to Jupiter.
> 26. Kindness is as natural to humanity as an artificial fire.[7]

Unfortunately for Geulincx, his popularity provoked a backlash among opponents of the new Cartesian philosophy, and the old guard closed ranks against the innovative thinker. Protective of Scholastic teaching, a group led by the respected medical professor Vopiscus Fortunatus Plempius (1601–71) fired the first of a series of shots across the bow in 1654 in the form of a letter soliciting a university-wide declaration against Cartesianism. The petition refrained from naming Geulincx explicitly, and it did not receive many signatures; Geulincx was still in a relatively powerful position within the Leuven academy as Dean of the Faculty of Arts from March to September of that same year. In 1657 he was designated for a canonry at the cathedral in Aix, but here his opponents were more successful, managing to keep him out of the esteemed position 'ostensibly because he did not succeed in proving the legitimacy of his parents' birth' (Land 1891, p. 227). From here Geulincx's misfortunes gathered pace, the most drastic of which was probably somehow connected to his marrying Susanna Strickers, who was either his cousin or niece. Most probably citing the frowned-upon relationship, as well as his growing popularity in teaching controversial new philosophy, opponents forced him from the University.[8]

With very little money, Geulincx and Susanna moved to the National University of Holland at Calvinist Leyden.[9] Here Geulincx managed to secure a position among a faculty more open to Cartesianism, though the new thinking still predominantly operated in secret. While certain of the faculty were well known as Cartesians, teaching of the new science was officially banned and it received only tacit support. Beckett himself summarized Geulincx's situation in this new university in a paragraph of the 'Philosophy Notes':

> Jansenists & Fathers of the Oratory, living in Augustinian-Scotist atmosphere, were friendly to new philosophy, while orthodox Peripatetics, and esp. Jesuits, opposed it violently. Thus old opposition between Augustinianism & Thomism was renewed in controversy over Cartesianism. To meet this attack the Cartesians (Louis de la Forge & Malebranche) insisted on connection with Augustine. (TCD MS 10967/189r)

Land concurs with appraising Geulincx's Augustinian connections, and later conversion:

> In later years, the learned adherents of Jansenius and of Descartes were mostly the same men; and we have every reason to suppose that Geulincx' occupation with that Augustinian theology prepared the way for his going over in his mature years to the reformed confession. (Land 1891, p. 225)

Although Geulincx would never regain the level of prestige he had held at Leuven, he did attain a measure of popularity at Leyden thanks to the substantial support he received from the professor of theology Abraham Heidanus (1597–1678), as well as from certain of his own students (to whom he would directly address parts of *Ethica* and who would edit his works posthumously).[10] By 1667 he managed, finally, to publish the first Tractate of *Ethica*.

This hard-won fame was not to last long. Sometime between 8 and 21 November 1669 Geulincx died of an unidentified plague, along with a number of other faculty at the university. While lamenting the early deaths of Geulincx and Susanna (who died the following January) Land argues that Geulincx did at least manage, with his death, to avoid encountering further misfortunes.[11] The remaining proponents of the new philosophy were steadily suppressed and their positions made vacant by the ascendant Orange party and the 'strict clericals' (Land 1891, p. 238) joined with it; even the highly respected Heidanus lost his office. The university produced a bronze medallion commemorating those from the faculty who had died in the 1669 plague, yet it makes no mention of the ever-controversial and original Geulincx. Consequently, there is no surviving image of him, and Land admits to being unable to find where he is buried.

Misfortunes, failures and their consequences pervade Geulincx's philosophy, and must surely derive in part from such experiences in his own life. As van Ruler describes him, 'Geulincx was an unhappy man and his philosophy an unhappy man's recipe for happiness' (*Et*, p. xxxii). H. J. de Vleeschauwer calls him 'the man of the serious word and the ungrateful life' (de Vleeschauwer 1957, p. 13). Exasperated rhetorical questions in *Ethics*, such as 'Why do so many and such great calamities conspire against me? Have I offended God in some way' (*Et*, p. 351), clearly display a tone of lamentation that is other than only logically systematic. When discussing his seventh ethical obligation, for example, concerning the onus upon the ethical novice to choose a good and pragmatic career, Geulincx refers specifically to an academic life as one 'in which study and a thousand tediums have to be endured, and which is subject to envy and criticism' (p. 273); he was intimately familiar with these as aspects of his own career.

Even without an accompanying detailed biographical commentary, Beckett could not fail to have noticed how such autobiographical passages frequently jut, at times quite sharply, into and out of *Ethica*. It is well known that Beckett was fascinated by the logical byways of seventeenth-century rationalist philosophy, as well as by the implications for such grand closed systems of contrasting moments of alterity and slippage, moments that accordingly have their parallels in Beckett's works. Arsene's moment off the ladder in *Watt*, for example, plays out a farcical paradigm of the ineffable intervening uninvited in the otherwise properly effable, where Arsene is surprised by the 'sentiment' – otherwise alien to his *quid pro quo* rationalism – 'that a change, other than a change of degree, had taken place' (*W*, p. 36). Similarly, the narrated protagonist of *Company* suddenly stands stock-still part way along a walk taken many times previously, his steps counted and the action repeated by a self that is bent on systematizing the experienced environment:

> You take the course you always take which is a beeline for the gap or ragged point in the quickset that forms the western fringe. Thither from your entering the pasture you need normally from eighteen hundred to two thousand paces depending on your humour and the state of the ground.

The scene is set for a difficult conjunction in the 'white pasture afrolic with lambs in spring and strewn with red placentae', where the sudden halt in the field, 'as never before' (*Co*, p. 23), bears no apparent relation to the narrator's usual numerical enfoldedness in the world. The stasis intrudes as one epistemology into another entirely irreconcilable with it, where a mysterious, ineffable weight has dragged the otherwise straight line across the fields down into a bowed curve, and an eventual halt:

> The foot falls unbidden in midstep or next for lift cleaves to the ground bringing the body to a stand. Then a speechlessness whereof the gist, Can they go on? Or better, Shall they go on? The barest gist. Stilled when finally as always hitherto they do. You lie in the dark with closed eyes and see the scene. As you could not at the time. The dark cope of sky. The dazzling land. You at a standstill in the midst. The quarterboots sunk to the tops. The skirts of the greatcoat resting on the snow. In the old bowed head in the old block hat speechless misgiving. Halfway across the pasture on your beeline to the gap. The unerring feet fast. You look behind you as you could not then and see their trail. A great swerve. Withershins. Almost as if all at once the heart too heavy. In the end too heavy. (pp. 24–5)

Geulincx's metaphysical and ethical systems cannot break free from personal selfhood and autobiography, from what is sometimes just 'too heavy' to not have to set down at some point, much as the abstract, frequently mathematical, systematizing of many of Beckett's protagonists cannot exist free of physical, tangible connections to an experienced, remembered and lived-in bodily and messy world, a world if not quite 'realist' then at once differently 'real'. It is a world that sometimes echoes moments of Beckett's own life; Beckett took walks with his father in the Wicklow mountains, for example, and these provide a partial basis for the imagery in *Company* (imagery that itself echoes a Cartesian and Occasionalist chasm between the 'head' and the 'heart'). There is also Beckett's confession to Charles Juliet in 1977 that 'Sometimes, when I am out walking, I find myself counting my steps' (cited in Juliet 1995, p. 162). Molloy proclaims of collisions between systems and self, with a characteristic mix of joy and spite as he counts his farts, that it is 'Extraordinary how mathematics helps you to know yourself' (*Mo*, p. 28). Mathematics does not, of course, in Beckett's fractured, sometimes-permeable closed systems, tend to help 'you' to know anything other than more mathematics. Something 'other than a change of degree' is required in order that something other than more degrees can be admitted.

There is a great deal more that Beckett found of interest in Geulincx's Occasionalism than this mix of real life and theorizing, as his repeated references to the ethical axiom attest, and as will be discussed in the following chapters. Yet it is worth emphasizing at the outset that Beckett recognized in Geulincx a complex, narcissistic, brilliantly intelligent, unhappy and individual figure. While Geulincx's reliance on his own lived life for his work was not the mystical *'flame* [. . .] *that burns away filthy logic'* (cited in Juliet 1995, p. 167) that Beckett admitted to liking in St John of the Cross, Meister Eckhart and Ruysbroeck, nevertheless it was an important way of confronting the tribulations of rationalism. For the young aspirant of the 1930s, with his own 'misery and solitude and apathy and the sneers' (SB to TM, 10 March 1935: *L1*, p. 258) as Beckett admitted to, lessons from a figure such as Geulincx in the importance of incapacity, restraint and humility when living in a world perceived as difficult and hostile, would have a striking effect.

Occasionalist Metaphysics

The following summary of Geulincx's philosophy takes its contours from *Metaphysica Vera* and *Ethica*. These are Geulincx's major works and the ones from which Beckett took the majority of his transcriptions.

Broadly speaking, Occasionalism arose among French and Dutch Cartesians of the second half of the seventeenth century. As Jean-Christophe Bardout describes:

> The occasionalist philosophy is usually thought of as a response to difficulties that its proponents see facing Cartesianism. In particular, the so-called 'mind-body problem': How can the real and absolute distinction between two such heterogeneous substances as mind and body be reconciled with the thesis of their substantial union in a human being? (Bardout 2002, p. 140)

Through consequences of the 'mind-body problem' inherited from Descartes, Beckett too first encountered the solutions offered by Occasionalism. However, Occasionalism has a much wider scope beyond its solution to mind–body interaction. That particular solution is merely implied by a much more ambitious aim of offering an account of the entirety of causal relations in all 'created nature' (p. 141). While none of the thinkers grouped under its heading actually adopted the 'dubious' title of 'Occasionalist', historically the term has come to denote a unifying, usually monotheistic thesis which seeks to prove that only one single agent causes interaction between a mind and body, between minds and other minds and between bodies and other bodies.[12] The movement's name derives from Descartes's unfinished *Treatise on Man*, published by Claude Clerselier in 1664 with notes by La Forge. In this *Treatise* the great progenitor of modern philosophy used the word 'occasion' during crucial discussions of mind–body interaction, and it struck certain of his followers that the theoretical, explanatory space the word occupied required explication. The *Treatise* contains phrases such as, for example, 'fibres cause a movement in the brain which gives occasion for the soul [. . .] to have the sensation of *pain*' (Descartes 1985, p. 103). To put the problem into the terms in which Beckett would later allude to it, the ill-defined word 'occasion' became the inheritance of later Cartesians seeking to account for the problems presented by a pineal gland that had (following *Murphy*) 'shrunk to nothing' (*Mu*, p. 6), having been drained of explanatory power via the uninformative but load-bearing term 'occasion'. In seeking to account for apparent schisms and connections between minds and bodies, however, Occasionalism was not always effective. La Forge was constrained by his fealty to Descartes, and despite Cordemoy striving to extricate himself from those same origins, both he and La Forge held in common a propensity to turn to the questions and solutions of Occasionalism via physics and attendant issues of bodily causation.[13] Geulincx distinguished himself among his peers by turning more resolutely towards epistemology and its consequences, in a broader hope for completion of the Cartesian project in an ethics, which led him in turn to affirm the radical incapacity and impotence of the human mind, and to counsel, as a result, the humility that so moved Beckett.

Geulincx begins *Metaphysica Vera* with the founding Cartesian motto that Beckett duly transcribed:

<u>Prima Scientia</u>. Cogito ergo sum. (TCD MS 10971/6/2r)[14]
Proposition 1. I think, therefore I exist. (*Met*, p. 31)

He then immediately begins his individual project by questioning the efficacy of this foundational conception of what it is to 'think', as Beckett noted:

<u>Secundo S</u>. Varios habeo cogitandi modos in infinitum.

Cogito ergo, et infinitis modis cogito; sed illae res quas cogito num sic sint ut cogito, adhuc nescio. (TCD MS 10971/6/2r)[15]

Proposition 2. I have innumerable modes of thought. [. . .]

Therefore I think, and think in innumerable modes. But whether the things I think really are exactly as I think of them, I still do not know. (*Met*, p. 32)

Geulincx's foregrounding of this 'nescio', a not knowing, is central to *Metaphysica Vera*, where it determines his epistemology before it has further important implications for his ethics. Ignorance and impotence are keystones of Geulincx's self-made 'Temple of Philosophy' (*Et*, p. 4). He argues from *Metaphysics*' 'Proposition 2' that the things I think, and which might not be 'exactly as I think of them', could in fact be very far from how they appear to me to be. Yet I, to my detriment, have no way of knowing whether things are as I perceive them to be or not. Specifically (and centrally as regards his legacy as an Occasionalist), Geulincx argues that as a result of this not knowing, no human can be said to cause actions in a physical world, and no human can cause thoughts to occur in other minds.

In seeking to stake a bridge across the mind–body divide, Geulincx first of all argues that the divide is just too great, too unknowable, for any human to cross. Even though it might appear to me as though I have capacities to cause movement in bodies, and even to cause thoughts in other minds, according to Geulincx I emphatically do not; in fact only God properly qualifies as a causal agent. These two conclusions (that I lack the aforementioned capacities, and that God alone has them) derive from the central metaphysical argument, the major argument that distinguishes Geulincx as a metaphysical epistemologist: in order to qualify as performing an action (or causing anything, including thoughts in minds) I must have *knowledge* of this action. Such knowledge must consist in being able to say, fully and with reason, *how* an action happens. If I cannot say how something happens, then, according to Geulincx, I cannot claim that it is my own action. The metaphysical axiom summarizing this argument appears in Beckett's transcriptions from both *Metaphysica Vera* and *Ethica*:

Quod nescis quomodo fiat, id non facis. (TCD MS 10971/6/2v)[16]

What you do not know how to do, is not your action (*Met*, p. 35)

If, as Geulincx wrote in dedicating *Ethics*, 'In the Temple of Wisdom Ethics is the ceiling and the roof' (*Et*, p. 311), then his metaphysical axiom gives the temple essential support; without it there could be no substantive building. Geulincx is at times so determined that his reader should accept this axiom that he contradicts himself, seemingly tripping over his own enthusiasm for it, asserting it to be so obvious that it does not require arguing, immediately prior to his arguing for it:

I have not claimed that *what you do not know how to do does not happen*, but: *what you do not know how to do is not your action*. [. . .] Nor is there any need for arguments here, only anyone's consciousness. . .I say. . .that if you are willing to describe yourself as the doer of anything that you do not know how to do, there is no reason why you should not believe that you have done or do anything that happens or has been done. If you do not know how motion is made in the organs of your body while being nevertheless quite sure that you made it, you could say with equal justification that you are the author of Homer's *Iliad*, or that you built the walls of Nineveh, or the Pyramids; you could say with equal justification that you make the sun rise and set for us all, and the succession of days and nights, and of winter and summer. (p. 330)

Geulincx takes his metaphysical arguments to their extreme, arguing that precisely and validly analogous with the impossibility of my causing the sun to rise and fall or my having built the Pyramids, is the impossibility of my causing my own arm to rise and fall, or picking up a single stone. The philosopher Steven Nadler has written on how Malebranche also introduced an epistemological criterion to what would otherwise have been a purely metaphysical theory of causation. Malebranche even imagines the criterion using the same metonymic imagery as Geulincx – the movement of an arm. During his comparison of the two thinkers, Nadler asks the fundamental question of all this extremism: 'Why would one think that there is an epistemic condition upon causality?' (Nadler 1999b, p. 269). He concludes that the only possible solution to the problems this condition raises that avoids category errors of confusing causation by volitional agents with causation by non-volitional agents, is to take 'volitional agency to be *the* paradigm of causality' (p. 270), and this is just what Geulincx does.[17]

In defining what might qualify as knowledge of an event, such that knowledge can be said to pass his stringent epistemic tests, Geulincx gives the example of an anatomist as a paradigm of the scientific knower; even such a rigorous, precise thinker as this, the reasoning goes, cannot properly say 'how' an arm is moved. According to the analogy, there is something fundamental missing from a purely physical account of movement, of the anatomist's descriptions of blood flow and what Geulincx calls (following Descartes) the movement of 'animal spirits'. Anatomy (and by extension all rational language) does not reach, cannot speak of, the ineffable *how* of causation. Geulincx describes such scientific knowledge as merely 'the knowledge not of an author but of a contemplator of an event [and thus it is] no more than a consciousness and perception of *the fact that* motion is taking place' (*Et*, p. 228, my italics). It is not a substantive explanation of *how* movement takes place.

This *how* is hugely important for Geulincx, for it is with its ineffability that he manages to distil and blend his otherwise contrasting impetuses as a rationalist Christian mystic. The *how* of causation is properly ineffable, for Geulincx, because it cannot be stated in rational discourse:

Something is said to be *ineffable* not because we cannot think or speak of it (for this would be *nothing*, *nothing* and *unthinkable* being the same . . .) but because we cannot think about or encompass with our reason how it is done.

As he writes, 'in the end an ineffable something is always missing' (p. 334); a residue of experience that is not exhausted by describing that experience 'with our reason' always remains. Only God can properly know such an ineffable realm, a realm that Arsene describes as 'what has so happily been called the unutterable or ineffable' (*W*, p. 52). For limited, non-knowing humanity, Geulincx would concur with the servant's appraisal 'that any attempt to utter or eff it is doomed to fail, doomed, doomed to fail' (p. 53).

Geulincx's metaphysics cohere, then, in a bringing together of two seemingly irreconcilable impetuses – the ultrarational and the ineffable. All that can properly be said to exist for humanity is what he calls, following Descartes, the 'occasion' of my willing an action to happen, and the 'occasion' (the moment) of that action happening.[18] If that action I have willed does indeed occur this is only because God has caused it, so actions I want to happen will only happen if I am making decisions that accord with what Geulincx calls 'the absolute, true, and strict will of God' (*Et*, p. 317). All humanity can do is hope, pray and ethically intend.

It can perhaps be seen already, even in these broad introductory terms, that Geulincx's world of ignorance and impotence bears comparison with Beckett's ideas on humanity experiencing the world. As, for example, these were expressed in an interview of 1956:

> I think anyone nowadays who pays the slightest attention to his own experience finds it the experience of a non-knower, a non-can-er [somebody who cannot]. The other type of artist – the Apollonian – is absolutely foreign to me. (Cited in Graver and Federman (eds) 1979, p. 162, editorial Graver and Federman's)

The third and final chapter of *Metaphysica Vera* is entitled 'Concerning God' (*Met*, p. 91). Here Geulincx asserts that God 'is an ineffable Father' (p. 97), 'Creator of the World' (p. 99), 'a powerful Creator and Mover' (p. 102) is 'a law unto Himself' (p. 108) and is 'supremely Perfect' (p. 120). These sections were certainly of some interest to Beckett, and he summarized all of them in three pages of notes. Yet the major part of Geulincx's thought inheres in his conceptions of metaphysical ignorance and impotence as these inform his ethics.

Occasionalist Ethics

Geulincx's emphasis on ignorance and impotence, his proposing humanity's total lack of agency, prompts his further step into ethics. According to which, the proper response to humanity's limited capacities and to the concomitant limitless capacities of God, is a particular kind of ethical humility. The transition is summarized in the following passage, which Beckett transcribed from *Metaphysica Vera*:

> Nothing ever happens to me, properly speaking, because I will it, but rather because the true Mover wills what I will, just as He sometimes does not will what I will [. . .] And here we reach the estuary of the moral river, where the coastline broadens out into Ethics: for it follows from what I have said, that when it is not our human destiny to have power to do anything, neither should we will anything. And because it involves the whole of morality, this principle is the first, the best, and the broadest foundation of Ethics, and the one most easily known to us by the light of nature: *Wherein you have no power, therein you should not will* [*Ubi nihil vales, ibi nihil velis*]. (*Met*, p. 44)[19]

Beckett cited Geulincx's foundational first principle of *Ethics* a number of times in personal correspondence as being a place from which commentary of his own work, for those in the unfortunate position of embarking on such an enterprise, might also begin. Taken out of the context of the whole of *Ethica*, the axiom's apparent advocation of will-lessness has led to accusations that Geulincx 'condemned man to passivity' (de Vleeschauwer 1957, p. 62), where as Beckett recorded it in his 'Philosophy Notes' 'Man has nothing to do in outer world' (TCD MS 10967/189v), and against which de Vleeschauwer rightly defends him. The necessity of humility when facing humanity's impotence does not, for Geulincx, entail a total withdrawal from the world into the mind, and although Beckett's earlier 'Philosophy Notes' appear to point towards this interpretation, the longer detailed transcriptions that derive directly from *Ethica* testify to a much more thorough and nuanced understanding of the axiom and how it coheres within and anchors Geulincx's whole system. Before progressing to a more detailed look at this coherence in *Ethics*, however, there are a number of things that should be noted about the axiom itself.

'*Ubi nihil vales, ibi nihil velis*' is the centrepiece of Geulincx's Occasionalism, and it is also the phrase-bomb to which Beckett repeatedly returns, throwing it out to correspondents and laying it in wait for readers of his prose. Just shy of symmetrical, *ubi nihil vales, ibi nihil velis* has the kind of balanced equilibrium that characterizes so many of Beckett's own sentences across the breadth of his oeuvre from *Watt* onwards. He discussed his propensity for such neatness in an interview with Harold Hobson in 1956, where he invoked the dialogue in *Waiting for Godot* between Vladimir and Estragon about the 'reasonable percentage' (*CDW*, p. 13) of one of the two thieves put up for crucifixion alongside Jesus being saved:

> I take no sides. I am interested in the shape of ideas. There is a wonderful sentence in Augustine: 'Do not despair, one of the thieves was saved. Do not presume, one of the thieves was damned'. That sentence has a

wonderful shape. It is the shape that matters. (Cited in Ackerley and Gontarski 2006, p. 593)[20]

Beckett returns repeatedly to many such little phrases throughout his works, echoing and repeating in a way comparable to the obsessional returns that Vinteuil's musical 'little phrase' makes throughout Proust's *À la recherche du temps perdu*; music and language brought if not fully together then into provocative proximity. As will be seen in the chapters that follow, however, Beckett also goes on to upset the 'wonderful shape' that Geulincx's little phrase displays, variously breaking it apart or flattening its incisiveness out to something barely recognizable, turning its appealing neatness against itself.

Uhlmann discusses the axiom's translation into English:

> 'Ubi nihil vales ibi nihil velis' has often been translated by Beckett scholars as: 'Where one is worth nothing one should want nothing'. The Latin, 'valeo', carries the meaning both of 'to be able to, to have force' and 'to be worth'.

As Uhlmann points out, Beckett makes use of both senses of the first part of the axiom, employing 'the formula where one is "worth nothing" in *Murphy*, and alternatively, where one "can do nothing" in *The Unnamable*' (*Et*, p. 305). Ackerley notes of his own translation that he 'chose to retain the second person singular and something of the assonance of the original: "where you are worth nothing, there you should want nothing"' (Ackerley 2008, p. 200). Martin Wilson translates it in *Ethics* as '*Wherein you have no power, therein you should not will*', retaining his own version from the earlier translation of *Metaphysics* (1999). As Ackerley points out, the different renderings of the axiom necessarily emphasize either the metaphysical or the ethical at the expense of the other, and he laments Wilson's retention of the earlier translation:

> The point that Wilson's translation misses, I feel, is the verbal relationship of the phrase not so much to the metaphysics of motion (for in that context his weighting seems most apposite) as to the virtue of *Humilitas*, for Geulincx the core of his entire ethical system: *Radix Ethices est humilitas* ('humility is the root of Ethics'). (Ackerley 2008, p. 201)

For Geulincx there is only one ethical axiom, and yet he was presumably well aware of its ability to capture the codependency between the metaphysical and the ethical where his Occasionalism thrives. For Geulincx, being 'worth nothing' was precisely a matter of being 'able to do nothing'. Tracing '*a literary fantasia*' uses Wilson's translation of the axiom. While Ackerley is surely correct in pointing to this version's lack of ethical overtones, Beckett's own uses of the axiom (except in *Murphy*) tend to correspond to the metaphysical emphasis of the axiom. Yet it is also clear, as will be seen in the axiom's variable deployments, that Beckett was also well aware of the multiplicity of this densely woven little phrase. Indeed, Geulincx's rather playful ambivalence in his axiom might go part of the way to accounting for how a rationalist might be, at the very core of his system, not so very rational.[21] The Latin *valeo* is well chosen by Geulincx, allowing him to firmly situate his metaphysics in the realm of incapacity, while also connoting a relationship already there between this incapacity and humility, thanks to *valeo*'s intimation of worthlessness. The axiom itself renders that turn onto what Geulincx calls the 'estuary of the moral river' – the route into ethics – as the transition from the first half of the axiom (the more strictly metaphysical half, whichever translation is used) to the second, ethical half.

Before Geulincx gets to the stage of stressing the importance of *ubi nihil vales, ibi nihil velis*, however, *Ethics* begins with a chapter on '*Virtue in General*', defined as 'the exclusive Love of right Reason' (*Et*, p. 312). This intertwining of Virtue and Reason sets the tone of *Ethics* to follow as one determined by a rationalist's belief in an ineffable God. Geulincx sought to build upon a Christian conception of the blessed life while incorporating the structuring rationalism of then-current thinking. However, as van Ruler points out, a historical narrative that accounts for *Ethica* solely in terms of 'the invention of a Christian philosophy of morals' (p. xvi) would fail to note the even wider ranging context out of which *Ethica* came to being. Christian conceptions of the blessed life had for more than a century and a half been admitting elements of classical thought, and *Ethica* also builds on these. Often critical of what he calls 'pagan' (p. 8) ways of thinking, Geulincx nevertheless constructs important parts of his system in frameworks comparable to those of Aristotle, whose ethics of the mean bears comparison with Geulincx's diagrammed middle ground between moral categories such as '*Vice of Excess, Vice of Defect*' (p. 324), for example. Van Ruler describes *Ethics* as in part 'an extraordinary attempt to reinvest the ancient approach to ethics with an input of a genuinely Christian flavour' (p. xvii).

In Chapter 1 of *Ethics* Geulincx discusses 'Virtue' in terms of 'Love', 'Reason' and 'Disposition'. While not as emphatically 'ineffable' as the realms of causation and God, those of 'Love' and 'Reason' are nevertheless both initially described as also beyond language's power. Of 'Love', for example, Geulincx writes (with what in the English translation sounds a little like a note of exasperation) 'What love is, does not need to be stated. . .There is often a certain ambiguity in a name when the thing itself is perfectly clear' (p. 313). Similarly, he adds of 'Reason', 'What Reason is, is sufficiently known because of the fact that it is known at some point' (p. 315). He goes on to claim that self-evidently Reason 'is sufficiently well known to all of us, as we have the distinction of being rational' (p. 316).

Another context – Geulincx's Augustinianism – partly accounts for his conception of 'Disposition', which shows him to be firmly an ethical intentionalist:

'*Whatever men do, they are all judged by their intention*' (p. 349). Here he breaks from classical influences, with 'Disposition' becoming for him something much more absolute then a '*disposition to act rightly, acquired by the frequent performance of good actions*' (p. 318).

Ethics goes on to enumerate 'the Cardinal Virtues' (p. 320). These are 'Diligence' (a 'perpetual grasping at Reason' (p. 321)), 'Obedience' to Reason (and a concomitant avoidance of 'what Reason forbids' (p. 322)), and 'Justice', which 'is the fair application of Reason' (p. 324). At the end of the section on cardinal virtues is the part that stuck Beckett so forcefully, and which he recommended to his friend and member of the Dublin literati, Arland Ussher, on 'Humility'. Geulincx writes:

> Humility is the most exalted of the Cardinal Virtues: when Virtue includes only Diligence, Obedience, and Justice, it is incomplete. Humility closes the circle: beyond it nothing more can be added to Virtue. (p. 326)

Humility consists (typically for a Geulingian concept) of further subdivisions. First, it requires 'Inspectio Sui' (TCD MS 10971/6/32)[22]/'*Inspection of Oneself*' (*Et*, p. 327). The section headed 'Inspectio Sui' is by far the most detailed of Beckett's *Ethica* notes. *Inspectio sui* corresponds to the first half of the ethical axiom *ubi nihil vales* [wherein you have no power]. Upon delving into ourselves, into what Geulincx describes as our 'innermost sanctum, in order to consult the sacred Oracle of Reason' (p. 19) as was similarly undertaken in *Metaphysica Vera* under the rubric of 'autology', we discover incapacity and ignorance. As it was in *Metaphysics*, Geulincx's central argument in *Ethics* is that I cannot cause a thing to happen because I do not know (I 'cannot think about or encompass with [. . .] reason') how I could do so. I realize upon inspecting myself that I have no capacity for action (*ubi nihil vales*), so I should not try to act (*ibi nihil velis*):

> *Wherein you have no power*; we read in this the inspection of oneself. . . *Therein you should not will*; we read in this. . . disregard of oneself, or neglect of oneself across the whole human condition, and resigning ourselves into the power of His hand, in which we are, indeed, whether we like it or not. [. . .] or what comes to the same thing, *Do nothing gratuitously, do nothing in vain*.

As already stated, Geulincx does not in fact counsel absconding Murphy-like into a little world of interiority as the only place in which one might influence anything. His hope that humanity might '*do nothing in vain*' is, as I read it, more a valiant, if doomed, attempt to 'eff the ineffable' and state a paradox at the heart of every ethical, indeed also every non-ethical, decision a person might make; you cannot go on, but you will, and must, go on.

Following his discussions of self-inspection and self-disregard, Geulincx details seven ethical obligations that are consequent upon this binary conception of humility. *Ethics* thereby becomes wider in scope by making a clear transition from a theoretical to a practical ethics. Obligations, Geulincx solemnly asserts, are the inevitable guiding rules to which one who lives a blessed life must adhere: 'I must labour not over my own happiness, blessedness, or repose, but over my obligations alone' (p. 337). Yet these obligations do not counsel stoic abstinence or solipsistic resignation. In detailing his sixth obligation, for instance, Geulincx describes how a loss of control over oneself when getting drunk can act as a sure way of revealing one's true ethical self, and so is to be encouraged as a good test: '*In vino veritas* [In wine there is truth]. Only a virtuous man, who never hides his true colours, comes out well here' (p. 349). The seven obligations are as follows:

(1) When God summons me from the living, and orders me to return to Him, I must not persist in refusal, but hold myself ready. (p. 338)

(2) [. . .] not to depart this life unless God has summoned you. (p. 339)

(3) The Third Obligation concerns the need to refresh the body. It arises from the Second Obligation; for if you do not refresh the body, it will fail; which the Second Obligation forbids. (p. 343)

(4) (1) Choice of mode of life; (2) Devotion to this mode of life; (3) Constancy in this mode of life; (4) The vicissitudes of this mode of life. (p. 346)

(5) To bear many things, to do many things; for sometimes I cannot find a mode of life that is productive and affords me sustenance. (p. 347)

(6) [. . .] the rule that one should frequently relax the mind, lest it become jaded by incessant business. (p. 348)

(7) I should look upon my birth as a good, never detest it, and never lament it. I must not rage with madness and impotence that I am punished by having been born. I must not revile those who engendered my body. (p. 350)

Beckett's notes begin to fade away towards the end of this section, after he records Geulincx's comments on original sin – a topic that Beckett also returns to throughout his oeuvre. He did not type up all the handwritten notes he produced on the seventh obligation, and there is one final manuscript section to the transcriptions. '*The Adminicule of Humility*' (p. 352) is Geulincx's admonition to flee from happiness in order that it might pursue you, arguing that a person will never attain happiness if pursuing it: 'Happiness is like a shadow: it flees from you when you pursue it; but pursues you when you flee from it' (p. 353). Geulincx's note of leave-taking appears to have also been Beckett's cue to take his leave from Geulincx.

Beckett's notes are all from Treatise 1 and its annotations. *Ethica* continues for a further five Treatises. Lest this gap in the transcriptions be taken as evidence that Beckett was only interested in Geulincx in a piecemeal way, it is important to point out that the first Treatise, which occupies around two-thirds of the final version, was published by Geulincx as a stand-alone edition in 1667 as *Van de Hooft-deuchden: De eerste Tucht-verhandeling*, and that many of the later sections of *Ethica* repeat material from Treatise 1. The later sections are accompanied by relatively few annotations, in contrast to the earlier, lengthy notes – a consequence of *Ethica* being partially edited posthumously by Geulincx's students. Treatises beyond the first include chapters on 'THE VIRTUES COMMONLY CALLED PARTICULAR' (p. 65), 'THE END AND THE GOOD' (p. 95), 'THE PASSIONS' (p. 109), 'THE REWARD OF VIRTUE' (p. 127) and 'PRUDENCE' (p. 151). In order to focus on the aspects of Geulincx that Beckett focused on (as well as for reasons of space), *Ethica*'s later treatises are not summarized here. Instead, the remainder of Chapter 1 is dedicated to empirical groundwork that establishes further connections between Geulincx and Beckett. My focus is first on aspects of the notes and transcriptions Beckett produced that refer to Geulincx, before turning to a detailed analysis of the revealing private correspondence in which Beckett discusses the philosopher.

Geulincx in the Early 1930s 'Philosophy Notes'

Beckett's first known encounter with Geulincx and Occasionalism was via Windelband's *A History of Philosophy*. Following Windelband's lead, Beckett took notes on Occasionalism's inheriting unresolved issues of mind/body dualism from Descartes. The notes describe a somewhat anthropomorphically insolent Cartesian dualism:

> The nature of man consists in the inner union, metaphysically incomprehensible, of two heterogeneous substances, mind and body, and this is the only instance of interaction between the conscious and spatial. Animals are mere bodies, but in humans the form of spiritus animales in pineal gland (conarium) disturbs the mental substance and gives rise to unclear and indistinct idea (emotion, passion, perturbation animi). (TCD MS 10967/189r)

Beckett then summarizes how a consequent 'theory of influxus physicus led to a revision of theory of causality'. This revision of 'psycho-physical' interaction argued that the:

> true functions in causal relation are not causae efficientes, but causae occasionales. The ultimate 'cause' for causal connection between stimuli and sensations, purpose and action, is God. This is occasionalism. (TCD MS 10967/189r)

Following Windelband, Beckett names Geulincx as the thinker who takes Occasionalism to its extreme:

> This furthest developed in <u>Ethics</u> of <u>Geulincx</u>. Illustration of the 2 Clocks which having once been synchronised by same artificer continue to move in perfect harmony, 'absque ulla causalitate qua alterum hoc in altero causat, sed propter meram dependentiam, qua utrumque ab eadem arte et simili industria constitutum est'.
>
> What anthropologism!
>
> Leibniz illustrated with same analogy his doctrine of 'preestablished harmony', characterised Cartesian conception by immediate and permanent interdependence of 2 clocks, and Occasionalist by constantly renewed regulation of clocks by clock master. (TCD MS 10967/189r–189v)[23]

The Latin quotation that Windelband gives from Geulincx is also translated in the italics of the following passage in Beckett's *Ethica* transcriptions.

> It is the same as if two clocks agree precisely with each other and with the daily course of the Sun: when one chimes and tells the hours, the other also chimes and likewise indicates the hour; *and all that without any causality in the sense of one having a causal effect on the other, but rather on account of mere dependence, inasmuch as both of them have been constructed with the same art and similar industry.* (*Et*, p. 332, my italics)

This historically important passage is the section in *Ethics* around which debate arose in the nineteenth century disputing the provenance of Leibniz's more famous clock simile.[24] The passage's duplication across Beckett's notes marks an important, precise point of continuity between the cribbing 'Philosophy Notes' of the early 1930s and later more in-depth study. The duplication also reveals, of course, Beckett's familiarity with the central tenet of Geulincx's metaphysics, with that which Geulincx takes 'furthest' and upon which he builds his ethics: his resolution of the problems of causality in the 'ultimate "cause"', the agency of God.

Beckett's early notes are only a glimpse of what was to come, gesturing towards the relations between Geulincx's epistemology, metaphysics and ethics. It was here that Beckett wrote out the axiom for the first time:

> Geulincx reduces self-activity to immanent mental activity in man. The 'autology' or <u>inspectio sui</u> is not only epistemological starting point, it is also ethical conclusion of his system. Man has nothing to do in outer world. <u>Ubi nihil vales, ibi nihil velis</u>. Highest virtue humility – <u>despectio sui</u>. (TCD MS 10967/189v)[25]

Just as Geulincx himself did, Beckett saw this axiom as holding all Geulincx's philosophy in its neatly balanced grasp. Though as has already been seen, a summary of Geulincx's philosophy as arising from the proposition that humanity 'has nothing to do in outer world' sells the practical aspects of Geulincx's system somewhat short. It would take a much more concerted effort on Beckett's part to address this inadequacy. Once behind TCD's gates in 1936 Beckett worked assiduously on his transcriptions. In order to gain a better appreciation of the work he was engaged in for a few months of that year, with a view to then being able to determine more accurately how this informs his literary work, attention turns to an archaeology of these surviving notes.

Geulincx in the 1936 Transcriptions: TCD MS 10971/6

Beckett transcribed only five sentences on a single folio from *Questiones Quodlibeticae*.[26] The 10 folios (recto and verso) of notes from *Metaphysica Vera* are much more thorough, summarizing as they do sections from the entire work.[27] The most extensive notes are from *Ethica*, some 40 sides of which survive as two typescripts and a manuscript.[28] The first fair copy comprises 18 typed sides,[29] the second fair copy a further 18,[30] the manuscript 4.[31] *Ethica* forms the major part of Land's final volume of the three-volume *Opera*, and Beckett's proportional focus on it indicates he was not reading the collected works exhaustively from start to finish but was concentrating instead on discrete works; one from each of the three volumes. Beckett's working process can be adduced with some confidence from the pages of the *Ethica* material, as scholars have noted.[32] For instance, a first fair copy includes a number of handwritten corrections, which are incorporated as typescript into a second fair copy. This second repeats the material of the first and extends it, the handwritten corrections of the first inserted where appropriate as typed text in the second. The final four handwritten foolscap pages begin, with a little overlap, where the second fair copy finishes.[33] This manuscript ends with roughly a quarter of a page left blank, near the end of *Ethica*'s Treatise 1, at '11. <u>Adminiculum Humilitatis</u>', suggesting this was the precise point at which, as Beckett admitted to MacGreevy, he 'could not quite finish the Ethic' (SB to TM, 9 April 1936)[34]. What appears beyond much doubt is that Beckett first took handwritten notes, presumably while in the library, and that he then typed these up adding handwritten corrections and insertions, before retyping this first fair copy, incorporating corrections into the text, and rearranging the order of some paragraphs to incorporate Geulincx's annotations into the body of the main text.[35] He then left aside a final few pages as manuscript, and thereby for a second time 'could not quite finish the Ethic'.

There is, however, an issue involving the composition of the notes that is less clear, and that has potentially important implications for thinking about how Beckett's interest in Geulincx might come through in his writing of this early period. Typically Beckett's research into Geulincx is thought to coincide exactly with his first mentioning it in correspondence to MacGreevy in early January 1936. Yet scholars have argued that there are anomalies in the notes that point to Beckett using an edition of Geulincx's works other than *Opera*, and/or earlier than this. The questions bear in turn on the extent to which Geulincx might be said to have influenced the composition of *Murphy*, because if Beckett's transcriptions were not all from *Opera*, then perhaps they are not all from TCD in 1936. Perhaps, that is, Beckett was reading Geulincx during earlier stages of *Murphy*'s composition. While the question of Beckett's research becoming one of precise dating – whether Beckett was reading Geulincx in London in 1935 – might appear somewhat esoteric, of little interest other than as a matter of biographical footnoting, it has wider ramifications for how *Murphy* (written between August 1935 and June 1936) can be characterized, as it frequently is, as a *philosophical* novel. The issue, that is, promises to take us closer towards understanding what exactly a philosophical novel was for Beckett in the 1930s.

One anomaly that might indicate Beckett's using different versions of *Ethica* is the variation among how Geulincx's name is spelled. Everett Frost and Jane Maxwell point out that Beckett's 'spelling [. . .] of "Arnoldus" and "Geulinx" (unusual but not unprecedented) may mean that he began his study in something other than the Land edition'. Land consistently spells the name throughout *Opera* as 'Arnoldi Geulincx', in large bold type on each volume's title page and throughout the edition. However, the attribution of Beckett's variant spelling to 'fols 1–15' (Frost and Maxwell 2006, p. 145) – the entire first fair copy – is inaccurate. Beckett does indeed write 'Geulinx' at the beginning of his notes, but on fol. 11v he uses the correct (or at least standardized by Land) spelling of 'Geulincx', where the name appears as one of very few interjections or marginalia added by Beckett to the otherwise faithfully transcribed notes. In a paragraph Geulincx addresses to a fictional ethical novitiate Philaretus (the moniker later adopted by Geulincx's student Cornelius Bontekoe when he edited Geulincx's works) Beckett notes: 'Geulincx's fictitious apostrophee [sic], virtuous but hasty' (TCD MS 10971/6/11v).[36] Undoubtedly it would be convenient had Beckett used a particular spelling in one fair copy, and another spelling for the second, leading as it might to the supposition that he was in a different location, transcribing from a different edition, when he produced each of the two sets of notes. Unfortunately, the identifications are not this neat.

Beckett did hold a ticket for the Reading Room of the British Museum. His application for it is dated 27/7/32[37] and it was renewed a number of times over the following few years while he was a resident in London (which he was between January and late December 1935[38]). Might he have consulted editions of *Ethica* other than Land's, or even other texts by Geulincx held at the British Museum? Geulincx's name is spelled in a number of different ways in publications the British Library (then housed in the British Museum) held on and by Geulincx in 1935–6. A version of *Physica Vera* (which includes *Metaphysica Vera*) published in the same edition as Bontekoe's own *Metaphysica* and edited by Bontekoe in 1688, has Bontekoe's name on the spine of the book but does refer, in the introductory essay a number of times, to 'Arnoldus Geulinx', the spelling that matches Beckett's initial variant. Bontekoe then uses 'Arnoldi Geulincx' on *Physica Vera*'s title page. The pattern of using a number of Latin cases in the same edition is also continued in the two editions of *Ethica* other than Land's that Beckett could have consulted in the British Museum in 1935. However, these editions also exhibit other variants. In the 1675 edition of *Ethica* the author is named on the title page as 'Arnoldi Geulincs'. Yet, in this edition's introductory chapter reference is made to 'Arnoldus Geulinxs', 'Arnoldi Geulinxs' and 'Arnoldus Geulinx', only this final a match for Beckett's. Other declensions and variants include 'Arnoldum', 'Geulingius', and 'Geulingi'. In the 1709 edition, again attributed on the title page to 'Arnoldi Geulincs', Geulincx's own *Dedicatio Auctoris* is signed 'A. Geulinck'. The conclusion all this leads to is that if Beckett did consult one of these other editions at all then the more likely candidate looks to be the 1675 *Ethica*, with Beckett first reading the introductory essay by Bontekoe and transcribing the spelling used there before correcting it when he later came to use Land. Yet this is far from convincing evidence that he used the earlier edition, and it also does nothing to settle the possibility of whether he consulted Land's *Opera* first in London.[39]

Leaving aside names, a second route of inquiry involves the typewriter Beckett used. Frost and Maxwell are certain that the first and second fair copies of *Ethica* notes:

> are from the same typewriter as used for TCD MS 10967 (Western philosophy), as evidenced by the offset figure '2' and left hand round bracket, and for typewritten correspondence originating variously from Dublin or Foxrock (for example, TCD MS 10402/25); but not the same typewriter as TCD MS 10971/5 (Mauthner). (Frost and Maxwell 2006, p. 142)

This is in contrast to the editors of *Ethics*, who advance the following:

> There is also some evidence that a different typewriter was used in preparing the second fair copy: the letter capital 'D' which occurs in words such as 'Deum', is at times barely visible in the second fair copy. (*Et*, p. 308)

What is of primary interest here, of course, is less the actual typewriter Beckett used than the location at which he typed up his notes, it being plausible that different typewriters were used in London and Dublin. Unfortunately, again no identifications this neat can be claimed. There is very little evidence of differences in idiosyncrasies caused by varying typewriters between the two fair copies. Van Ruler, Uhlmann and Wilson appear to overstate any discrepancies between the two typescripts. Indeed the similarity (noted by Frost and Maxwell) of the left open bracket in each typescript looks to settle this issue on its own. Wider at the top than the bottom, this bracket, and the less often used numerical '2' which appears with a faint shadow of itself and at a slight angle, both clearly look to come from a single typewriter. The capital letter 'D', cited by van Ruler, Uhlmann and Wilson as a reason for positing a second typewriter, is very rarely distinct from its appearance in the first fair copy.

Perhaps Beckett's method of organizing his material on the page might offer some assistance. In the *Ethica* notes he organizes the paragraphs according to capital letters. These letters correspond to Geulincx's Arabic numerals (with lowercase 'a' added by Beckett where relevant to indicate that a portion is taken from an annotation); Beckett notes 'C' in the margin as corresponding to a section in *Ethica* Geulincx titles '3'. It is a difference that may derive from Beckett's seeing, in earlier editions of *Ethica* than *Opera*'s, the book subdivided into lettered sections. For example, located between the main text and the annotations (recto only) in earlier editions is a capital letter. 'A' begins the sequence and the next five pages are labelled respectively 'A2', 'A3', 'A4', 'A5' and 'A6'. The six pages in the sequence after this have neither letter nor numerical indicator, prior to the next sequence beginning with the following alphabetical letter. Yet the sequencing is a mark of an outmoded publishing convention required by a book's being bound with multiple folded sheets, and so requiring some way of correlating a large single sheet's sections with page order (i.e. sheet A is a single sheet of paper, while the numbers indicate the order that sections of this sheet should appear in when folded correctly). Potentially Beckett saw this system in the opening pages of *Ethica* where there is a coincidence of paragraph numbers and the pagination system, and began to follow the use of the capital letters. He then simply continued with this system after he would have realized the coincidence only lasts the few opening pages. But again the issue cannot be settled. Beckett's organization of Geulincx's paragraphs is surely less likely due to this technical and archaic pagination system than it is to a shuttling back and forth among the book's well-organized sections, Beckett reading the annotations as he went (as they are indicated in the main text) and transcribing them in the order that matched his reading, and thereby avoiding being what *Murphy*'s narrator dismissively calls a 'gentle skimmer' (*Mu*, p. 54).

The strongest evidence for claiming Beckett consulted a version of *Ethica* other than that in *Opera* is the divergence the notes take from verbatim transcriptions of Land's text. Such differences are numerous, with many occurring on a single page. To take just fol. 7r (the first page of *Ethica* notes), variations include the following:

Land: 'Igitur in Sapientae fano' (*Op* vol. 3, p. 4)

Beckett: 'In Sapientae fano' (TCD MS 10971/6/7r)

Land: 'Imo fine Ethica' (*Op* vol. 3, p. 4)

Beckett: 'Sine Ethica' (TCD MS 10971/6/7r)

Land: 'Non enim eaedem mihi *Virtutes*' (*Op* vol. 3, p. 6)

Beckett: 'Non mihi <u>Virtutes</u>' (TCD MS 10971/6/7r)

Land: 'At vero nullum' (*Op* vol. 3, p. 6)

Beckett: 'Vero nullum' (TCD MS 10971/6/7r)

What these variants indicate, however, rather than an edition other than Land's, is Beckett's excellent command of Latin. They reveal that he knew where he could condense his transcriptions without losing the text's meaning. Often, as in these few examples, the paraphrasing amounted to little more than missing out either the first word of a sentence or the occasional conjunction. Beckett had studied Latin as one of the privileges of a Protestant upper-middle-class education at Portora Royal School, where it was a compulsory course taught first by, as James Knowlson reports, the 'much respected Mr A. T. M. Murfet' and then by the Headmaster (Reverend Ernest G. Seale), also 'a good classical scholar' (Knowlson 1996, p. 41).[40] Both earlier editions of *Ethica* held at the British Library correspond to Land's text much more closely than they do to Beckett's variants (indeed, none of these missing words from Beckett's transcriptions are also missing from either earlier version). Consequently, while it must remain a remote possibility that Beckett consulted Geulincx in London prior to his Christmas 1935 move to Dublin, it seems beyond much reasonable doubt that if he did then he consulted Land's *Opera* as he would at TCD, and there is little if any reason to suppose that he even did this. Claims such as 'It seems more likely that Beckett began reading Geulincx in London' (Frost and Maxwell 2006, p. 145) cannot be strongly maintained without evidence, however much we might wish onto Beckett a longer initial period of engagement with Geulincx's texts. The deviations from *Opera* surely derive from his confidence with Latin rather than another edition. Such a conclusion, combined with evidence about the typewriter, indicates that the familiar story is indeed the most likely if less exciting one; Beckett first came into contact with Geulincx's original texts in TCD, in January 1936, when he was already well on with *Murphy*.

The Correspondence (1936–67)

Beckett wrote to critics and friends on the subject of Geulincx at regular, if infrequent, intervals over a 31-year period. In these letters Beckett either gave the name of the philosopher, quoted the axiom or used other terminology central to Geulincx's metaphysics or ethics. The correspondence that covers this lengthy period, which began alongside writing *Murphy*, has never previously been compiled in one place, some of it remaining unpublished until now. Along with the variously concealed or open allusions to and direct quotations from Geulincx appearing throughout the prose and drama, it forms a fundamental basis for any investigation into Geulincx's various influences upon Beckett's creative work and critical and philosophical thinking.

The first mention of Geulincx in Beckett's correspondence is in a letter to MacGreevy of 9 January 1936 where Beckett writes of his new research:

> I put my foot within the abhorred gates for the first time since the escape, on a commission from Ruddy. And I fear I shall have to penetrate more deeply, in search of Geulincx, who does not exist in the National [Library], but does in TCD. (SB to TM, 9 January 1936)[41]

'Ruddy' (Thomas Rudmose-Brown), professor of Romance Languages at TCD and Beckett's tutor and friend, appears in *Dream of Fair to Middling Women* as the Polar Bear, a caricature among others that Beckett came to regret given his indebtedness to Rudmose-Brown's encouragement and interest, the tutor fostering Beckett's wide-ranging literary education while at TCD.[42] The 'escape' refers to Beckett's difficult decision to resign from a teaching post at the college,[43] while the 'And' most likely implies that the 'commission from Ruddy' and being 'in search of Geulincx' are not one and the same task. Motivation for the latter derived from somewhere else, and although it is difficult to determine exactly where, Beckett gave a clue in a letter to Reavey written the same day:

> I said i [sic] was not keen on doing more translations, but would if necessary. He [Brian Coffey] appears to want to make the philosophical series very serious & Fach. But my Geulincx could only be a literary fantasia. (SB to GR, 9 January 1936: *L1*, p. 295)

According to the editors of Beckett's selected letters, Coffey was planning to publish a series of philosophical monographs, and had asked Beckett to produce one such book on Geulincx. Martha Fehsenfeld and Lois Overbeck write that 'Coffey encouraged SB to read Geulincx for a possible monograph in a Philosophy series he envisioned' (*L1*, p. 692), and assert even more directly that 'he [Coffey] had proposed that SB prepare a monograph on Geulincx' (*L1*,

p. 309). Such a 'commission' would explain why Beckett ventured so 'deeply, in search of Geulincx', but importantly there appears to be no extant evidence to substantiate the claim that he had seriously considered writing this book. While Coffey may indeed have been planning a series of monographs, there are few surviving letters between Beckett and Coffey that could bear on the issue of any planned contribution from Beckett.[44] Mark Nixon, one among a number of scholars sceptical of this monograph rumour, concludes that such an extrapolation 'is a misinterpretation of the "literary fantasia" quotation'.[45]

There are precedents for Coffey's involvement in Beckett's philosophical reading. Coffey lent Beckett Spinoza's *Ethics* in 1936, for example, a work that Beckett had some trouble with.[46] Yet had Coffey also been the person to direct Beckett to Geulincx it is likely this would have received mention in Coffey's memoir of his involvement with Beckett in the 1930s and the concomitant composition of *Murphy*. Yet all Coffey records in *Memory's Murphy Maker* (1962, reprinted 1991) is the following, which appears in the context of a discussion of the Descartes of 'Whoroscope':

> As a consequence of the original *distinction* (of body and soul), post-Cartesian thinking reached curious positions of involvement with theology. One such thinker was Geulincx, concerning whom I had a p.c. from Beckett asking questions. (Coffey 1991, p. 3)

Beckett mentions what was probably this personal *communiqué* or postcard. In a letter of 29 January 1936 he told MacGreevy that he has not heard from Coffey, who had 'promised me Geulincx & Eluard informations' (SB to TM, 29 January 1936: *L1*, p. 305).

This issue of whether or not Beckett's interest in Geulincx was rekindled by Coffey, and to what ends, cannot be definitively resolved. As Garin Dowd has pointed out in an argument against the imposition of strict empiricist boundaries on readings of Beckett's texts, the 1936 Geulincx transcriptions are fundamentally 'of uncertain status' (Dowd 2008, p. 387). We cannot say, that is, *why* Beckett produced them. There are a number of possibilities, many of which are persuasive. Yet despite attempts to settle this issue as far as it can be settled, it remains stubbornly elusive. Dowd argues that this important elusiveness reminds readers how it can be impossible to trace the entirety of the literary act to a concomitant verifiable location in a world of physicality, of philosophical transcriptions, notebooks, correspondence and draft material. However, an argument that admits the elusiveness of Beckett's Geulincx transcriptions only as a result of missing empirical evidence would somewhat miss the point that is made by Dowd. The transcriptions will remain 'of uncertain status', even if, for example, rumours about Beckett planning a Geulincx monograph can at some point be definitively settled. It is an uncertainty that is made even less stable when we consider in more detail the terms in which

Beckett described his research. For instance, the 9 January letter to Reavey describing 'my Geulincx' as 'a literary fantasia' is fundamental to a consideration of Beckett's interest in Geulincx; Beckett's contrast, rendered in musical terms between 'Fach' and 'fantasia', is highly resonant. Colloquially meaning compartment or subject, the Fach system delineates an opera singer's voice category, classifying it according to range and tone. It is a system of strict though not always mutually exclusive musical boundaries, and it predominantly correlates with English classifications of Soprano, Contralto, Tenor, Baritone, Bass and their subcategories. A particular singer graded according to a certain Fach will be called upon to perform a given role written for a specific style of voice (which might not necessarily correspond to a single Fach). The word Beckett chooses to contrast with Fach, 'fantasia', is usefully defined by Grove Music as follows:

> A term adopted in the Renaissance for an instrumental composition whose form and invention spring 'solely from the fantasy and skill of the author who created it' (Luis de Milán, 1535–36). From the 16th century to the 19th the fantasia tended to retain this subjective licence, and its formal and stylistic characteristics may consequently vary widely from free, improvisatory types to strictly contrapuntal and more or less standard sectional forms.[47]

While there is not the requisite space here to detail the many historical changes to the expansive and mutable musical 'fantasia' form, the emphasis across its history on a 'subjective licence' that is potentially 'improvisatory' is crucial to bear in mind. As well as the capacity of the term to refer to what might be 'more or less standard' forms, the fantasia also, by virtue of its essential mutability, stands in stark contrast to a strictly categorized Fach system. Beckett's Geulincx, regardless of whether this was a critical monograph to be edited by Coffey, or a Geulincx of Beckett's imagination yet to be rendered in any form, is a Geulincx of whom Beckett asserts his own 'subjective licence'; 'my Geulincx' might 'vary widely' from anyone else's reading of the philosopher. However, 'my Geulincx' might also bear a close resemblance to a 'more or less standard' rendering of the philosopher. By denoting Geulincx as a 'fantasia' these become equally valid possibilities, underwriting the individuality and the viability of Beckett's own reading. Beckett shifts the ground away from the possibility of properly asking of his philosophical reading whether it might be correct and accurate or not, and thereby also opens the possibility for a Geulincx that is, as well as the notes on him, 'of uncertain status'.[48]

This musical contrast Beckett sets up in relation to Geulincx is not dissimilar to references he also made to Schopenhauer. In a 1932 letter to MacGreevy, for example, he described reading this other favoured philosopher of abstention and will-lessness in terms that evidenced the extrication of his reading from a predetermined, Fach-style framework:

> I am not reading philosophy, nor caring whether he is right or wrong or a good or worthless metaphysician. An intellectual justification of unhappiness – the greatest that has ever been attempted – is worth the examination of one who is interested in Leopardi & Proust rather than in Carducci & Barrès. (SB to TM, c. 18–25 July 1930: *L1*, p. 33)

Similarly, 7 years later Beckett wrote that while he had been ill 'the only thing I could read was Schopenhauer [. . .] it is a pleasure also to find a philosopher that can be read like a poet, with an entire indifference to the apriori forms of verification' (SB to TM, 21 September 1937: *L1*, p. 550). In these letters Beckett's responses to philosophy extend beyond the bounds of analytic accuracy; Beckett does not hear the philosophical voice of Schopenhauer as one to be strictly classified in a Fach-styled analysis. The voice Beckett hears is one that speaks poetically and intellectually about emotional and psychological experience, a voice with a range that extends beyond pre-assigned, in this case strictly philosophical, categories. Such an interdisciplinary conception of Schopenhauer, however, his 'my Schopenhauer', also owes a debt to a hard-tasking autodidacticism, as is also the case with Geulincx. That is to say, these assessments of the poetic philosopher are far from flippant or callow. They are informed by deep research as well as a poetic sensibility. The description of 'a philosopher that can be read like a poet', for example, echoes the 'Philosophy Notes' of a few years earlier:

> Schopenhauer became – leaving the weaknesses of his system aside – one of the greatest philosophical writers because – in contrast to Hegel – he put the world back in its rightful place, because he attempted to think perspicuously. One reads him therefore with the admiration with which one once read Plato. Whoever demands from philosophy no more than the highest conceivable perspicuity, the liveliest metaphorical representation of abstract concepts, must call him a tremendous thinker-poet. (TCD MS 10967/478)

Beckett's own thoughts about these ethical philosophers of will and abstention, then, are simultaneously owed to the hard work of philosophical investigation, as well as to the freeform associations of fantasy. The two are not necessarily mutually exclusive; there is 'Fach' within Beckett's 'fantasia'.

Beckett might also have had Giambattista Vico's ideas of 'fantasia' in mind when he wrote of a 'literary fantasia'. He had researched Vico for work on Joyce's then-titled *Work in Progress*, and may well have come across Vico's conception of fantasia as a form of imagination. Fantasia for Vico exists as a stage between *memoria*, which merely remembers things, and *ingegno*, which can be called 'invention when it gives them a new turn or puts them into proper arrangement and relationship' (Vico 1988, p. 819). As David Walter Price describes it, for Vico fantasia is 'the essence of the poetic wisdom of the ancients', and without it 'meaning is impossible' (Price 1999, p. 68). Similarly to a musical sense of the word it involves change, and comes midway between a conservative and an unprecedentedly new sense of something. It implies adherence at the same time as breaking free, requiring 'the active construction of images in pursuit of a mimetic or an expressive mode of re-presenting to the mind what took place in the past' (p. 65). As will be argued in chapters that follow, memory has important parts to play in Beckett's returning to Geulincx.[49]

Following the 'fantasia' letter to Reavey, in further private correspondence Beckett began to quote Geulincx's ethical axiom repeatedly, in what might be termed the *basse fondamentale* or the root note of his semi-improvisatory incorporations of Geulincx. It is evidence that he was starting to get to grips with the substance of this philosophy:

> No news from Coffey since I saw him here. I shall have to go into TCD after Geulincx, as he does not exist in National Library. I suddenly see that Murphy is break down between his ubi nihil vales ibi nihil velis (positive) and Malraux's Il est difficile à celui qui vit hors du monde de ne pas rechercher les siens (negation). (SB to TM, 16 January 1936: *L1*, p. 299)[50]

As he frequently does when citing the axiom in correspondence, Beckett contrasts it with a further 'phrase-bomb', here a quotation from Malraux's *La Condition Humaine* ('it is difficult for one who lives isolated from the everyday world not to seek others like himself'[51]). The perspective adapted from Malraux is that of Tchen (Ch'en in the English translation), a political activist who plans to blow himself up in an act of terrorism, and requires solitude to organize this despite the temptations of company. Nixon describes Beckett's use of Malraux's politically minded Tchen:

> Unsurprisingly, Beckett removes the references to the committed man, thus obscuring a complexity that pertains to his own thinking at both this and a later time. For Beckett, the artist is as committed as the political activist, although the investment of energy is directed inwards rather than outwards. (Nixon 2011, p. 56)

At the beginning of March 1936 Beckett was deeply engaged with the Geulincx research as well as with thinking about its causes and consequences, as his most complex letter about the work attests:

> I have been reading Geulincx in T.C.D., without knowing why exactly. Perhaps because the text is so hard to come by. But that is rationalisation & my instinct

is right & the work worth doing, because of its saturation in the conviction that the <u>sub specie aeternitatis</u> [from the perspective of eternity] vision is the only excuse for remaining alive. (SB to TM, 5 March 1936: *L1*, pp. 318–19)

Beckett's enthusiasm for his research is clear, and the letter speaks of its personal importance to him. He goes on in the letter to situate Geulincx's central principles of *inspectio sui* and *despectio sui*, the inward looking at self and the outward looking at the world, in relation to a range of classical mythological and modern literary and philosophical references:

He does not put out his eyes on that account, as Heraclitus did & Rimbaud began to, nor like the terrified Berkeley repudiate them. One feels them very patiently turned outward, & without Schwärmerei turned in-ward, Janus or Telephus eyes, like those of Frenhofer in the <u>Chef d'Oeuvre Inconnu</u>, when he shall have forgotten Mabuse & ceased to barbouiller. (SB to TM, 5 March 1936: *L1*, p. 319)

In different ways George Berkeley, Arthur Rimbaud and Heraclitus all turned away from reality or otherwise stopped their eyes from seeing. Berkeley's importance to Beckett is evidenced by, as one example among a number, *Film* (1964) exploring for purposes of merely 'structural and dramatic convenience' (*CDW*, p. 323) Berkeley's axiom *Esse est percipi* [to be is to be perceived]. Berkeley's idealist contention that no objects of the perceived world exist except but in the mind of their perceiver is also employed as a 'dramatic convenience' in other of Beckett's works, but it finds particular and explicit focus in *Film*.[52] Rimbaud's, as Beckett called it in 1931, 'eye-suicide – <u>pour des visions</u> [for the visions]' (SB to TM, 11 March 1931: *L1*, p. 73), was an exploration of poetic vision by a child who in 'Les Poètes de sept ans' [The Seven-Year-Old Poets] squeezes his eyes to produce hallucinogenic, hypnagogic visions:

En passant il tirait la langue, les deux poings
À l'aine, et dans ses yeux fermés voyait des points.
Une porte s'ouvrait sur le soir: à la lampe
On le voyait, là-haut, qui râlait sur la rampe,
Sous un golfe de jour pendent du toit.   (Rimbaud 2009, p. 96)

He'd run by, sticking out his tongue, fists
In crotch, eyes shut tight, seeing stars.
A door opened onto evening; up
There among the banisters he'd rant
And rave in a pool of ceiling light.   (p. 97)

This concept of the sightless seer, which has a precedent in Beckett's earlier interest in (and translations of) Rimbaud, was also an important motif in later years.[53]

As Shane Weller has pointed out of what he describes as 'an early form of the "pseudocouple"' (Weller 2005, p. 2), Heraclitus (c. 540–480 BC) the 'weeping philosopher' is frequently paired with Democritus (c. 460–370 BC) the 'laughing philosopher' by Beckett, but also by thinkers as far back as antiquity, re-emerging in the sixteenth century. Heraclitus 'put out his eyes', then, by weeping in empathy for humankind. Heraclitus's legacy to Beckett's oeuvre is also partly in terms of the doctrine of flux, according to which all things are in a state of change. Consequently, pause, a stilled moment, is impossible. Such impossibility does not, however, prevent many of Beckett's protagonists from attempting it.[54]

According to Beckett's comparisons, Geulincx's eyes are able patiently and with discipline to face the vicissitudes of an outward world without turning away or closing, in awareness too that an inner world offers little real refuge. Like the two-faced Roman God Janus, Geulincx offers a gaze that simultaneously and without 'Schwärmerei' [fanaticism, or raving] can look in these two directions. Beckett's reference to Telephus is similarly to a narrative of doubled self; it is to the myth of Telephus's stab wound received from Achilles, a wound that would not heal unless Telephus scraped pieces of the very spear that had caused the injury into his wound. The wound could only be cured by a return to its own origin. Analogously, Geulincx's *inspectio sui* only finds its proper conclusion and resolution in a return to the world from which the philosopher originally withdrew, a return to origins Geulincx characterizes as *despectio sui*.[55]

The name Frenhoffer derives from Balzac's *Le Chef d'oeuvre inconnu* [*The Unknown Masterpiece*] (1832). In the short story the elderly painter Frenhoffer reveals a secretive portrait he has been working on for 10 years to two younger painters (Poussin and Porbus) in exchange for the opportunity to paint Poussin's beautiful lover. Yet in a legacy of Mabuse, who had been Frenhoffer's teacher and had only ever taught this one student, Frenhoffer has laboured too long on a single thing – the picture he mistakenly believes to be his masterpiece. The less experienced painters point out that the portrait has been obscured to such a degree by perpetual layering ('barbouiller' – to daub, or smear) that barely a foot of the sitter is recognizable. In *Le Chef d'oeuvre inconnu* Frenhoffer never finds freedom from his teacher's legacy, never having 'forgotten Mabuse'. He realizes his spectacular failure, and dies after burning his canvasses. All of Frenhoffer's eloquent criticism of art as a visionary incarnation of nature, rather than a mere following of its contours, according to which 'The mission of art is not to copy nature, but to give expression to it' (Balzac 2007, p. 12), comes to nothing. According to Beckett, in contrast to Frenhoffer Geulincx does manage to free himself from a burdensome legacy, and achieves a freedom in turning (towards the world) from the accreted layers of redoing the same old thing (looking at the self). If we are to find one single point at which many of the ways in which Geulincx's ethical lessons of humility, self-inspection and turning again towards the world operated for Beckett in the mid-thirties, it is in this single letter where Beckett also claims to have found a personal justification, indeed according to this letter the only justification possible, for being in the world. This answer to original sin, a notable and continual preoccupation of Beckett's throughout the course of his writing, comes couched in a range of reference that lays out the interdisciplinary nature of Beckett's interwar self-education, while at the same time this 'work worth doing' already shows itself to bear on his other, literary work, *Murphy*.

Twenty days after this March letter Beckett briefly mentioned his research to MacGreevy, along with his lassitude at the family home:

> The days pass pearly, mild and tolerable. I seldom go to town, unless to read Geulincx in Trinity or do a pressing tot or square for Frank when hard beset. (SB to TM, 25 March 1936: *L1*, pp. 323–4)

Another letter was addressed to Arland Ussher and it also speaks of Beckett's enthusiasm:

> I am obliged to read in Trinity College Library, as Arnoldus Geulincx is not available elsewhere. I recommend him to you most heartily, especially his Ethica, and above all the second section of the second chapter of the first tractate, where he disquires on his fourth cardinal virtue, Humility, contemptus negativus sui ipsius [comprising its own contemptible negation].
>
> Humiliter, Simpliciter, Fideliter,
>
> Sam (SB to AU, 25 March 1936: *L1*, p. 329)

Despite this enthusiasm, Beckett did eventually run out of energy for the work, as he confessed to MacGreevy on 9 April:

> I could not quite finish the Ethic of Geulincx, à l'impossible nul n'est tenu [no one can be expected to achieve the impossible], not even in Lent. (SB to TM, 9 April 1936)[56]

Beckett's playing with a French proverb here relies a little on MacGreevy knowing something of Geulincx's ethics of abstinence. Being unable to fully follow Geulincx 'even in Lent' makes a joke not only of Beckett as a very 'dirty low-church P.[rotestant]' (SB to TM, 18 October 1932: *L1*, p. 134), but also of Geulincx's ethical lessons about the impossibility of achievement as themselves impossible to achieve, even given favourable circumstances. By the time Beckett wrote this he had taken notes from *Questiones Quodlibeticae*, *Metaphysica Vera* and approximately two-thirds of *Ethica*, and had stopped where the posthumously edited sections of *Ethica* begin. However, Beckett did not stop writing about Geulincx to correspondents once he was again free from TCD in 1936.

Two letters to Georges Duthuit from spring 1949 refer to Geulincx.[57] In the first, the ethical axiom is again cited in relation to *Murphy*:

> C'est vraiment très simple, mon cher Georges, et pas métaphysique ni mystique pour un liard, ce que nous avons pigé. C'est même le sens commun, bon et rond comme le dos de d'Alembert. Dans la vieille phrase de Geulincx citée dans <u>Murphy</u>, un peu à l'aveuglette il est vrai, tout est dit: <u>Ubi nihil vales, ibi nihil velis</u>. Il s'agit seulement de s'entendre sur le domaine où l'on ne vaut rien. On ne risque guère d'en exagérer l'étendue.
>
> What you and I have managed to get hold of, Georges my old friend, is very simple and not the least little bit metaphysical or mystical; indeed it is common sense, good and round, like d'Alembert's back. It is all in the old sentence from Geulincx quoted in *Murphy*, admittedly a little hastily: *Ubi nihil vales ibi nihil velis*. The only point is to be clear about the domain in which one is worth nothing. There is little risk of anyone's exaggerating its extent. (SB to GD, on or after 30 April, before 26 May 1949: *L2*, pp. 148–50)

In a second letter to Duthuit, Beckett describes Bram van Velde and an art of non-relation using the term 'autology', which he had transcribed from the title to *Metaphysica Vera*'s Chapter 1.[58] He applies the term to creativity, to the artist who 'indulges now and then in a small seance [sic] of autology with a greedy sucking sound'.[59] The word 'autology' dates from the mid-seventeenth century and is used by Geulincx in *Metaphysica Vera* to refer to what in *Ethica* is described via *inspectio sui*.[60]

Four years later he again referred a correspondent to Geulincx's axiom, quoting it to the author of the first essay to bring Beckett's work to the wide attention of an American public, Niall Montgomery, on 2 December 1953. Montgomery's 'No Symbols where None Intended' essay was published in the fifth volume of the respected periodical *New World Writing* the following year, where it appeared alongside the opening part of the English translation of *Molloy*. Beckett writes that 'The heart of the matter, if it has one, is perhaps rather in the <u>Naught more real than nothing</u> and the <u>ubi nihil vales</u>, already in <u>Murphy</u> – I imagine so' (SB to Niall Montgomery, 2 December 1953: *L2*, p. 427).

In 1954, the German translator of *Molloy*, Erich Franzen, asked Beckett about the passage in *Molloy* that names Geulincx:

> I who had loved the image of old Geulincx, dead young, who left me free, on the black boat of Ulysses, to crawl towards the East, along the deck. (*Mo*, p. 50)

As Uhlmann has revealed, Beckett sent the following in reply:

> This passage is suggested (a) by a passage in the <u>Ethics</u> of Geulincx where he compares human freedom to that of a man, on board a boat carrying

him irresistibly westward, free to move eastward within the limits of the boat itself, as far as the stern; and (b) by Ulysses' relation in Dante (Inf. 26) of his second voyage (a medieval tradition) to and beyond the Pillars of Hercules, his shipwreck and death. I do not understand very well your difficulty in reconciling this passage with 'Das ist eine grosse Freiheit für jemanden etc.' I imagine a member of the crew who does not share the adventurous spirit of Ulysses and is at least at liberty to crawl homewards (nach Osten) along the brief deck. (SB to EF, 17 February 1954: *L2*, p. 458)[61]

Such valiant (because doomed) effort is, Molloy opines, 'a great measure of freedom, for him who has not the pioneering spirit' (*Mo*, p. 50). This Geulingian image of the man on a ship recurs in *L'Innommable/The Unnamable* and again, reduced and barely recognizable, in *Comment c'est/How It Is*. Beckett could not understand why Franzen was having difficulty 'reconciling this' with Dante's presence in the passage, and sought to set the translator on the right path.

Two years later, Beckett wrote to the writer and lifelong friend of T. S. Eliot, Mary Hutchinson[62]:

> I feel more and more something that is almost if not quite a loathing for almost everything I have written and simply cannot bear to go back over it and into it. If there is a queer real there somewhere it is the Abderite's [sic] mentioned in <u>Murphy</u>, complicated by – ibidem – the Geulincx 'Ubi nihil vales etc.' I suppose these are its foci and where a commentary might take its rise. But I really do not know myself – and don't want to know – par quel bout le prendre, and can't help anyone. (SB to MH, 7 November 1956: *L2*, pp. 668–9)[63]

Beckett and Hutchinson corresponded a little further on the subject of Geulincx, Beckett referring to the difficulties 20 years earlier of finding *Ethica* in Dublin, and describing Geulincx's world of incapacity and dependence on God as a world where man is a puppet (a 'guignol', a French forerunner of the English Punch[64]):

> Geulincx hard to come by. I read him in TCD library, the National Library didn't boast the Ethics. Frightful kitchen Latin but fascinating guignol world. (SB to MH, 28 November 1956 (HRHRC))[65]

This letter complicates the admiration voiced in *Murphy* for Geulincx's 'Beautiful Belgo-Latin'. Even more intriguing is Beckett's description of Geulincx's world as 'guignol', as a world of puppetry and cruelty, the implications of which I discuss in Chapter 6.

The most widely quoted reference to Geulincx in Beckett's correspondence is in fact his final one. In a 1967 letter to Sighle Kennedy, Beckett responded to questions about his work forming part of a Modernist lineage that included the oeuvres of Joyce and Proust, as revealed by early critical statements about form and content in *Dante...Bruno.Vico..Joyce*:

> Do the critical statements in your essay '*Dante...Bruno.Vico..Joyce*' – with their open admiration for the 'practical... roundheaded... scientific... rational... empirical' in thought, and their repeated admiration for writing which 'is not *about* something; *it is that something itself*' – do these statements in your early essay serve as a valid yardstick for measurement of your later work? (SK to SB, 7 May 1967)[66]

Beckett attempted to steer Kennedy away from these literary authors, with whom he was of course intimately familiar, and onto more minor yet apparently more viable routes of enquiry:

> I simply do not feel the presence in my writings as a whole of the Joyce & Proust situations you evoke. If I were in the unenviable position of having to study my work my points of departure would be the 'Naught is more real...' and the 'Ubi nihil vales...' both already in *Murphy* and neither very rational. (SB to SK, 14 June 1967: *Dis*, p. 113)

As Weller has argued of Beckett's response to Kennedy, Beckett's double nothingness presents 'philosophy countering literature' (Weller 2005, p. 3), the high Modernists if not quite in the service of the philosophies from which they drew so much, then at least evoking less of an affinitive 'feel' in Beckett as regards how he thought of *Murphy* than the obscurer philosophies.

A further striking aspect of this letter is its description of the rationalist Geulincx as not very rational. This is surely a self-deprecating joke about Beckett's own decision to employ Geulincx and Democritus in *Murphy*, but is it also something more? Is Beckett also hinting that these axioms, or even their authors themselves, are inherently not very rational? As will be argued in Chapter 2, these axioms (and many other borrowings) that appear in *Murphy* are extensively altered, bent if not entirely out of shape then reworked enough that they become more amenable to Beckett's own immediate ends in utilizing what he called his intertextual 'bits of pipe' (cited in Knowlson 1983, p. 16), in a process of deliberate misappropriation comparable with Murphy's own faux-adoption of astrology. In this sense the deployment within texts of fragmentary quotations such as these axioms might be productively described as not very rational; they are transformed, severed from their original contexts, and made, in Poundian Modernist parlance, 'new'.

In 1967 Beckett was writing about *Murphy* with 30-plus years' worth of hindsight. The lineage of correspondence establishes beyond doubt that the well-known 1967 letter to Kennedy is far from an anomaly. Rather, it is the final part in a regular and remarkably consistent series of correspondence pointing to the importance of Geulincx, a series that includes correspondence with MacGreevy, Reavey, Ussher, Duthuit, Montgomery, Franzen, Hutchinson and Kennedy, and that should also include Lawrence Harvey. In 1970 Harvey paraphrased a remark made by Beckett in interview that repeats the substance of comments to Hutchinson and Kennedy:

> In 1962 Beckett remarked that if he were a critic setting out to write on the works of Beckett (and he thanked heaven he was not), he would start out with two quotations, one by Geulincx: 'Ubi nihil valis [sic] ibi nihil velis,' and one by Democritus: 'Nothing is more real than nothing.' The first suggests that to Murphy (and perhaps to a lesser extent to Beckett), the body, that part of him which exists in the macrocosm, is of negligible value. Indeed, it is primarily a source of suffering. And where no value is attached, no desire is possible. (Harvey 1970, p. 267)

One final empirical fragment should be noted that extends the importance of the correspondence. Left in Beckett's Paris flat at his death in 1989 was a copy of Berkeley's *A New Theory of Vision, and Other Writings* (Berkeley 1926 [1910]). In the margin of p.146 of this edition, alongside propositions LXVI–LXVII of Berkeley's *Principles of Human Knowledge*, Beckett annotated in his often-used blue pencil (such as he used to confirm corrections to parts of *Watt*'s composition in notebooks) the two words 'Against Geulincx?' He also connected the paragraphs of the two propositions with an undulating line in the text's margin. *Principles of Human Knowledge* is the work in which Berkeley argues for the defining axiom that Beckett utilizes in *Film*. The propositions that struck Beckett in relation to Geulincx bear clear comparison to Occasionalist metaphysics. For example, Berkeley writes in proposition LXVI – '*Proper employment of the natural philosopher*':

> Hence it is evident, that those *things* which, *under the notion of a cause co-operating* or concurring *to the production of effects, are altogether inexplicable*, and run us into great absurdities, may be very naturally explained, and have a proper and obvious use assigned them, when they are considered only as marks or signs for our information.

Berkeley goes on to say that the proper employment of a natural philosopher is therefore to search after and understand 'this language' (Berkeley 1926 [1910]), p. 146) of marks and signs, rather than attributing it to external causal agency (as Geulincx would, thereby getting us into what Berkeley calls 'great absurdities'). Berkeley writes that 'The *fire* which I see is not the cause of the pain I suffer upon my approaching it, but the mark that forewarns me of it' (p. 145). Not so far removed from Occasionalism but crucially opposed to the logical validity of matter in general, Berkeley's argument posits idealist informational systematization where Geulincx sees divine causal agency. In proposition LXVII Berkeley highlights consequences of how certain (unnamed) philosophers leave out of their accounts of matter important qualities: 'the positive ideas of extension, figure, solidity, and motion' (p. 146), and this has the consequence of necessitating an *'occasion of our ideas,* or [. . .] the presence whereof God is pleased to excite ideas in us' (p. 147). While it might be prudent to not extrapolate too far with Beckett's annotation, it is nevertheless worth noting that far from all of Beckett's influential early sources of fascination are accounted for in this library. If the annotation is from decades earlier than Beckett's death in 1989, it survived much longer than many of his other important books.[67]

Chapter 2

Murphy and 'Mechanical Writing'

In Chapter 1, empirical materials from Beckett's so-called grey canon of correspondence, marginalia, notes and transcriptions that bear on his interest in Geulincx were laid open and explored. The series of correspondence that mentions Geulincx was read for what it has to reveal about Beckett's interdisciplinary thinking about philosophy, his enthusiasm for Geulincx in particular and the consistency with which he held to certain ways of thinking about Geulincx based in the axiom. The notes and transcriptions deriving from Geulincx were analysed, and these in turn had much to say about Beckett's developing understanding of Occasionalism, his expertise in Latin, and his dedication to 1936's research project. Also, the chapter set out the fundamentals of Geulincx's particular Occasionalism, showing how the philosophy is more immersed in the real, 'big' world than Geulincx is often given credit for, both in its turn to a practical ethics of the everyday, and in a rootedness in first-hand experiences of a number of 'vicissitudes' of real life lived. Given that there is no extant evidence that Beckett would ever again turn directly to Geulincx's works after the short, intense few months of 1936, the parameters Chapter 1 set out form a boundary within which it might be expected that Beckett's fascination, his 'fantasia', would roam. With these materials to hand, therefore, the question abides – the fundamental question of this book – how does Beckett's thinking about these materials inform his literary work? In turning to this question, the majority of scholars have focused on *Murphy*, and with good reasons for doing so.

A first reason to begin with *Murphy* is the consistency of Beckett's own specific and repeated references to *Murphy* when discussing Geulincx in correspondence. He repeatedly singles out this novel and its protagonist as bearing relation to the philosopher: '<u>Murphy</u> is break down between his <u>ubi nihil vales ibi nihil velis</u>'; 'Dans la vieille phrase de Geulincx citée dans <u>Murphy</u>'; 'If there is a queer real there somewhere it is the Abderites, mentioned in <u>Murphy</u>, complicated by – ibidem – the Geulincx'; 'already in <u>Murphy</u>'. Beckett never quotes Geulincx's axiom in relation to any other work; it is always *Murphy* that must somehow bear the weight of the obscure relation, though, of course, he does not detail *how* the novel might do so.

Murphy *and 'Mechanical Writing'*

Second, there are the arguments made by scholars such as Knowlson and Matthew Feldman that indicate the likely relevance of Geulincx to whatever Beckett would have been writing in or around 1936, due to 'Beckett's general practice of drawing upon his contemporaneous reading in his writings' (Feldman 2009a, p. 43). This 'general practice' is the case with much of Beckett's early, Joycean method of filling notebooks with entries from his reading, often not referenced, before integrating the fragmentary quotations into his prose and poetry. Knowlson summarizes this process that was partly a legacy of Joyce:

> Beckett's notebooks show [. . .] that he too plundered the books that he was reading or studying for material that he could then incorporate into his own writing. Beckett copied out striking, memorable or witty phrases into his notebooks. Such quotations or near quotations were then woven into the dense fabric of his early prose. It is what could be called a 'grafting' technique that runs at times almost wild. He even ticked them in his private notebooks once they had been incorporated into his own work. (Knowlson 1996, p. 106)

Knowlson and Feldman's research builds on Beckett's own description of his early work as being 'soiled [. . .] with the old demon of notesnatching' (SB to TM, (undated) 1931)[1]. Beckett would find ways to move out of the shadow of this 'old demon', but it was a significant shadow cast in large part by what he later called the 'epic, heroic'[2] and encyclopaedic world-affirming inclusiveness of Joyce's 'apotheosis of the word' (SB to Axel Kaun, 9 July 1937: *Dis*, p. 172). In 1936, when Beckett was struggling to complete *Murphy* and researching Geulincx, his disciplined methodology was still in part determined by this approach, which also had something of an air of habit, that 'great deadener' (*CDW*, p. 84), as Vladimir calls habit in his final soliloquy (his soliloquy on finality) in *Waiting for Godot*. As John Pilling points out, notes in the 'Whoroscope' notebook from the 1930s, derived from English Literature and explicitly headed 'For Interpolation', reveal that Beckett may well have noticed a problem with notesnatching, such that it 'was actually deferring the moment when he could "put down last words of first version"' of *Murphy* (Pilling 2006b, p. 207). Nevertheless, in 1936 Beckett was still working with and from compilations of quotations. A proper assessment of his uses of the Geulincx notes for the prose of 1936, then, has the potential to deepen our understanding of Beckett's broader relationship with 'notesnatching' and 'phrase-hunting' (SB to TM, 25 January 1931: *L1*, p. 62). Does Geulincx reveal anything new about how Beckett changed his working methodologies around this time?

Third, the thorny matter of *why* Beckett was so interested in Geulincx in 1936 should be considered, not least because the consensus on this matter tends to underwrite how Geulincx is seen to operate in *Murphy*. A number of scholars have convincingly narrated Beckett's early literary development (roughly taken to be up until World War Two) as deeply intertwined with a personal evolution from what Knowlson calls the 'arrogant, disturbed, narcissistic, young man of the 1930s' to one later famed for his 'extraordinary kindness, courtesy, concern, generosity, and almost saintly "good works"' (Knowlson 1996, p. 179). This psychological evolution is in turn seen as a change that partly found its footholds in psychoanalytic and psychotherapeutic, as well as literary and philosophical explorations of interiority and, specifically, quietism. The narrative thereby offers a picture of the maturing Beckett as not only immersed in, but thoroughly determined by and hence at one with, his aesthetic interests and practical poetics. Ackerley, Nixon, Feldman and Knowlson all locate what Knowlson first called Beckett's 'quietistic impulse' (p. 353) of the period as bound in with a rejection of 'the primary transcendental element of [Thomas à] Kempis's ethics' (Nixon 2011, p. 51), while at the same time nevertheless retaining his commitment to what Pilling described in 1978 as a 'qualified humanism' (Pilling 1978, p. 24); Beckett's difficult departure from the possibilities and consolations of the transcendent leaves him with what Feldman calls an 'agnostic quietism' (Feldman 2009, p. 183), much as Murphy is 'an Occasionalist without at the same time being a Deist', as Ackerley and David Hesla call him. Prompted by MacGreevy enquiring about Beckett's responses to Thomas's *De imitation Christi* [The Imitation of Christ] in 1935, Beckett self-diagnosed this productive turmoil:

> All I ever got from the Imitation went to confirm & reinforce my own way of living, a way of living that tried to be a solution & failed. I found quantities of phrases like qui melius scit pati majorem tenebit pacem [he that can well suffer shall find most peace], or, Nolle consolari ab aliqua creatura magnae puritatis signum est [For a man not to wish to be comforted by any creature is a token of great purity], or the lovely per viam pacis ad patriam perpetuae claritatis [direct him by the way of peace to the country of everlasting clearness], that seemed to be made for me and which I have never forgotten. Amg [sic] many others. But they all conduced to the isolationism that was not to prove very splendid. What is one to make of 'seldom we come home without hurting of conscience' and 'the glad going out & the sorrowful coming home' and 'be ye sorry in your chambers' but a quietism of the sparrow alone upon the housetop & the solitary bird under the eaves? An abject self-referring quietism indeed, beside the alert quiet of one who always had Jesus for his darling, but the only kind that I, who seem never to have had the least faculty or disposition for the supernatural, could elicit from the text, and then only by means of a substitution of terms very different from the one you propose. I mean that I replaced the plenitude that he calls 'God', not by 'goodness', but by a pleroma only to be sought among my own feathers or

entrails, a principle of self the possession of which was to provide a rationale & the communion by which a sense of Grace. [. . .] And I know that now I would be no more capable of approaching its hypostatics & analogies 'meekly, simply & truly', than when I first twisted them into a programme of self-sufficiency. (SB to TM, 10 March 1935: *L1*, pp. 256–7)

The argument that Beckett's 'truce' (Nixon 2011, p. 37) between an agnosticism and the transcendental aspects of his 'quietistic impulse' was brought about by his previous substitution of the Godly terms of Christian mysticism with his own 'feathers or entrails', which, following the truncation of his psychotherapy in 1935, he needed to reject in favour of a resignation to the earthly life of 'the waste that splutters most', and the 'heart [that] still bubbles' (SB to TM, 10 March 1935: *L1*, p. 259), is persuasive. Nevertheless, Beckett was in fact capable, on his own terms, of again 'approaching' Thomas's humble 'meekly, simply & truly'. For it would not be long until the Geulincx research rekindled the faint hope, a hope that in 1935 Beckett was willing to let fade out, that 'there [might be] some way of devoting pain & monstrosity & incapacitation to the service of a deserving cause' (p. 258). As noted in Chapter 1, Beckett signed off a March 1936 letter to Ussher, a letter in which he enthused about just how deserving a cause Geulincx's humility is, with a return to these very words of Thomas: 'Humiliter, Simpliciter, Fideliter'. Beckett's invocation of this trinity in 1936, an invocation that was also a return to his use of the terms in *Dream of Fair to Middling Women* (where the Alba 'will do this thing, she will, she will be the belle, gladly, gravely and carefully, humiliter, simpliciter, fideliter, and not merely because she might just as well' (*Dr*, pp. 208–9)), appears then as something of a surprise given his rejection of it 12 months earlier. So, while it is certainly consistent to think of Beckett's research into the *inspectio sui* of Occasionalism as a logical progression of his own explorations in psychotherapy and Christian mysticism, these were both avenues of enquiry that by late 1935 Beckett had come to see as embroiled in too many concomitant compromises. The progression to Geulincx, then, is also a turning back. Ackerley may be right to argue that Beckett found a way to accommodate Thomas's ethics with Geulincx's in 'the fundamental unheroic' (an idea noted in his diary while visiting Germany), a 'surrender' inwards to self rather than a questing journey out for it (a journeying that Beckett was frustrated to find in the German literature he was reading at the time). But such rekindled facility for these mystical 'analogies' must have taken Beckett by surprise.

These issues of Beckett's progressing ideas about psychological inner space, as well as his note-taking habits of the period and his references to *Murphy* in correspondence, underlie the consensus of approaches to *Murphy* as the work that most evidently bears out Beckett's interests in Geulincx. As early as 1960 Ruby Cohn summarized the critical orthodoxy that predominates to the present day: '*Murphy* is the most Geulincxian of the works' (Cohn 1960, pp. 93–4). In stating this Cohn was offering a précis of Samuel Mintz's article in Cohn's own edited special issue of *Transition* (1959), in which Mintz had stated the following:

> My point is that Beckett used Cartesianism in much the same way that Joyce used Vico: to give his novel structure, action, and meaning and not merely to exercise his own intellectual ingenuity. In *Murphy* the system employed is the Occasionalist doctrine of the Belgian Cartesian Arnold Geulincx [. . .] *Murphy* is inexplicable except by reference to it. (Mintz 1959, p. 156)

Few would go so far these days, and the deepening understanding of how Geulincx does operate in *Murphy* over subsequent years is partly a lessening of the strength of Mintz's claims. Mintz reads the indispensible Geulincx as stoically introspective: 'Geulincx exhorted his readers to renounce the world and to cultivate the inner life, the only place where the self is effectual' (p. 159). As has been shown in Chapter 1, this is not strictly true of Geulincx. Nevertheless, such a reading of Geulincx in relation to *Murphy* has proved influential, even if it has also come to be increasingly problematized.

Psychological interiority as adjacent to but not wholly concomitant with the physical body was of course a familiar idea to Beckett before he read Geulincx's idiosyncratic formulations about the inner self. *Dream of Fair to Middling Women*, completed 4 years prior to Beckett's Geulincx research, finds Belacqua 'nesting in a strange place' (*Dr*, p. 43), where for 2 months he 'lay lapped in a beatitude of indolence', in sympathy with his namesake's purgatorial stasis. During this restful phase of Belacqua's otherwise hectic schedule his internal state is described in a passage that foreshadows Murphy's mind:

> If that is what is meant by going back into one's heart, could anything be better, in this world or the next? The mind, dim and hushed like a sick-room, like a chapelle ardente, thronged with shades; the mind at last its own asylum, disinterested, indifferent, its miserable erethisms and discriminations and futile sallies suppressed; the mind suddenly reprieved, ceasing to be an annex of the restless body, the glare of understanding switched off. (p. 44)

The point hardly needs making that it was not in Geulincx's works that Beckett first discovered categories or imagery of the mind as a closed space or a mortuary chamber that might be 'an annex of the restless body'. On the surface, at least, it would seem possible to take a rather un-grand tour starting from Belacqua's resting place, to Murphy's mind and travelling through the room in which Malone too lays 'lapped' in bed, and on to the closed space short later works such as *Company* with 'one on his back in the dark' (*Co*, p. 3), without noticing the need for much, if any, recourse to Geulincx at all. But just as his return to Thomas's mystical trinity must have taken Beckett unawares, so too a critical and historicizing return to Geulincx in relation to *Murphy* can be surprising, posing difficulties for long-established orthodoxies and altering familiar routes.

Murphy's Composition

Dating the composition of *Murphy* can become crucial here. With the previous chapter having fixed the dates of the Geulincx research at TCD as accurately as possible, it is incumbent to map these onto *Murphy*'s composition such that a tentative identification of the point at which Geulincx might come to enter the novel's composition process can be asserted. Then it should be possible to see anew how such a chronologically determined *Murphy* tallies with Beckett's repeated references to the philosopher's presence in the novel. In turn, it will be possible to reappraise that broad consensus held for so long, though in differing ways, that *Murphy* is 'the most Geulincxian of the works'.

The important question of at what precise point Geulincx comes to Beckett's sphere of possible influence with regard to *Murphy* is, however, significantly hampered by the fact that the *Sasha Murphy* manuscript, the six notebooks comprising some 800 pages in which Beckett drafted and made notes towards *Murphy*, is privately owned and unavailable to scholarly consultation. The extent to which the Geulincx research influenced any rewriting, or even the production of whole new sections of *Murphy* is paradigmatic of the difficulties scholars have faced with many questions of source-incorporation in, and redrafting processes of, *Murphy*. Ackerley (who has attempted the most exhaustive exploration of the novel's sources and references with the painstaking annotations of *Demented Particulars: the Annotated Murphy*) suggests that *Sasha Murphy* would probably 'not vary *significantly* from the typescript' held at HRHRC, given the timeframe in which the novel was composed. (Ackerley 2004a, p. 12). This is in contrast to Knowlson's assessment of the manuscript's comparison with the final novel, according to which *Sasha Murphy* 'differs radically from the finished text at many points' (Knowlson 1996, p. 743, n. 32).[3] With this unknown quantity noted, some guiding lines can nevertheless be inferred about *Murphy*'s composition. Knowlson reveals that *Sasha Murphy* was begun on 20 August 1935.[4] A month later Beckett wrote to MacGreevy with details of the work's fitful progress: 'I have been forcing myself to keep at the book, & it crawls forward. I have done about 9000 words' (SB to TM, 22 September 1935: *L1*, p. 277). By 8 October he would report further strain, along with his hope for the work's future completion:

I have been working hard at the book & it goes very slowly, but I do not think there is any doubt now that it will be finished sooner or later. The feeling that I must jettison the whole thing has passed, only the labour of writing the remainder is left. There is little excitement attached to it, each chapter loses its colour & interest as soon as the next is begun. I have done about 20 000 words. (SB to TM, 8 October 1935: *L1*, p. 283)

On February 6 1936 Beckett wrote to MacGreevy with what must have been some relief, as well as of further difficulties: 'There only remain three chapters of mechanical writing, which I haven't the courage to begin' (SB to TM, 6 February 1936: *L1*, p. 312). By this time Beckett had travelled back to Ireland from London (where *Murphy* is primarily set), had recovered from his Christmas bout of pleurisy, and was visiting TCD library to research Geulincx. Completing *Murphy* was still to be a fraught business. On 5 March, in the same letter in which Beckett went into such detail about Geulincx, he told MacGreevy that 'Murphy will not budge' (SB to TM, 5 March 1936: *L1*, p. 320), and 20 days later it was all going 'from bad to worse' (SB to TM, 25 March 1936: *L1*, p. 324); indeed so much worse that he had made a speculative effort to leave Europe and literature altogether, having applied to study cinematography under Sergei Eisenstein at the Moscow State School of Cinematography.[5]

Nonetheless, only 2 months after Beckett 'could not quite finish the Ethic of Geulincx' he did manage in early April to finish the more pressing *Murphy*, finalizing a draft by 7 June and getting it ready to send off to publishers over the following 3 weeks. While he described his composition of this novel from start to finish as a struggle, the coincidence of dates indicates that if Geulincx is bound in some ways to *Murphy*, this came about during the final stages of composition, and may even have provided some significant help towards completing the novel.

Correspondence beyond that which gives Beckett's progress in page numbers also indicates that for the most part *Murphy* was written chronologically – a broadly uncontroversial likelihood but one that is vital when tracing Geulincx's presences in the novel. For instance, Beckett 'went round the wards for the first time' (SB to TM, 22 September 1935: *L1*, p. 277) of the Bethlem Royal Hospital in September 1935 with his friend Geoffrey Thompson, a research trip that manifests as Murphy's employment at the Magdalen Mental Mercyseat (MMM), and which is first mentioned in *Murphy*'s Chapter 5 when Austin Ticklepenny introduces himself and offers to arrange Murphy's ultimately ungainful employment. Shortly after this, on 2 October 1935, Beckett attended Jung's third Tavistock lecture. As Ackerley has argued, the lecture provided material that found its way into 'Murphy's mind' (*Mu*, p. 69) of Chapter 6.[6] Nearly 6 months later and close to the end of the novel's period of composition, in a letter of 25 March 1936 Beckett describes a trip to Galway with his brother Frank, a trip that Ackerley argues becomes incorporated into the 'Clonmachnois' in Neary's vision following the protagonist's death.[7] If these chronological inductions are accurate they imply that concurrent with his Geulincx research, when Beckett wrote on February 6 1936 that 'There only remain three chapters of mechanical writing', the specific, if somehow semi-automated, work he was doing on *Murphy* was on what became the last few of the 13-chapter novel. The following two sections reassess some of the more familiar arguments about *Murphy* in this chronological, historicizing context, before I go on to offer some newer appraisals of Geulincx's importance for the novel.

Murphy's Occasional Dualism

Without the caveats of a chronologically determined assessment of how Beckett's Geulincx research might interact with the novel, scholars have been bolder in asserting the importance of Occasionalism in *Murphy* relatively early in the novel. Chapter 6, simultaneously the novel's abstract dead centre and the only bit where Murphy is properly alive, describes Murphy's self-perception of his own mind in terms of a dualist, somewhat Occasionalist, schism:

> Thus Murphy felt himself split in two, a body and a mind. They had intercourse apparently, otherwise he could not have known that they had anything in common. But he felt his mind to be bodytight and did not understand through what channel intercourse was effected nor how the two experiences came to overlap. He was satisfied that neither followed from the other. He neither thought a kick because he felt one nor felt a kick because he thought one. Perhaps the knowledge was related to the fact of the kick as two magnitudes to a third. Perhaps there was, outside space and time, a non-mental non-physical Kick from all eternity, dimly revealed to Murphy in its correlated modes of consciousness and extension, the kick *in intellectu* and the kick *in re*. But where then was the supreme Caress? (p. 70)

Murphy is (and feels that he is) constituted by an embodied, separated though connected mind, a mind locked 'bodytight'. Certainly, Murphy's ignorance about interaction between his thoughts and his body echoes Geulincx. For example, Beckett had transcribed the following from *Metaphysics*' section on 'Autology':

> Proposition 8. Body, and its motions, have no natural capacity to arouse thoughts in my mind. [. . .]
>
> In whatever way bodies come together, they do not pass into my mind. I am a thing free of parts, as was said above; and one cannot pass into something that has no parts. (*Met*, p. 40)

Such perceptions continue into *Ethics*, where they retain their similarity to Murphy's:

> I do not know how, and through which nerves and other channels, motion is directed from my brain into my limbs; nor do I know how motion reaches the brain, or even whether it reaches the brain at all. (*Et*, p. 33)

Even with the Platonic mathematical inflections that Beckett gives to Murphy's mind – his 'Kick from all eternity' – that distinguish Murphy's definitions of the physical from Geulincx's, it might be tempting to posit that this earlier section of the novel was rewritten following Beckett's Geulincx research. One could note, for instance, that Chapter 6 is a relatively discrete, stand-alone chapter, and arguably would not have needed to be written in chronological order. However, any such rewriting cannot be confirmed and must, perhaps until *Sasha Murphy* sees the light of day, remain speculation. Murphy himself cares little about solving the issues that have led him to see himself in Occasionalist terms:

> The problem was of little interest. Any solution would do that did not clash with the feeling, growing stronger as Murphy grew older, that his mind was a closed system, subject to no principle of change but its own, self-sufficient and impermeable to the vicissitudes of the body. Of infinitely more interest than how this came to be so was the manner in which it might be exploited. (*Mu*, p. 70)

Most critical discussions of *Murphy*'s difficult and ambiguous Chapter 6 appropriately exploit the congruencies between Geulincx's Occasionalism and Murphy's mind via a focus on the rocking chair. For it is only in this chair that Murphy is able to take leave of his body and access his deepest modes of mind. With a Cartesian conarium that 'has shrunk to nothing', not knowing 'through what channel intercourse was effected nor how the two experiences came to overlap', Murphy relies on the machinery of the chair to transport his mind away from his stilled body and exploit his dualism. This chair is the first in Beckett's oeuvre in a lineage of mechanized props that mediate interaction between a person and their little world. Uhlmann has attempted the most sustained interpretation of Murphy's chair in relation to Geulincx, by locating parallels between the chair and one of Geulincx's central analogies in *Ethics*, a child's cradle.[8] Geulincx argues that just as a child, crying for its cradle to be rocked, will infer a principle of causation between crying and the cradle being rocked, unaware as it must be of the actual intervening cause (its 'mother or nursemaid' (*Et*, p. 340)), so too a person habitually thinks of him/herself as causing things to happen by inferring comparable connections between willing something to happen and that thing's happening. When in reality all there is,

Murphy *and 'Mechanical Writing'*

according to Geulincx, is the disconnected and potentially disappointed 'occasion' of willing, and the separate 'occasion' of an action. According to Geulincx, when humanity fails to recognize the validity of Occasionalism, when it does not take account of the invisible hand that must belong to God, it is in a comparable position to the baby in the cradle. Geulincx discusses the cradle analogy in a number of places, and it occurs in two distinct places in Beckett's notes.[9]

In the second of these descriptions Geulincx qualifies the analogy, stepping back from the dangers of too neat or complete identifications:

> The analogy of the baby and his mother on the one hand, and of God and me on the other hand, is a lame one. . .(God makes motion, the mother does not make it; the baby moves his mother to move, I do not move God). But the whole force and energy of the analogy turns on this, that just as the motion or rocking of the cradle is made with the baby willing it, though this motion is not made by the baby, so equally, motion is often made with me willing it, though I never make it. (*Et*, pp. 340–1)

Uhlmann tracks the reappearances of rocking chairs in Beckett's later works *Rockaby* and *Film* back to this cradle in Geulincx. His argument is that in 'occluded' ways these later chairs form part of a genealogy that includes Geulincx's cradle. The argument is bolstered by Geulincx employing the image in the context of an argument about the impossibility of suicide. Suicide in *Ethics* functions as a synecdoche illustrating the impossibility of action; because any action is impossible unless God wills it to happen, then so too is an extreme action, an ultimate say over oneself, such as suicide. Uhlmann points out that rocking chairs in Beckett's works often appear in a comparable context of some relation between comfort and death (the death of Murphy, for example, the 'apparent death of "O" in *Film*, and the imminent death of "w" in *Rockaby*' (Uhlmann 2006a, p. 85)).[10] He summarizes the project of identifying these occluded imagistic congruencies:

> The 'discovery' of the genealogy of such images clearly brings something new to the texts, without in any sense solving them. The images will always remain in some ways occluded, as it is impossible to completely locate or circumscribe their meaning. That is, the identification of points of resonance such as this allows new elements of the image to powerfully unfold, without in any sense exhausting their potential. (Uhlmann 2006b, p. 94)

A question lingers over Uhlmann's account, however, given the chronology of *Murphy*'s composition outlined above, of whether or not such a 'genealogy' can validly invoke the scientific term which, even with its connotations of unpredictable mutation, must also be taken to imply chronological, progressive development. As seen above, Beckett began work on *Murphy* in August

1935, the very opening scene of which finds the protagonist ensconced in his chair. In turn this chair is so vital to the novel's development, so thoroughly enmeshed in Murphy's own activities and sense of his self that it would be very surprising were it something that Beckett inserted during redrafting. Ackerley has addressed just this issue as informed by the even earlier 'Whoroscope' notebook:

> The image of the central character ('X') thus bound into his chair was present in the earliest drafts of the novel (in the Whoroscope Notebook), long before Beckett's intensive reading of Geulincx; the question abides, therefore, as to precisely how and how far an Occasionalist reading is possible. (Ackerley 2008, p. 204)[11]

Offering a different insight into how Murphy's chair functions as part of a mind–body binary, Weller has described how, like Mr. Endon's 'reliance' (Weller 2005, p. 88) upon chess, the chair is a symptom of dependence on precisely that which it seeks to negate – the outer reality. The chair is irreducibly a part of the physical, big world, while it is also a kind of bridge to Murphy's inner world.[12] Similarly, Ackerley refers to Geulincx's assertion 'I am a mere spectator of a machine whose workings I can neither adjust nor readjust' (*Et*, p. 333) to compare Murphy's chair with Geulincx's description of the surrounding world as a machine on which one depends: 'In the "Annotata" [§21, 212], the machinery is identified as the world; in the novel the chair is referred to as a machine' (Ackerley 2004a, p. 29).

Authors other than Beckett have turned more explicitly to Geulincx's Occasionalist disconnection conceived in terms of a fusion or codependency between man and machine. In a novel Beckett was unlikely to ever come across – Fred Saberhagen's 1979 science fiction novel *Berserker Man* – a small group of soldiers place their hopes in a Christ-like saviour child called Michael Geulincx, who due to the circumstances of his almost-immaculate conception is part human and part machine. Similarly to how Murphy seeks what he thinks of as 'the best of himself' (*Mu*, p. 46) within his man/machine hybridized little world, where he becomes what Beckett calls 'the entire machine' (p. 21), so too Saberhagen's Michael Geulincx can only fulfil his potential as humanity's saving grace when he is combined with a further machine, in his case a special kind of space suit, one sympathetic to its context as both human (it is skin-like, self-healing) and machine (it has various kinds of life support systems and weapons). The suit ('Lancelot') provides Michael Geulincx access to a realm of experiences otherwise beyond his reach, comparable to how Murphy can only access his deepest zones of mind in the chair:

> Again Lancelot guided him into the realm that seemed to lie beyond time. And now Michael began for the first time to feel fully the stresses that

Lancelot could impose upon a connected human mind. (Saberhagen 1988, p. 117)

This 'realm that seemed to lie beyond time', accessible only when plugged in to the machine to become more than the sum of its parts – 'the entire machine' – is for both Michael Geulincx and for Murphy, the 'best' of themselves. That Michael Geulincx can access such a 'realm' as a 'connected human mind' might just save all humanity. That Murphy is able will not even save Murphy, who hopes for outcomes that are far more narcissistic. Indeed, narcissism is fundamental to Murphy's sense of self and his Occasionalist experiences in the chair, and this narcissism is borne out partly via Beckett's subversion of Spinoza, a subversion that relates to Geulincx's presence in the novel in intriguing ways.

Murphy and Spinozan Self-Inspection

In his chair where he is free from the vicissitudes of bodily immersion in the big world, Murphy seeks a kind of acquaintance with himself, pursuing inner explorations that at first sight could appear, to the reader unconcerned with historicizing the novel's composition and contexts, as more than merely analogous with Geulincx's *inspectio sui*. For instance, this immersion hinges on a freedom from contingency, Murphy being 'hermetically closed to the universe without', though not thereby stuck in 'the idealist tar', where his 'mental experience was cut off from the physical experience' (*Mu*, p. 69). This experience depends on his stilling the big world: 'But motion in this world depended on rest in the world outside'. Just as Geulincx's Cartesian investigation of the *cogito* also does, Murphy's 'sphere full of light fading into dark' (p. 70) purports to make itself available to the discovery of, rather than to proscribe, the limits of selfhood as defined epistemologically. A reader might be inclined, therefore, to think of Murphy as a kind of philosopher, as a lover and explorer of wisdom. Yet the only thing Murphy is interested in is 'what he had not ceased to seek from the moment of his being strangled into a state of respiration – the best of himself' (p. 46). Murphy is neither a questing voyager of 'the pioneering spirit' (which Molloy describes as also lacking in the Geulingian seafaring adventurer), yet nor is he a do-gooding self-improver. This 'best' Murphy cannot find venturing out in a world (unless parts of the big world are seen by him as proxies, as with the patients at the MMM). Instead, he gathers himself together in the chair, and seeks to find the 'best of himself' deep within his own free-floating depths. In this self-inspection, Murphy gives himself up in 'surrender to the thongs of self, a simple materialisation of self-bondage, acceptance of which is the fundamental unheroic' (German Diary 4, UoR[13]), as Beckett described it in a diary entry of 18 January 1937. All of this can appear broadly like Murphy is bearing out Geulincx's summary of *inspectio sui*: 'it is nothing other than that celebrated saying of the Ancients, KNOW THYSELF' (*Et*, p. 328).

But a significant qualification should be appended to any attempt to co-opt Murphy's inner explorations as Geulingian *inspectio sui*. Importantly, it is in terms of Spinoza, not Geulincx, that Murphy's self-regard is framed in the epigraph to Chapter 6 that subverts Spinoza's description of God:

> *Amor intellectualis quo Murphy se ipsum amat.*
> [The intellectual love with which Murphy loves himself.] (*Mu*, p. 69)

By tying Murphy's love of self into Spinoza's love of God, Beckett not only raises Murphy's narcissistic impulse to a higher realm, he simultaneously brings Spinoza's dictum (*Deus se ipsum amore intellectuali infinito amat* [God loves himself with an infinite intellectual love][14]) down to earth via Murphy's hubris. It is clear to see why Spinoza's formulation provided a template that Beckett could twist 'into a programme' if not of liveable 'self-sufficiency' for himself then at least for Murphy, and thus of one available to literature. For Spinoza, knowing of the love that God must have for himself leads to the further knowledge that in order to secure salvation, humanity should do the same:

> Hence it follows that God, in so far as he loves himself, loves mankind, and, consequently, that the love of God towards men and the mind's intellectual love towards God are one and the same. [. . .] From this we clearly understand in what our salvation or blessedness or freedom consists, namely, in the constant and eternal love towards God, that is, in God's name towards men. This love or blessedness is called glory in the Holy Scriptures, and rightly so. (Spinoza 1992, p. 219)[15]

Murphy misrepresents Spinoza's insight, and follows its light by loving himself, as God does, not by loving God. He thereby cuts God out of the equation completely, so there will be no 'salvation' resulting from the 'love towards' that is directly towards himself. It is a self-regarding love that is, one might say, more masturbatory than procreative, and thus Murphy's ignominious *petite mort* at the end of the novel is a logical consequence of this being ensconced in his little world. Ackerley argues of the epigraph:

> Spinoza thus subverted is a convenient formulation for the rejection of the rationalist tradition, although Beckett finally relies more upon the very different *Ethica* of Geulincx, in which, however, the opposition of Ratio (reason) and Philautia (self-love) is a constant theme. (Ackerley 2004a, p. 116)

There are interesting interrelations between Beckett's uses of Occasionalism and Spinoza here, even if Beckett 'finally relies more upon' Geulincx. Geulincx elucidates a breakdown of 'Love' into two divisions: 'pleasant love, and effective love'. Pleasant love is itself composed of two further divisions: 'sensible or corporeal love [. . .] and spiritual love', while effective love 'is either benevolent love, [. . .] concupiscent love, [. . .] or obedient love' (*Et*, p. 312). Self-love or *Philautia* (in Wilson's translation 'concupiscent love') functions as this middle subdivision of effective love. As Beckett transcribed, 'Concupiscent Love. . .it is nothing other than Self-Love or Philautia. . .it is the tinder of Sin, or rather Sin its very own self' (p. 315). In Chapter 10 of *Murphy*, Wylie, former pupil of the Newtonian, Pythagorean Neary, asserts his own Geulingian prerogative in similar terms:

'My attitude,' said Wylie, 'being the auscultation, execution and adequation of the voices, or rather voice, of Reason and Philautia, does not change.' (*Mu*, p. 134)

Beckett annotated his Geulincx notes on Philautia with a summary phrase added in English (here in bold):

Humility foreign to the ancients. . . But self-love seduced them all; and here I excuse no-one, not even great Plato. (*Et*, p. 311)[16]

Humility is also foreign to Murphy, who cares little for compromises and 'adequation', and the self-love that blocks humility also seduces Murphy in such a way that it can be seen to owe interwoven debts to Spinoza and Occasionalism that date back to Beckett's 'Philosophy Notes'. These notes reveal Beckett describing Malebranche's concept of universal reason as interchangeable with Spinoza's epigraph-to-be: '(amor intellectualis quo deus se ipsum amat = raison universelle of Malebranche)' (TCD MS 10967/188). Beckett had also noted the precise word *Philautia* earlier than from Geulincx. It appears in the 'Dream' notebook as entry no. 779, where it is snatched from Robert Burton's *Anatomy of Melancholy* as part of the initially misspelled entry 'inexorable & supercilious & arrogant & eminent ~~philolau~~ philautia' (Beckett 1999a, p. 111). Much like Beckett's own mind was in 1936, Murphy's brims with refracted analects, navigable but not always reducible to any single overriding origin. As Ackerley points out, Chapter 6, 'brief as it is, represents a compression and distillation of his years of reading' (Ackerley 2004a, p. 116). From some perspectives Murphy's mind might resemble an Occasionalist's, but on closer 'inspection' even those aspects that appear most clearly Occasionalist are problematic.

Geulincx in Pieces – Late Chapters

Building on the evidence that points to Geulincx as a presence that would appear predominantly in *Murphy*'s later chapters, the novel's final few chapters are discussed here. Geulincx is named and his axiom quoted in Chapter 9, at the moment Murphy claims to commit himself to the 'little world' of his interiority in seeking to avoid the somewhat Occasionalist 'occasions of fiasco' of the 'big world':

> His vote was cast. 'I am not of the big world, I am of the little world' was an old refrain with Murphy, and a conviction, two convictions, the negative first. How should he tolerate, let alone cultivate, the occasions of fiasco, having once beheld the beatific idols of his cave? In the beautiful Belgo-Latin of Arnold Geulincx: *Ubi nihil vales, ibi nihil velis.* (*Mu*, p. 112)[17]

In a 1993 article Rupert Wood made an important observation about this invocation:

> It is unclear whether this particular conviction, as expressed by Geulincx, forms part of Murphy's credo, or whether the line is simply a piece of narratorial intervention.

This lack of clarity is 'symptomatic', for Wood, 'of the general uneasiness about the intrusion of the philosopher, as name or figure, that pervades Beckett's writing' (Wood 1993, p.32). However, Wood's description of a 'general uneasiness' sidesteps the fact that such moments of 'narratorial intervention', or assertions of a character's 'credo', are discrete and they alter dramatically throughout Beckett's oeuvre; there is no 'general' uneasiness, though there are many specific instances of uneasiness. Similarly, if this is 'narratorial intervention' it might be far from being 'simply' so. It is complicated, for instance (and admittedly in retrospect), by Beckett's description to Hutchinson in 1956 of Geulincx writing in a 'frightful kitchen Latin'. The 1956 description indicates that whoever is speaking in the earlier *Murphy*, whether free-indirect protagonist or narrator, they might well be speaking with a tongue-in-cheek. While Wood is undoubtedly correct in imputing to Beckett's work a frequency of uneasy moments of 'intrusion' from philosophers, by speaking only of 'general' uneasiness Wood runs the danger of missing what distinguishes this novel's particular moments of Geulincx. Indeed, in *Murphy* Beckett appears a great deal less uneasy about the incorporation of this or many other 'name[s] or figure[s]' than in later works. While he was certainly determined to keep a number of these hidden from the reader (as his noting 'Choose "layers" carefully, on some such principle as V.'s [Virgil's] distribution of sins and punishments. But keep whole Dantesque analogy out of sight'[18] in the 'Whoroscope' notebook reveals), nevertheless there are many more incorporations of names, places, quotations and titles in *Murphy* that are much more warmly welcomed.

Taking this first mention of Geulincx in Chapter 9 as pivotal, I want to argue that there are a number of important consequences to the fact that Beckett researched Geulincx while already well on with the composition of *Murphy*, too late to use the research to drive larger aspects of the narrative throughout the novel, such that any influence of the research earlier in the novel than Chapter 9 would largely be a matter of extensive revising and redrafting, which in turn appears unlikely. And while this late 'intrusion' is not the 'key' to the novel Bair describes, it is welcomed by Beckett, who grasps Geulincx as a source he can use to underwrite allusions and broader themes that were, in fact, already present in the then-unfinished novel. More controversially, however, the evidence appears to point not to Beckett using Geulincx to significantly deepen themes or narrative arcs in line with the complexity of his newly detailed knowledge of Geulincx. Rather, for the most part, the Geulincx that Beckett invokes and refers to in *Murphy* can be seen as a reading of the philosopher that would have been entirely derivable from the earlier 'Philosophy Notes', a reading according to which Geulincx's only categorical and stark conclusion is that 'Man has nothing to do in outer world'.

Yet that is not the whole story. It is also clear that the 1936 turn to Geulincx also gave Beckett some confidence in his ideas about this strange philosopher, as well as the impetus to deploy them, and tracing Geulincx's appearances in later chapters of *Murphy* becomes a matter of tracing Beckett's developing uses of his notes for his prose. The uses and abuses of Geulincx for *Murphy* trace a progression from surface to depth, from a borrowed or stolen word here or there, thrown into or at the text in a similar fashion to *Dream*'s many-coloured fabric, to a much more subtle and integrated incorporation. If Geulincx is, as Bair stated in 1978, a 'key' to open the complex lock of the wide-ranging *Murphy*, then it is one that can do so only by opening a view onto the contours, achievements and constraints of this novel more broadly.

The impression that for the most part a relatively straightforward conception of Geulincx predominantly determines the incorporations into *Murphy* is strengthened by noting something regarding Beckett's letter of 16 January 1936, where he describes the realization about his protagonist, 'I suddenly see that Murphy is break down between his ubi nihil vales ibi nihil velis (positive) and Malraux's Il est difficile à celui qui vit hors du monde de ne pas rechercher les siens (negation)'. Interestingly, Beckett appears to have 'suddenly' seen this 'break down' before he was extensively engaged in the research, as the letter describes the research as still planned, not yet undertaken: 'I *shall have to go* into TCD after Geulincx' (my italics). While Beckett did know that TCD held a copy of Geulincx's works, even if he had looked at *Opera* by mid-January he seems unlikely to have got very far with the transcriptions, given how long he was visiting the library for and how far his transcriptions run. He was drawing broad conclusions about *Murphy* via Geulincx, then, without actually having transcribed the majority of the deeper notes that he would go on to produce in the weeks and months that followed.

The compliment to Geulincx's 'beautiful Belgo-Latin' arises in the context of what the novel's narrator intimates is Murphy's mistaken, naïve and narcissistic appraisal of the patients' sufferings at the MMM:

> The frequent expressions apparently of pain, rage, despair and in fact all the usual, to which some patients gave vent, suggesting a fly somewhere in the ointment of Microcosmos, Murphy either disregarded or muted to mean what he wanted. (*Mu*, pp. 112–13)

Murphy believes that the patients have achieved a persistence of that singular state he loves in himself when ensconced in his chair or collapsed in reveries in the grass of Hyde Park, where he indeed 'has nothing to do in outer world'. Accordingly, Murphy hopes to one day attain the same level of exemption the patients seem to have 'from the big world's precocious ejaculations of thought, word and deed' (p. 115). The patients have managed, so Murphy believes, to escape the everyday outer world's contingencies and have ascended to a plane of pure inner self. In consequence 'Murphy presupposed them, one and all, to be having a glorious time' (p. 113). Murphy is popular with these patients, and whatever sympathetic magic might be at work in that affection he refuses to ascribe it to the 'occasions of fiasco' and disasters of the out-of-control astrology of Suk's stars. Instead Murphy hoards this happy outcome as a consequence of his own dark depths, believing the patients 'felt in him what they had been and he in them what he would be' (p. 115). But despite hopes of attaining the patients' state, of being able to 'clinch' the matter, he is too tied to a world of physicality, too dependent on and distracted by the minor hedonistic pleasures of the big world, 'as witness his deplorable susceptibility to Celia, ginger, and so on'. He is too narcissistic to forgo the possibility that certain things he desires, which might appear to him to happen as a consequence of his agency, are not in fact due to him. Consequently, for Murphy, it:

> was not enough to want nothing where he was worth nothing, nor even to take the further step of renouncing all that lay outside the intellectual love in which alone he could love himself, because there alone he was lovable. It had not been enough and showed no signs of being enough. These dispositions and others ancillary, pressing every available means (e.g. the rocking-chair) into their service, could sway the issue in the desired direction, but not clinch it. (p. 112)

The approach Geulincx offers to Murphy, to 'want nothing where he is worth nothing', is insufficient. That is, Murphy still desires things of the big world even though he might be capable of very little there. Tenuously, but persistently,

Murphy is tied into a world he does not love and wherein he is also not lovable. The narrator does not claim that Murphy wants nothing in the big world and yet this wanting nothing is itself insufficient. Rather it is the case that Murphy cannot bring himself to want nothing in the big world. This is how the ascription of beauty to Geulincx's 'Belgo-Latin' can be accounted for (as well as in terms of its neatly balanced equilibrium); it speaks of the unattainable, a futile hope of freedom.

The passage that quotes Geulincx's axiom appears towards the end of Chapter 9, the first of the three chapters that draw most directly from Geulincx, the others being Chapters 10 and 11. Chapters 12 and 13 rely for their narrative propulsion and scenic dénouements on the other characters finding Murphy burnt to a cinder, before leavening their regrets in the short and near-pastoral conclusion of Chapter 13. It is predominantly, though not exclusively, where the late chapters focus on Murphy himself that Geulincx becomes most useful to Beckett, as it is the 'seedy solipsist' (p. 53) himself who was already suffering from the particular symptoms of Occasionalism. In Chapter 9, for example, Murphy questions 'the etymology of gas', wondering whether gas might 'turn a neurotic into a psychotic'. He concludes:

> No. Only God could do that. Let there be Heaven in the midst of the waters, let it divide the waters from the waters. The Chaos and Waters Facilities Act. (*Mu*, p. 110)

These wonderings are narrated as Murphy drifts off into himself in his chair, the narration slipping from narrator to Murphy and back again as Murphy loses control over himself and slips off into reveries. They appear as a flourish of free indirect style comparable to what Beckett had described in Joyce's then-titled *Work in Progress* 7 years earlier, where the writing '*is that something itself*': 'When the sense is sleep, the word go to sleep' (*Dis*, p. 27). The words are murmured by the semi-conscious Murphy, bubbling and gurgling just like his own mind will shortly do, with chaos and primal waters. Murphy thinks in fragments of remembered knowledge, revolving what Beckett called 'obsessional' (cited in Knowlson 1996, p. 29) images rather than resolving their unknowns. Their intimation of an Occasionalist God who is the only agent capable of causation, who continually sticks his oar in between 'Chaos and Waters', is one of the first hints in the novel's later chapters that Geulincx is entering their peripheries as an ephemeral presence, one that will become more fully cohered with characterization in later sections.

In Chapter 10 Neary's hope that he can 'count on the Almighty to pull off the rest' after 'the ice has been broken' (*Mu*, p. 138) in his hoped for relationship with Miss Counihan renders human wishes in terms of the deistic agency of Occasionalism. As does the description of the sleeping patients at the beginning of Chapter 11:

> Those that slept did so in the frozen attitudes of Herculaneum, as though sleep had pounced upon them like an act of God. And those that did not did not by the obvious grace of the same authority.

However, these are still fragmentary, somewhat piecemeal incorporations, and while they enable a level of irony they do not drive any major aspects of narrative, and little of the novel's deeper characterization relies upon such interjections. It is often in single words, those that were note-snatched and perhaps also ticked off somewhere other than TCD MS 10971/6 (*Sasha Murphy*, perhaps), that Geulincx shows up. Yet, as we move further into the novel, Geulingian incorporations can with more confidence be said to derive from the 1936 transcriptions, such as with the word 'adminicles' that appears in Chapter 11. In the quiet of a dark night Murphy feels himself subject to a rather Manichean division in his being cut adrift from all his bright and sunny daytime involvement with the hospital patients, and he thinks of and viscerally feels this gulf:

> There were the patients themselves, circulating through the wards and in the gardens. He could mix with them, touch them, speak to them, watch them, imagine himself one of them. But in the night of Skinner's there were none of these adminicles, no loathing to love from, no kick from the world that was not his, no illusion of caress from the world that might be. (p. 149)

In an atmosphere of night ordained by the radical behaviourist psychologist B. F. Skinner, whose theories prioritized an individual's private experience (which more traditional theories of behaviourism necessarily lacked), Murphy's own singular and private experience lacks the support of daytime distractions, the consolations of illusory interaction with the patients.[19] Following the section in *Ethics* on the seven ethical obligations that proceed from an acceptance of humility and the *ubi nihil vales, ibi nihil velis* axiom, is the penultimate section of Treatise 1, the final section of Beckett's transcriptions, which concerns what Geulincx calls '*The Adminicle of Humility*' (*Et*, p. 352). Beckett's transcriptions from this section are all contained in the handwritten manuscript that constitutes the final few pages of TCD MS 10971/6. This word *adminicle*, derived from *adminiculum* and meaning prop or support, summarizes Geulincx's thoughts on humility as it pertains to happiness:

> Happiness is like a shadow: it flees from you when you pursue it; but pursues you when you flee from it. But you should be aware that it may not always pursue you when you flee; for if you learn cunning in the ways of Happiness and flee from it in order that it may pursue you, it will not pursue you.

Geulincx insists on humanity finding a way to become compelled solely to follow its ethical obligations, so as to avoid frantically pursuing temporary satisfactions. This way involves fleeing happiness not only because following the dictates of Reason alone, according to Geulincx, is the right thing to do but also because pursuing happiness is futile anyway, given that 'it flees from you' when you do so. It is Geulincx's final lesson in Treatise 1 deriving from the instruction not to attempt what you cannot attain (*ubi nihil vales, ibi nihil velis*), and it is asserted with an emphatic floridity that Beckett recorded:

> Let us forsake these inauspicious standards behind which with such great pomp, such great consent and concourse, so many impediments and burdens of studies and counsels, the human race marches. Day and night they seek Happiness; it is the Palladium for whose capture they compete. . .Nor are they ashamed of such disgraceful service, or rather servitude. . .Their watchword is public, and in the mouths of all: *Let us be happy and prosper!*

Instead of marching in a public crowd behind flags proclaiming all our happiness, Geulincx counsels, we should rather be 'found' (p. 353) individually by happiness, while labouring over our dedication to our obligations, much as Murphy surrenders rather than quests. Conceptions of searching without moving will become increasingly important to Beckett in works after *Murphy*. But what can be said at this stage about the precise function the word 'adminicles' has as a quotation in the context of *Murphy*? I want to suggest that it manifests a kind of middle ground as regards the 'notesnatching' of fragmentary words and phrases from Geulincx. As has been seen, a number of earlier allusions to Occasionalism in the novel do not depend upon any strong integration between the reference and its context in the novel. Yet the later 'adminicules' aligns Geulincx's description of happiness (as only being possible in a turning away from happiness, in the hope that it might follow) with Murphy's involvement with the patients at the hospital, those whom Murphy pursues but who rarely pursue him. However, the word still sits in the text a little awkwardly, showing off its author's expertise in Latin philosophy by manifesting a precision of intellectualism at odds with the novel's more determinedly ambiguous drives (such as bring about the more elusive Chapter 6). The word's deployment is thus comparable to those few sections of the novel that Uhlmann critiques as lapsing into an overly 'dogmatic' use of philosophy, such as when Murphy's arrogance comes to the fore in the garret when confronting Ticklepenny.[20] The use of 'adminicules' reveals, as do the infrequent but striking shifts into a tone in which the reader might feel just as hectored as Ticklepenny, that Beckett's philosophical reading in Geulincx, his borrowing fragments of the obscure Latinate voice, was still partly a hindrance to his firmly establishing his *own* voice. Beckett's Geulincx research provided a wellspring of complex concepts and 'hard words'. But in a number of the instances in which the research finds its way onto the pages of *Murphy*, Beckett betrays signs of struggling with how to incorporate it in a way that is distinct from the older ready-mades in *More Pricks than Kicks* or *Dream of Fair to Middling Women*.

The Failure of 'Vicarious Autology' – The Chess Game

There is arguably an exception to these compromises of the middle ground, however, a place where Geulincx does not jut out obviously and where his Occasionalism underscores an important whole section of the novel's dramatic structure and characterization. This is in the chess game of Chapter 11. The chess game is even more important, however, as it instantiates the first of what would become many scenes in Beckett's works in which his comic talents would find a suitable form to accommodate the chaotic – in the ludic aspects of closed systems.

Murphy is flattered that he appears to the pot-poet Ticklepenny to have 'a great look of [the patient] Clarke'. Clarke had been in a 'katatonic' [sic] stupor for three weeks, and 'would repeat for hours the phrase: "Mr. Endon is *very* superior"' (*Mu*, p. 121). Murphy is flattered by the apparent resemblance because he thinks the same about the patients at the MMM, and about Mr. Endon in particular. To Murphy the patients are, like his own mind, a 'Matrix of surds [. . .] missile[s] without provenance or target, caught up in a tumult of non-Newtonian motion' (p. 72). They are of interest to Murphy only in so far as they reflect (he hopes, precisely mirror) his own sense of self. And for Murphy, Mr. Endon is the apotheosis of this, the pinnacle of achievement of a self-inspection, staring at one's own inner depths (as is often pointed out in regard to Mr. Endon's name, the Greek preposition *endon* means 'within').[21] Mr. Endon apparently suffers (though this may be such suffering that suffering is not the word, for he is numb and inviolable, not raging or in any apparent pain) from 'a psychosis so limpid and imperturbable that Murphy felt drawn to it as Narcissus to his fountain' (p. 116). But in advance of their game, to give the signal that there will be a game, Murphy peers with an impatient eye through the betraying 'judas' window into the little world of Mr. Endon's cell, and the discrepancy between the two is made clear:

> [. . .] the sad truth was, that while Mr. Endon for Murphy was no less than bliss, Murphy for Mr. Endon was no more than chess. Murphy's eye? Say rather, the chessy eye. Mr. Endon had vibrated to the chessy eye upon him and made his preparations accordingly. (p. 150)

In a farce as ridiculous as the monkeys playing chess Beckett wanted as a frontispiece for the novel,[22] the frustratedly stuck-in-the-big-world Murphy and the unwittingly stuck-in-the-little-world Mr. Endon will play out between themselves the 'ethical yoyo' (p. 69) through Beckett's favourite game of closed-space abstraction.[23] For it is Murphy's failure to heed the axiom from *Ethics* during this game that is his undoing. Even though he earlier rejected it, all he had really rejected in Chapter 9 was the possibility of living entirely within the little world. In the chess game, Murphy does not realize he has no power to cause any response in Mr. Endon, despite Mr. Endon being 'voted by one and all the most biddable little gaga in the entire institution' (p. 149), and he persists with wilful determination, unable to cast his eyes with humility on the unbridgeable gulf between himself and his opponent.

Murphy's first move in the game is pawn to king's fourth, a move Beckett had also described in his first published prose text, the short story 'Assumption', written 7 years prior to *Murphy*:

> He spoke little, and then almost huskily, with the low-voiced timidity of a man who shrinks from argument, who can reply confidently to Pawn to King's fourth, but whose faculties are frozen into bewildered suspension by Pawn to Rook's third [. . .] He indeed was not such a man, but his voice was of such a man. (*CSP*, p. 3.)

In the earlier story Beckett inscribes two specific moves of chess with the capacity to reveal personality, a hint that a reader might be on a right track in thinking of Murphy's self as similarly inscribed in his game. Mr. Endon's first move, a confident reply, is knight to king's rook third. Less confidently Murphy tries mirroring Mr. Endon; and his third, fourth, sixth and seventh moves all also mirror those of Mr. Endon. In the one instance of the game where Mr. Endon repeats a move that Murphy has made (Mr. Endon's eighth, though this repeating only really follows Murphy's pre-empting), he thereby brings his pieces back to exactly the same positions they held when the game began. Without playing the game out, or being able to visualize the moves as they are narrated, the annotation to Mr. Endon's eighth move that describes it as 'An ingenious and beautiful début, sometimes called the Pipe-opener', might well be taken as a straightforward description of a specialized opening. In fact it is a comment on Mr. Endon's mania for symmetry and his solipsism; he has merely rearranged his pieces in a monochrome visual pattern. After Murphy's ninth move the board is left just as it was after Murphy's opening move. With the hindsight offered by this intervening series a reader can see that Murphy's opening move being 'the primary cause of all White's subsequent difficulties' (*Mu*, p. 152) is solely because it is the first move, the original sin of Murphy's necessary assertion of self that he cannot take back. The primary cause of Murphy's difficulties is himself; his sanity and normality in playing pawn to king's fourth, and this sanity's rootedness in the world he longs to escape.

In a series of moves calculated to solicit recognition of them, to force Mr. Endon to recognize Murphy as a causational and thus an existing and equal agent, Murphy also takes a different approach to that of imitating moves (technically Mr. Endon's moves follow Murphy's because Murphy opened the game), and he tries desperately to give up his pieces. He moves a knight into a losing position three times and tries valiantly with what the narrator annotates as 'the ingenuity of despair' at move 27 to sacrifice his queen, trying again at 41, but still Mr. Endon's non-reaction is unshakeable. Neither approach causes Mr. Endon to try anything like a recognizably competitive move. Just as Mr. Endon sees not Murphy at his window but only the signifying 'chessy eye', so he follows the rules of chess in a further abstraction, adhering to them only in so far as they allow him, without actually breaking any, to monomaniacally rearrange a monochrome visual pattern according to a strict plan of symmetry. Mr. Endon is toying with a closed system, and it is his manipulation of the pieces to rearrange symmetry that is the single most determining factor in his moves. He manoeuvres his pieces into a different symmetrical pattern on six different occasions (at moves 8, 21, 23, 27, 39 and 41).

Mr. Endon's turns taken, the claim being that they cannot really be called his responses, during Murphy's abject begging for quittance, are described as his 'irresistible game' (p. 153) when rather than taking Murphy's queen he returns a knight to a corner square, revealing his pieces in the comic symmetry of move 27. Murphy's pieces end in utter disarray, an indication of the real chaos of his own mind. Murphy is by turns confused, imitative, desperate, seemingly random, then suicidal, giving up the ghost entirely when forced into a winning position by Mr. Endon's most likely (but illegal) 44th move that would establish his pieces in a seventh occurrence of symmetry. Murphy's narcissism cannot bear the realization that Mr. Endon does not see him as an opponent, a partner or an equal. So Murphy 'surrenders' (p. 152): 'Further solicitation would be frivolous and vexatious, and Murphy, with fool's mate in his soul, retires' (p. 153).

Geulincx wrote in *Ethics*:

> we have no power to affect either our own or any other body; this is perfectly obvious from our consciousness alone, and no sane man would deny it. (*Et*, p. 328)

Murphy does not realize that he has no power to affect Mr. Endon. Instead, his hubris prolongs the fruitless manoeuvres in a game he can only pointlessly win or concede, and in his consequent frustration we might well hear an echo of Geulincx's realization that 'I am a mere spectator of a machine whose workings I can neither adjust nor readjust. I neither construct nor demolish anything here: the whole thing is someone else's affair' (p. 333). If only Murphy would try the alternative approach of Geulingian restraint he might come closer to beating this catatonic at his own game. If Murphy would cast his eyes with humility upon his impotence and realize that where he cannot act, where he is worth nothing, he should not try to act, then he might at least stand a chance of failing this game in a better way.

Regardless, Murphy is not a humble man. Geulincx asks rhetorically 'How will [a humble man] listen to what Reason says if he listens only to what he himself says, that is, to what concerns his convenience and pleasure?' (p. 220). Besotted with his own company, just like Malraux's solitary terrorist Murphy seeks out only those others who are like himself, listening only to himself or, as the narrator of *The Unnamable* will put it some years later, to a suitable 'vice-exister' (*U*, p. 26). Thereby he forces the oblivion. Presaging Beckett's use of Geulincx's terminology when writing to Duthuit 10 years later as well as during the composition of *Watt*, Murphy had been transfixed by a 'vicarious autology that he had been enjoying [. . .] in little Mr. Endon and all the other proxies' (*Mu*, p. 118). However, Murphy's self-regard will get the better of him, and when his own little inferno engulfs him later it will be while he is still in thrall to himself and his own 'autology'.[24]

As with Geulincx's Cartesian inheritance, Beckett first transcribed Geulincx's term 'autology' as filtered through Windelband in the 'Philosophy Notes', as seen in Chapter 1:

> Geulincx reduces self-activity to immanent mental activity in man. The 'autology' or *inspectio sui* is not only epistemological starting point, it is also ethical conclusion of his system.

In the 'Philosophy Notes' 'autology' is identified with *Ethica*'s *inspectio sui*, and Geulincx also points to the terms as related when he writes that 'I discussed the kind of inspection that I called *Autology*' (*Et*, p. 241) in the earlier *Metaphysics*. Autology is the first stage (the 'epistemological starting point') in its being interchangeable with *inspectio sui*. It establishes the *humilitas* in the 'ethical conclusion' that Beckett found so enthralling in the turn from self, from the discovery that self is comprised of ignorance and impotence, to God and the world. Beckett records the word, in the single instance in which it appears in his 1936 Geulincx notes, in Greek, following Land's convention in *Opera*, noting the title of Chapter 1 of *Metaphysica Vera*:

Pars Prima: De Me Ipso, sive ΑΥΤΟΛΟΓΙΑ (TCD MS 10971/6/2r)[25]

PART ONE Concerning Myself, or AUTOLOGY (*Met*, p. 29)

As described above, it is due to the epistemological inspection of the self that Geulincx's Occasionalism culminates in the assertion of *nescience*: humanity as ignorant and impotent in the face of God. And despite the infrequency with which Beckett records the word itself, the legacy of this single word throughout *Metaphysics* and even *Ethics* is immense. Beckett recorded some of Geulincx's most emphatic assertions about the agency of self as derived from *autology*, such as 'I am a thing one and simple' (p. 33)[26], 'I have thoughts that do not depend on me' (p. 34)[27] and 'My human condition is completely independent of me' (p. 43)[28]. He also used the term in a letter to MacGreevy in August 1936 where he wrote of his reading *Faust* that he could understand how '"keep on keeping on" [could function] as a "social prophylactic, but not at all as a light in the autological darkness, or the theological"' (SB to TM, 19 August 1936: *L1*, p. 368).

Following the collapse of the quasi-autological chess game, Murphy stares into the unresponsive cornea of Mr. Endon and finally sees a version of himself reflected. He literally sees 'horribly reduced, obscured and distorted, his own image' (*Mu*, p. 156). This instant of non-perception has been described as a 'Geulincxian critique of the Proustian moment, which redeems nothing' (Ackerley 2004a, p. 202). Murphy is horrifyingly still himself, unable to let go of his sanity's rootedness in the big world. Recalling the terms of Murphy's attraction to Mr. Endon, O'Hara has described Murphy here as reproducing 'the pose of Narcissus, bent over the stream to see himself' (O'Hara 1997, p. 60). This is the point at which Murphy in his narcissistic way blooms. To pursue this analogy briefly (leaving O'Hara's Freud to one side in favour of Ovid, whose *Metamorphoses* Beckett was fond of), if Mr. Endon is Murphy's Echo, with his psychosis perhaps a little of Juno's curse, this is only after Murphy has in vain and in vanity tried to sound the echo of Mr. Endon's moves in the game. However, Murphy will be 'melted, consumed by the fire inside him' (Ovid 2004, p. 16), as is the fate of Narcissus, rather than turn to stone. The game has unmasked him as the selfish Narcissus, not the selfless Echo. Staring into these 'Waters' reveals only his own 'Chaos' and its messy consequences. By the following day he will be dead and dust, even more literally 'a speck in Mr. Endon's unseen' (*Mu*, p. 156). Unable to resign himself to the Geulingian knowledge that 'whatever I do stays within me; and that nothing I do passes into my body, or any other body, or anything else' (*Et*, p. 331), Murphy persists with his misguided belief that there might be something to achieve in this game. There is not, and for Murphy as anyone else Geulincx would offer the simple restraint: 'It is vain for me to attempt what I cannot undertake' (p. 339). Murphy cannot properly seek out the company of others like himself, as he sees Mr. Endon to be, yet nor can he sufficiently stick only to his own. He will indeed 'break down', as Beckett described it, between the two poles of Malraux and Geulincx by dying while tied to the chair, stranded between here and there, neither wholly of the big world nor of the little.

Murphy's chess game was hugely important to Beckett. Through all the difficulties trying to get the novel published Beckett remained steadfast in refusing to alter this section, and had even considered 'putting the game of chess there in a section by itself' (SB to TM, 7 July 1936: *L1*, p. 350). On 13 November

Murphy *and 'Mechanical Writing'*

1936, for example, he flatly pointed out his frustration and incredulity at a publisher's wish to cut some of the book:

> I can't imagine what they want me to take out. I refuse to touch the section entitled Amor Intellectualis quo M. se ipsum amat. And I refuse also to touch the game of chess. The Horoscope chapter is also essential. But I am anxious for the book to be published and therefore cannot afford to reply with a blank refusal to cut anything. (SB to GR, 13 November 1936: *L1*, p. 380)

Nearly 30 years later when *Murphy* was reprinted by John Calder's Jupiter imprint Beckett can again be found involved with this chess game, altering Mr. Endon's penultimate move, number 42. Ackerley describes how 'in many editions of *Murphy* Mr. Endon's move 42 is incorrect, being printed as K – Q2, an illegal final move into check', and continues:

> The Routledge original, the Grove Press printing and the French translation are correct; the error crept in when the novel was reset for the 1963 Jupiter edition, and was replicated in the Picador version where it went unnoticed even by those (Taylor and Loughery, 1989; myself, 1998) writing specifically on the game. (Ackerley 2004, p. 195)

Ackerley could not have been aware when publishing this statement in 2004, as Beckett's correspondence with Barbara Bray was not made available for consultation by TCD until 2006, that Beckett makes reference to this very alteration in his correspondence with Bray, and to how the game itself is one big, if 'feeble', joke:

> Checked Murphy's game of chess and made a small change. Mr. Endon's 42nd move: K – Q2 instead of K – K2. Pretty feeble joke the whole thing. Could do it a little better now – but not much. (SB to BB, 7 February 1962, TCD MS 10948/1/170)[29]

The publishing error, therefore, appears to be in reprinting the earlier K – K2.

However, the new move (K – Q2) would place Mr. Endon's king at the mercy of Murphy's queen on an adjacent square, an illegal move. There is therefore an argument to be made that Beckett's change was itself made in error, as it is the only move in the game that would break the rules of chess, and Beckett may have realized as much and retracted it. In a letter to Bray of early the following year Beckett reports that he had looked again at '<u>Murphy</u> proofs', and writes 'I thought there was an error in the Endon affence, but there does not seem to be, or I could not find it' (SB to BB, undated [January 1963] (TCD MS 10948/1/219)).[30] With either move, however, the central point remains that

Murphy refuses to end the game by making winning moves, though K – Q2 would make the 'feeble joke' of Mr. Endon's lack of recognition that much more explicit, while retaining the possibility that his next move would complete a symmetry.

Occasional(ist) Reviews

Early reviews of *Murphy* provide interesting examples of the reception of the Geulingian aspects of Beckett's oeuvre not usually considered by studies on the topic. If Beckett's critics came to recognize and make explicit certain Occasionalist impetuses of *Murphy* in 1959–60, they were still slower than a small number of reviewers by some 20-plus years, the reviewers more implicitly pointing to these traits. In 1938 Coffey wrote a review of *Murphy* that presumably, according to J. C. C. Mays, pleased Beckett enough to have been a major reason for his gifting Coffey the novel's manuscript (the now privately owned *Sasha Murphy* discussed above, which Coffey later sold). In the allusion-heavy 'review' Coffey asserts the chess game to be the novel's climax, and writes of the scene following the game's collapse:

> Communication – the crash together in space of two granite blocks – ends at the finger-nails. He does not undesire but through pain of loss. The experiment failed again. (Coffey 1938. Reproduced in Mays 2010, p. 89)

For Coffey, as for Beckett, the chess game is the novel's climactic 'crash together in space', revealing Murphy as the protagonist had studiously avoided seeing himself – as having 'failed'. How this climax comes about for Coffey, who frames the issue in terms of 'Communication', is through the very Geulingian concept of 'undesire'. The realization of the failure of Murphy's 'experiment' in the asylum is a consequence of his inability to 'undesire', to undo his desires, to 'want nothing'. Of course Coffey was one of a small number of people intimately acquainted with Beckett's philosophical interests of this period, as records of his involvement with Beckett (discussed in Chapter 1) show. So it comes as little surprise that Occasionalist undercurrents might shift around among the many layers of Coffey's only very recently published text. But what of reviewers who had little or no inside knowledge of Beckett's working methodologies?

In a predominantly negative review, published in the same year as Coffey's, Dylan Thomas delivered his verdict that '"Murphy" is difficult, serious, and wrong' (Thomas 1938, p. 454). This was due in part to Beckett's own world of '*Quid pro quo*' (*Mu*, p. 3), his selling what Thomas calls 'his bluffs over the double counter'. However, Thomas did at least admit the work's intelligence, calling *Murphy*'s author 'a great legpuller and an enemy of obviousness'. But these traits of its author were not enough to redeem the novel, and the review concludes that *Murphy* 'fails':

> It fails in its purpose because the minds and the bodies of these characters are almost utterly without relation to each other. (Thomas 1938, p. 454)[31]

Thomas thereby states his central criticism of the novel in terms that evoke *Murphy*'s Occasionalism. The disconnection between mind and body, residing in the novel as a 'problem [. . .] of little interest' neither to be solved or even necessarily neatly rendered, but rather variously 'exploited', appears for Thomas as a disconnect that also distances the reader, asking too much of them if it expects them to be interested in what Thomas calls 'walking, gesticulating brains' (Thomas 1938, p. 454). The imagery is suited to a caricatured depiction of Geulingian Occasionalism. A 'walking, gesticulating' brain is a viable picture of what for Geulincx is the essential ineffable mystery of all human life: given that I have a brain and that I appear to do things (like walk and gesticulate, examples that Geulincx even uses[32]), what is there constituting me but these two separate events upon which, with no rational justification, I impose a causal relation? If I reflect 'with Reason' then I will see that this causal relation is entirely unknowable, and is thus nothing to do with me. According to Geulincx, in a sense we are indeed just such 'walking, gesticulating brains'. Like Coffey, Thomas gets to the heart of *Murphy* as a novel founded on or climaxing in Occasionalist disconnection. For Coffey this is a disconnection between minds, between Mr. Endon and Murphy's and it instances the brilliance of the novel's climactic non-climax. For Thomas it is between minds and bodies and it thereby reveals the flaws in what he thinks of as the novel's unconvincingness.

This chapter has argued that, based on the evidence available, Beckett's substantial research into Geulincx appears to have been undertaken too late into the composition of *Murphy* to have a significant influence upon earlier stages of the novel that would not be the result of extensive, unlikely revisions. A corollary is that when Geulincx does come to the fore, as revealed in the chess game, this is an important underlying presence that sets a precedent for Beckett's later ways of incorporating his wide reading. Might it therefore be possible, even necessary, to think of the importance of Geulincx for Beckett in terms of how Beckett might have made use of his research after completing *Murphy*? If Geulincx was 'already' in *Murphy*, as Beckett told Kennedy in 1967, then Geulincx would likely be, this 'already' hints, in other works. The transcriptions produced in 1936 remained with Beckett all his life, in contrast to many other papers donated to archives at Reading or elsewhere, hinting that, as Uhlmann has indeed suggested, 'they were made [. . .] for works he might write after *Murphy*' (*Et*, p. 303). While Uhlmann's strong assertion of what the notes might have been made 'for' is at an opposite end of a spectrum from Dowd's description of the notes as being irreducibly 'of uncertain status', nevertheless the proposed chronology of how the transcriptions map onto *Murphy*'s composition, if even close to accurate, can have identifiable implications far beyond a reading of this novel. That Geulincx does arguably come to play an important role in the novel's final stages, as climax rather than 'key', a ghost in the 'mechanical writing' if not 'the entire machine', holds out the tantalizing prospect that works beyond *Murphy* might also be composed, in sympathy perhaps more than in overt synchronicity, with aspects of Geulincx's philosophy more complex than those Beckett deployed as underwriting the stark Occasionalist schisms of *Murphy*. The following chapter explores this prospect, and argues that Beckett's Geulincx research informed a new way of working, characterized by a shift away from 'notesnatching' and 'phrase-hunting', to become important to the complex composition processes of the transitional novel *Watt*.

Chapter 3

Watt: Ineffable Forces

The previous chapter argued that there are good reasons for not expecting *Murphy* to be what Cohn called 'the most Geulincxian of the works'. It analysed the available chronology of *Murphy*'s composition alongside the novel's allusions to Geulincx, and argued that these allusions change, as the late chapters progress, from surface level textual quotation to something more deeply ingrained and integrated with characterization and narrative game playing. Fundamentally, Chapter 2 argued that for the most part the Geulincx of *Murphy* is closer to a Geulincx of Beckett's 'Philosophy Notes' than to the 1936 transcriptions, and so it concluded by asking the same question Uhlmann has asked of Beckett's transcriptions; might it be they were put to use in, or were even made for, 'works he might write after *Murphy*'? In addressing this question the current chapter focuses on *Watt*, the novel Beckett turned to after *Murphy* was published. This is not with a view to arguing that *Watt* is a work Beckett purposefully kept his notes for, but rather that elements of *Watt*'s composition can be seen to owe variously subtle and minor, though sometimes deeply embedded, debts to Geulincx that reveal how Geulincx was becoming integrated with other aspects of Beckett's thinking. While *Watt* is far from what might be called a Geulingian novel, the traces of Beckett's interests and reading, what Ackerley refers to as the 'ghosts and fluxions' (Ackerley 2005a, p. 26), that found their way into this novel's composition, have the capacity, when unearthed, to reveal new aspects of this multifaceted novel.

In 1994, in a chapter in which he also argued for the importance of Spinoza to *Murphy*, P. J. Murphy wrote of Beckett's enigmatic English-language novel *Watt*, written over a protracted period between 1941 and 1945 and the last work Beckett would complete in English until *From an Abandoned Work* (1954–5), '*Watt* is perhaps the decisive work for reappraising Beckett's relationship to the philosophical tradition'. Murphy focuses the claim, however, to substantiate the narrower argument that '*Watt* is a Kantian novel' (Murphy 1994, p. 229). *Watt* has also been read as detective fiction, as a *cryptic* text, a farce of cruelty and absurdity and, as influential initial critical studies had it, as a parody of Cartesian rationality.[1] There have been many other readings.[2]

Despite the diversity of approaches, a certain persuasive critical consensus has come to obtain in recent years regarding the strange and difficult object that is *Watt*, a consensus that reflects a more nuanced version of a view such as P. J. Murphy's. According to this historicizing reconceptualization, *Watt* is a vitally important point of transition in Beckett's oeuvre in the contexts of his relationships with philosophy and psychology and how these interact with a changing working methodology as regards source incorporation. In 2009 Feldman wrote, for example, and while criticizing P. J. Murphy's going too far with Kant, that '*Watt* may be seen as *the* pivotal novel in Beckett's oeuvre' (Feldman 2009b, p. 13). In the specific context of Feldman's phenomenological analysis, Beckett's phenomenology is key to broader shifts in his writing, and *Watt* was Beckett's breakthrough in 'beginning to write phenomenologically' (p. 14). Similarly, Weller argues for the transitional status of *Watt* in its new ways of enacting and performing its concerns as this novel's defining characteristic. According to Weller, *Watt* is the point at which Beckett achieves 'an actualization', rather than (as was the case in earlier works, particularly *Murphy*) 'the thematization' of what Weller calls 'the Schizoid voice' (Weller 2009, p. 43).

Beckett himself had a characteristically more diffident view when it came to assessing the novel he is often said to have referred to as his 'ugly duckling'.[3] Harvey quotes Beckett saying *Watt* was '"a game". . .a means of "staying sane", and a way "to keep [his] hand in"' (Harvey 1970, p. 222).[4] In 1947, while Reavey was acting as agent and having great difficulty placing the work with a publisher, Beckett described how historical circumstances had imposed compromises on a novel that he would come to recall, when it did eventually find a willing publisher, as 'our old misery' (SB to GR, 12 May 1953: *L2*, p. 376):

> It is an unsatisfactory book, written in dribs and drabs, first on the run, then of an evening after the clodhopping, during the occupation. But it has its place in the series, as will perhaps appear in time. (SB to GR, 14 May 1947: *L2*, p. 55)

As the studies by Feldman, Weller and others show, *Watt*'s 'place' in Beckett's oeuvre, an oeuvre that Beckett himself thought of as a 'series', has indeed been appearing in time.[5]

Watt is not only part of a series of completed or published works, but it manifests seriality in a number of distinct yet interrelated ways. The first part of the novel is taken up with Watt's coming to the house, whereupon another servant, Arsene, departs, and Watt thereby plays his part in what the novel's sole extant typescript describes as 'the series of servants' (*Watt* Typescript, p. 353[6]). Once Watt is inside the house, as one in the series of replenished and replenishing servants who come to and depart from the house, his movements – between levels of the house, for example – are also part of serial processes. And while on a particular level of the house, on an even more micro level, Watt's thought processes at these various stages themselves involve the management of numerous serial processes. Indeed, it is the novel's serial enumerative and sometimes entropic reasoning – that which Deleuze subtitled the *'Langue I'* of Beckett – that gives the novel's comic critiques of rationalism such intensity,[7] its particular 'Cartesian dimension' that Ackerley rightly argues 'should not be ignored' (Ackerley 2005a, p. 13).

Also vital to a consideration of *Watt* as manifesting seriality is how the work was drafted and redrafted across some 4 years, in the 'dribs and drabs' of semi-discrete scenes and evolutionary stages that Beckett mentions. This serial compositional existence – whereby characters, places and scenes emerge through a number of transitions, amendments and mathematical permutations – is preserved (for the most part, given that certain important compositional stages are missing) in what Carlton Lake called the 'white whale' (Lake 1984, p. 76) of Beckett scholarship: the stages through which the novel came to fruition in the six notebooks and single typescript held at HRHRC and commonly referred to as the Ur-*Watt*. A playful, visible residue of the protracted and experimental processes of *Watt*'s composition is retained as the published novel's addenda, where the partially jettisoned material is a kind of synecdoche that connects the novel to its own prior existences.

This multiplicity of transitions and serial existences is of direct relevance to Geulincx's importance to the composition of *Watt*. For the importance of memory – how one version of a thing becomes another, whether in a Viconian trinity or otherwise – has also come to the fore in studies of the novel, an importance that derives from its being written 'during the occupation'.[8] As scholars such as Knowlson and Ackerley have noted, Beckett worked for the most part on *Watt* without straightforward recourse to his lengthy 'Philosophy Notes', 'Whoroscope' notebook, the transcriptions from Geulincx or most other sets of notes, having been forced to leave behind many of his belongings in Paris in August 1942 following a hasty telegrammed warning from Mania Péron, whose husband Alfred had been arrested by the Gestapo. The possibility of Geulincx's presence in *Watt*, therefore, provides an intriguing case study of what would happen to Beckett's philosophical and 'notesnatching' impetuses when he was forced to work without direct recourse to his transcriptions, notes and books. That is, when working from memory.

This chapter argues that, as a memorialized presence, one utilized in ways that did not derive from direct reference to notes such as TCD MS 10971/6, Geulincx features more in the protracted processes of composition – in the Ur-*Watt*'s serial stages – than in the final published novel where much of this presence is alternately subsumed, consumed, sublimated or discarded. Tracing this fleeting and background presence as it develops from composition to published novel throws light on the issue of *Watt*'s place in the oeuvre as 'series': unpacking Geulincx's, albeit minor, presence in the Ur-*Watt* opens up a number of important moments at which broader preoccupations of Beckett's – conceptions of psychological interiority, and the inevitability of humanity's insatiable needs, for example – found new ways and means in their being mapped onto literary and linguistic explorations of communicative possibility. In the parts he plays in these shifting foci, Geulincx is important to Beckett's 'series' conceived as progressive stages moving from description to performance, from 'thematization' to 'actualization' in a number of ways that involve memory and philosophy. The almost-ineffable, phantasmal presence of Geulincx in *Watt* confirms the appraisal of this novel as an important step, albeit at times a faltering one not dissimilar to Watt's own stilted way of walking, on the way towards the abstracted voices of Beckett's middle period works, and also that the problems attendant upon an unreliable memory paradoxically instilled in Beckett a confidence to progress further down the road that would differentiate him from Joyce. Beckett told Knowlson that he realized how Joyce 'had gone as far as one could in the direction of knowing more, [being] in control of one's material. [. . .] I realised that my own way was in impoverishment, in lack of knowledge and in taking away, in subtracting rather than adding' (cited in Knowlson 1996, p. 352). In beginning to work with fragmentary shards of knowledge, Beckett managed to turn a situation of very real 'impoverishment' to a difficult but vital creative advantage.

Autology in *Watt*

As Chapter 2 discussed, psychological interiority, its pleasures and (what *Ohio Impromptu* sarcastically calls) its 'profounds' (*CDW*, p. 448), were central both literally and figuratively to *Murphy*. *Watt* is a very different work, and it might seem surprising that any legacy Geulincx has for this novel would be framed in the context of a term that at first sight might not seem especially productive. Insofar as *Watt* is 'a game', a ludic puzzle or ultrarationalist's satirical nightmare, it is frequently a game played with surfaces, with the appearances of things and their positions in the world. If Watt were to look inside himself to inspect what he knows of himself, 'in a careful enquiry into the nature, condition, and origin of oneself' (*Et*, p. 329) as Geulincx describes self-inspection, he (and we) might not expect to discover very much. Certainly any force of personality Watt has is as bland as the milk Mr Hackett believes is all he lives on. Early in the novel Watt finds that he cannot hear Mr Spiro's responses to the question of what should be done with a rat that '*eats of a consecrated wafer*'. He cannot hear 'because of other voices, singing, crying, stating, murmuring, things unintelligible, in his ear' (*W*, p. 22). Sometimes, of these voices, 'Watt understood all, and sometimes he understood much, and sometimes he understood little, and sometimes he understood nothing, as now' (p. 23). Such are the less than coherent sounds of Watt's interior, inner self.

Bearing out a broad conception of 'the series', and of the composition of the Ur-*Watt*'s stages specifically, as characterized by turning away from more overt uses of philosophical and psychological vocabulary as are found in *Murphy*, the first-person plural narrator of the *Watt* typescript bears a stronger similarity in this regard to Murphy. When asked, for example, where exactly it is the narrator plans to 'get along' to following his proposed departure from Arsene, the narrator replies:

> "To some other place" we said, "some other scene, some other field of activity."
> "Nothing more definite than that?" said Arsene. "Think well before you reply."
> We thought well and then we replied. "Perhaps deep down in our unconscious mind –"
> Arsene rubbed his hands. "Ah" he said. "the unconscious mind! What a subject for a short story!"
> "Perhaps deep down in those paleozoic profounds, midst mammoth Old Red Sandstone phalli and carboniferous pudenda, lurked the timid wish to leave you."
> "More!" cried Arsene. "Again! Again! Further! Deeper! The Upper Silurian! The Lower Silurian! The truth! The truth!" (*Watt* Typescript, p. 149)

Ackerley has discussed how in drafts of *Watt* such explorations of an ancient stratified mental world were 'defined as "auto-speliology" [*sic*]' (Ackerley 2005a, p. 24), and how this psychological geological zoning is related to the elemental imagery of mud, rocks and geographical zones in the Beckett Country.[9] The neologism also recalls Geulincx's subtitle of *Metaphysics*' Chapter 1 'Autology'. Yet this word that Beckett uses to name the parsing of one's own sedimented layers is removed from the novel before its final version.

'Arsie', as the narrator nicknames Arsene, wills the narrator onward to delve through these rocky domains: 'Dig! Delve! Deeper! Deeper! The Cambrian! The uterine! The pre-uterine!' (*Watt* Typescript, p. 149) The narrator has a limit, however, replying that this pre-uterine is a stage too far.[10] The later Watt's mind in the published novel has become, in contrast to these zones of stony penises, coal-bearing arses and womb-ages, a jumble of voices. Watt has lost whatever capacity this earlier narrator had for an awareness of, or at least vocabulary for, his 'unconscious mind'.[11] The later Watt instead turns his attention more fully towards the world, to his role as servant within it, in what might be characterized as a form of *despectio sui*, where a servant must disregard personal desires to function more properly in their given, somewhat impotent and obligatory role.

Beckett's imagining boundaries of psychological space according to geological periods is hinted at earlier in the 'Whoroscope' notebook, where he noted 'the geology of conscience – cambrian experience, cainozoic [sic] judgements'[12], immediately prior to listing a table of Geological Eras. Rocky memories which are, as Pilling details, derived in part from Jean-Paul Sartre's *L'Imagination*: 'Sartre (141, 144ff) speaks of a "géometrie" in Husserl; Beckett is using "conscience" in the French sense, to mean sensibility' (Pilling 2005, p. 46). Beckett, then, transforms a derivation from the initial Sartrean origins of its first appearance in the 'Whoroscope' notebook, reconfiguring it with an autological inflection during the composition of *Watt*.

Unlike the later Mr Knott, James Quin (an early incarnation of the novel-to-be's protagonist but who gradually through the Ur-*Watt* becomes Mr Knott) did have some interest in autology. Quin's internal depths are primarily determined by what is called a 'prevailing sensation [. . .] of nothingness' (*Watt* Typescript, pp. 53–5), and Beckett wrote a long passage on 'The Nothingness' (p. 55) as it pertains to Quin's interiority, with 'The Sky' (p. 61) above and 'The Waste' (p. 63) below, between which Quin abides as 'a dark nothing between the dark thing above and the dark thing beneath' (p. 61):

> The feeling of nothingness, born in Quin with the first beat of his heart, if not before, died in him with the last, and not before. (p. 55)

Ackerley describes the world of *Watt* as a world 'not of mathematics (the Idea) nor biology (unaccomodated man), but of physics, in the Greek sense of that word ("*physis*") as defined by Windelband (73) in terms of the relationship between the unchanging order of things and the world of change' (Ackerley 2005a, p. 25). Unwittingly posed on the middle ground of such a world, Quin's ability to inspect these depths of 'nothingness' is limited by a number of factors, one of which recalls a neologism that was noted as entry no. 1123 in the 'Dream' notebook, 'Autopornography' (Beckett 1999a, p. 161):

> Not that Quin, regarding this and other traits of his nature, was quite devoid of curiosity. But each time he set himself to give it satisfaction, he was filled with that selfsame chagrin as is the man, the woman, or the child, who seeks to obtain, without the aid of a reflector, a clear view of his or her own anus. (*Watt* Typescript, p. 55)[13]

Quin not only suffers from a sense of nothingness, he cannot even glimpse this nothingness. Such doubled incapacity, here in a man literally and comically doubled over, echoes the incapacity that Geulincx argues characterises the self's autological investigations. Not only can we do nothing, but we also cannot even properly comprehend our lack of agency because such agency is the ineffable domain of God alone. We can reason that we can do nothing, but we cannot properly know this nothingness: 'I understand only that I can never understand it' (*Et*, p. 334). We simply watch the world, and do nothing in it, even though paradoxically we must do things in it. The congruency recalls a note in the 'Whoroscope' notebook, where in a series of fragmentary philosophical part-quotations that include mention of Socrates, Spinoza, Kant and Bacon, Beckett writes 'Not only did he know nothing, but he was ignorant of the fact' (UoR MS 3000). Geulincx, however, manages at times to contrive some degree of consolation from this apparently self-contradictory impotence of invested spectatorship. Beckett transcribed the following from a summary of how 'I am but a spectator of the World':

> God alone can produce that spectacle. [. . .] And He does so in such an ineffable and incomprehensible manner that among all the stupendous miracles with which God favours me on this scene, I myself, the spectator, am His greatest and most enduring miracle. (*Et*, p. 336)

For Quin, despite insurmountable obstacles, lack of proper tools or any religiosity he might harbour, compulsion to his own version of self-inspection is somewhat less 'stupendous' and is merely, unfortunately, inevitable:

> And the time comes, alas, in the life of each one of us, however godfearing that life may have been, and wholesome, and upright, when a clear view of that part, if without synecdoche it may be called a part, would more than Baiae's [sic] Strand, the Vale of Avoca, or the Lakes of Killarney, gratify the eye. (*Watt* Typescript, pp. 55)[14]

But before there was 'nothingness' in the Ur-*Watt*, there was the more down to earth notion of death. In the first notebook Quin thinks about death so much that it engenders a 'feeling of weakness or fatigue', and this 'caused Quin ^to go^ at an early hour to bed' and to forgo an outer world of 'the precincts of his home and garden'. Quin's weary resignation sounds echoes of Murphy's dark inner zones, but given an even more explicit Occasionalist frame: 'The feeling of weakness or fatigue, in so far as it was a matter at all, was as dark a matter as what has ^sometimes^ been called the occasional kind' (*Watt* notebook 1, pp. 47–9). As discussed in Chapter 2, interiority was Murphy's *raison d'être*. The only thing Murphy finds worthwhile is his dark zones of 'the best of himself', a 'best' he finds via compromises and caveats (the chair of the big world, and his being powerless to prevent even the tiniest of big world events, such as the ringing of a telephone, from happening), but which nevertheless exists for him as the only worthwhile possibility for self. Belacqua too had few reservations about his own 'wombtomb', whose interiority 'was real thought and real living, living thought' (*Dr*, p. 45). However, there was to be no comparable 'best' of any character's interiority after 1936 when Beckett read Geulincx, and little of any characters' interiorities at all in the final version of *Watt*. While it would be rash to assert a directly causal, formative connection between the 1936 research and the turn away from interiority as relief, nevertheless it is productive to think of Geulincx's *humilitas* as having its part to play in this turn, given how much Beckett was impressed by the ethical idea. It seems reasonable to postulate that it is highly unlikely Beckett was especially preoccupied with the metaphysics of seventeenth-century Occasionalism as he and Suzanne fled south from Nazi persecution during the early phase of *Watt*'s composition. Yet, as the ideas he once paid such detailed, assiduous attention to themselves became sedimented in memory, the Geulingian conception of self-investigation as futile – because it is an exploration that can find only accreted layers, and no ultimate 'bedrock of assurance' (Ackerley 2005a, p. 25) – was playing a part in Beckett's developing aesthetic thinking. Whereas Murphy's occasional access to his Occasionalist nothingness was an index of his freedom, the desolate 'nothingness' in the Ur-*Watt* evinces a shift into interiority as a different kind of emptiness, as an unmasterable ignorance and impotence that comes after Beckett transcribed his lengthy notes on Geulincx's own convictions about such exploration. Geulincx summarizes these discoveries of incapacity and ignorance in the following: 'I cannot get beyond *I do not know*, there is nothing I can add to this *I do not know*. I do not know how I came to this condition. . .What is lacking is the knowledge of how I came to this condition' (*Et*, p. 334). For Quin too, autological inspection is the impossible inspection of a void; Quin too does not know, and cannot 'get beyond' or 'add to' this.

This theory – that Geulincx has a part to play in Beckett's conceptions of failed interior investigation, but a part that is not necessarily wholly formative – is itself somewhat Occasionalist. Naturally there were many other factors at work in Beckett's thinking about thinking and about himself around the time of composing both *Murphy* and *Watt*. To take just one early example, it is well known that he underwent psychoanalysis in London in 1934–5. A 'truncated analysis' (Connor 2008, p. 12), but that is no less significant for its being severed or for its being an autobiographical self-exploration. Along with the reading in psychology and notes undertaken alongside it, Beckett's analysis attests to the complications and complicities among his various familiarities with delving into a self, either on his own or accompanied by another (Wilfred Bion acting as Beckett's Virgilian guide in the Tavistock clinic). However, there are textual specificities that allow the divide to be more confidently bridged.

In the third Ur-*Watt* notebook Beckett explicitly uses the term 'autology' to describe Watt's thinking about the abstract and, for him, the inexplicable

Mondrian-style circle and dot painting he discovers in Erskine's room (and which in the novel brings him to a state of tears resulting from discovery, difficult for the ultrarationalist to face, of the infinite and irresolvable):

> As to whether the formation was the fixity of self-indifference or – Watt sought for a word, found one, found two, three, four, approved them, related them, approved the relation, disapproved them, disapproved the relation, let them stand and was discontent – the regulated turmoil of autology's autoscopy, the loss in each case was the same, because it was the loss of all. (*Watt* notebook 3)[15]

Pilling describes how this scene of Watt's impotent language before the striking image also bears on the novel's broader, linguistic concerns:

> This anticipates the moment in *Watt* when Watt can find no words to assuage his 'need of semantic succour' (79). But *Watt* as a whole is the product of the tensions dramatized here. [. . .] With every intention of creating 'regulated turmoil', Beckett is nevertheless obliged to content himself, or discontent himself, with the 'fixity' which any 'formation' – visual or verbal – confers upon its constituent ingredients. (Pilling 1997, p. 180)

Though left out of the final novel, the use of Geulincx's term in what would have been a part of Chapter 2 reveals a conception of Watt's own communicative possibilities conceived in Geulingian terms, where a linguistic manifestation of 'autology's autoscopy', a language of self-critique, is a critique that comes up against its own limits in being incapable of seeing through its own 'veil' (*Dis*, p. 171) (as Beckett described literary language to Axel Kaun in 1937) because it is constructed in that self-same language. Even a minimal language is full of 'turmoil', and in seeking to regulate it Beckett juxtaposes his narrator's fluid and ranging vocabulary alongside the comic need for precision about the bathetic focus of that vocabulary. A form of irony, then, becomes a vital autological implement during *Watt*'s composition:

> The word marsh would perhaps better render than the word waste, and perhaps even better than the word marsh the word bog, the precise shade of meaning intended in the present connexion.
> For the word waste, therefore, wherever in the present connexion it has been used, or wherever similarly hereinafter by unavoidable inadvertence it shall be used, the word marsh may perhaps be substituted with advantage; or, with perhaps even greater advantage, the word bog.
> So much for the sky and the wa - -, pardon!, the bog. (*Watt* Typescript, p. 63)

Although there are numerous other points in the final novel as well as in the notebooks and typescript that bear on the capacities of language to communicate meaning – to accurately convey, or even to performatively change, the status of something in the world – the transition from metaphysics to epistemology implied in a linguistic autology instances Beckett's 'series' developing the ways in which the possibilities of an autological analysis of language can at least be framed, if not satisfactorily resolved, in terms that owe a debt to Geulincx.

Beckett had noted a similar word to 'autology' some years earlier in the 'Whoroscope' notebook, which was 'autolysis'.[16] Autolysis is a physical process whereby cells of the body are destroyed by their own enzymes, and is more commonly referred to in the way Beckett also defines it, as 'self-digestion' (UoR MS 3000). It is a process not dissimilar to Watt's own self-induced communicative entropy that manifests in the asylum. Watt's entrapment in his fatalist philosophical method drives him eventually to that refuge which is even more lowly that his status as a servant for Mr Knott, where his inability to look into his own working methods with those self-same working methods is shown to be as flawed an enterprise as Quin's attempts without the aid of an autoscope to look up his own arse and see his nothingness. Watt's predicament here is the logical conclusion of the impossibility of 'autology's autoscopy', of critiquing the confines of his critique from within. It can be read as a more linguistic version of Geulincx's insistence upon the impossibility of discovering a self that is capable of agency from within that same self, and its being located in relation to this use of 'autology' in the Ur-*Watt* is evidence that, for Beckett, Geulincx's Occasionalist philosophy was becoming increasingly malleable, amenable to a more 'fantasia'-style interweaving even as it existed only as fragments in memory.

Coming, Being, Going I

In the first single-authored full-length critical study of Beckett, Hugh Kenner argued that instances of the 'partially congruent' (Kenner 1961, p. 83) in Beckett's oeuvre bear a mark of Geulincx in their playing out the central epistemological concern of Occasionalist metaphysics – a lack of knowledge of causation. According to Kenner, examples of Geulingian partial congruence in *Watt*, movements that in their being 'partially' congruent might come to life through a shrunken conarium rather than through one entirely dissipated, include Watt's shambling way of walking and the frog song where 'each frog attends only to its private schedule of croaks' (p. 86). In situations such as these a harmony of sorts appears to occur. However, such harmony is established by accident rather than preordained design. Watt does progress forward, but this is coincidence, a lucky result. And although the frogs do not intend to produce a coherent 'song', Watt hears the sounds of the Fibonacci sequence the frogs produce as systematized music. These are instances of a 'pre-established arbitrary' (*W*, p. 114) rather than a harmonious Leibnizian alternative. According to Kenner, such an almost-connect between events and the perception of these events is what 'qualifies him [Geulincx] for repeated mention in the Beckett canon'. This is because, according to Kenner, such incongruity derives from Geulincx's 'doctrine of a "bodytight" mental world, attached to which the body performs its gyrations according to laws the mind need not attempt to fathom' (Kenner 1961, p. 83). In 1961 Kenner could not have known, but Beckett even transcribed specific examples that bear out these arguments. Recalling Watt's 'headline tardigrade' (*W*, p. 24) Geulincx wrote, for example, 'These feet are not moved because I wish to go on my way, but because another wishes what I wish' (*Et*, p. 332), in the same arguments in which he set out the cradle analogy.

However, I want to argue here that Watt's disconnected movements also derive from a broader imagistic legacy of Cartesian and post-Cartesian thought. In making the case that *Watt* is a philosophical novel in a more performative sense than *Murphy* is, and duly recognizing how a Cartesian rationalist 'spirit of system' (*U*, p. 2) that the narrator of *The Unnamable* so despises thoroughly pervades *Watt*'s methodological digressions, it should also be noted how Beckett's philosophical imaginings in this novel are not confined to explicit enumerative reasoning. They also pervade something as visual, and even viscerally realist, as Watt's way of walking. For Watt's way of walking is not just a method of perambulation, it is a *méthode*, a 'way of advancing' (*W*, p. 23) to get him to refuge:

> Watt's way of advancing due east, for example, was to turn his bust as far as possible towards the north and at the same time to fling out his right leg as far as possible towards the south, and then to turn his bust as far as possible towards the south and at the same time to fling out his left leg as far as possible towards the north, and then again to turn his bust as far as possible towards the north and to fling out his right leg as far as possible towards the south, and then again to turn his bust as far as possible towards the south and to fling out his left leg as far as possible towards the north, and so on, over and over again, many many times, until he reached his destination, and could sit down. So, standing first on one leg, and then on the other, he moved forward, a headlong tardigrade, in a straight line. (pp. 23–4)

In his very first published poem 'Whoroscope' Beckett had included biographical details culled from J. P. Mahaffy's *Descartes* (1901) with a view to winning first prize in Nancy Cunard's poetry competition, and he was duly successful. 'Whoroscope' references the famous sequence of dreams Descartes had on the night of 10 November 1619 (as Beckett's annotations to 'Whoroscope' have it, lines 45–53 of the poem refer to Descartes's 'visions and pilgrimage to Loretto' (*SP*, p. 7)). Down the years, scholarship on these dreams frequently paints them as ghostly, unknowable shadows coupled to and darkening the otherwise rational system, and in the first of his three dreams Descartes has similar perambulatory problems to those of Watt. In Norman Kemp-Smith's partial translation of Adrien Baillet's biography (Baillet relates the dreams from Descartes's 'Olympica' notebook) the event is recorded as follows:

> After he had fallen asleep his imagination was strongly impressed with certain phantoms which appeared before him and terrified him in such wise that, while walking, as he fancied, through the streets, he was obliged to turn himself over to his left side so as to be able to advance to the place where he wished to go, feeling, as he did, a great weakness in his right side which disabled him from leaning on it. Ashamed of walking in that manner he made an effort to straighten himself, but felt an impetuous wind which, catching him up in a kind of whirlwind, made him revolve three or four times on his left foot. But what really frightened him was something more: the difficulty he had in dragging himself along made him think he was failing at every step, until finally perceiving on his path a college with open gate he entered, seeking there a refuge and a remedy for his trouble. (Kemp Smith, 1963, pp. 33–4.)

But it is not only the way of walking that bears comparison with Watt's. John Cole describes the significance of the fact that Descartes's difficulties take place on a street:

> The street scene is almost by definition a 'method scene.' Etymologically, the term 'method' and its cognates in French and Latin go back to the Greek meta ('according to') and hodos ('the way, path, or road').
>
> The 'way' or 'road' in French voire or chemin and in Latin via or iter, was to become one of Descartes's most characteristic and insistent images in his later writing, where le droit chemin suggests 'the right method.' (Cole 1992, p. 134)

Across the breadth of Beckett's oeuvre roads suggest comparable methodological pathways and routes of coherence – something Chapter 1 discussed as operating in *Company*. The 'country road' where the non-action of *Waiting for Godot* is set suggests and fixes Vladimir and Estragon's very stuck-ness: emphatically they do not progress along this road. It is Pozzo and Lucky who whirl round the two protagonists, much as prior ciphers traverse the nowhere space around the owl-eyed vantage point of *The Unnamable*'s narrator. A road also serves to mediate understanding by physical distance for Molloy when he sees A and B, but darkly. From the more realist routes taken by Belacqua and

Murphy through Dublin and London respectively to the otherworldly muddy decrepitude of *Comment c'est/How It Is*, roads and routes form an important part of the philosophical content in Beckett's oeuvre. In the late short text *The Way* (1981) we find, as Lake describes it, 'the distillation of all the journeys made by all of Beckett's eternal wanderers' (Lake 1984, p. 174), in an infinite repetition of wandering that traces the figure '8', an everlasting glad going out and sorrowful coming home. Watt's very disconnected Cartesian wanderings, then, are an important stage in these philosophical journeys.[17]

To return to Kenner's specific arguments about disconnections, it should probably be counterargued against them that broken or partial connections appear throughout Beckett's oeuvre in many divergent guises. Kenner marshals these as all equally Geulingian, and while this grouping does find a way to track the possible influence of Geulincx on Beckett that stands the important test of cogency when brought to bear on different works, and thereby hints at repercussions across the oeuvre of the importance of Geulincx, it also makes too neat and complete a comparison of Geulincx. The viability of Kenner's reading across various works is at the cost of making Geulincx an equivalent force in manifestations of causal incongruity or partial congruence across all these works, and it thereby offers little in the way of a strategy for distinguishing between widely divergent forms of disconnect. Reading Watt's walking along the road in relation to Descartes's dreams, however, reveals certain broader philosophical underpinnings of Beckett's slapstick humour. Nonetheless, Kenner's enumeration of the implications for Beckett's works of Geulincx's '"bodytight" mental world' reveals something that has both far-reaching and yet more clearly identifiable boundaries and specificities than that of just dualist disconnections. In his discussion of how 'Geulincx and his school are driven to a treatment of motion as grotesquely analytic as the work sheets of a Disney animator' (Kenner 1961, p. 87),[18] Kenner quotes Geulincx on the importance of *abitus, transitus* and *aditus*, citing the following from *Physica Vera* and *Annotata ad Metaphysicam*:

> Watt's way of walking is less something his body does than something we can observe his body doing. 'Sicut in omni corpora sunt tres dimensiones,' writes Geulincx, 'as in all bodies there are three dimensions, so in all motion three tendencies, *abitus, transitus, aditus*; for in all movement there is a parting from somewhere, a passage somewhere, a going to somewhere..... But there is no departure without transit and arrival, no transit without departure and arrival, etc.' (pp. 87–8)

As a specific type of non-causal narrative, Geulincx's metaphysics of *abitus, transitus, aditus* – of coming, being and going – are vital to *Watt*. Geulincx emphasizes the importance of coming, being and going in *Ethica* where it appears in the section on humility that Beckett lauded, arguing (in a passage which in its English translation retains Beckett-like brevity) that in relation to God:

> totus sum (totus huc veniendo, totus hic agendo, totus hinc abeundo) (TCD MS 10971/6/25)[19]
>
> I have my whole being (in coming hither, acting here, departing hence). (*Et*, p. 337)

Such a tripartite existence is, in relation to the house of Mr Knott, Watt's. If there is a narrative trajectory to be spoken of in the novel, it is surely this. That is to say, Watt's (as per *Watt*'s) whole being is determined by his status as coming hither, acting here or departing hence, his being one in 'the series of servants'; Watt comes to the house with the intention of becoming a servant, he acts at the house as a servant and then he departs having been a servant. Yet this coming hither, acting here and departing hence is non-causal; it is only 'partially' congruent. Inside the house, where the servants move from one floor to another, where 'every going, every being, every coming consisting with a being and a coming, a coming and a going, a going and a being', Watt has an impression of cause and effect. But this impression is misleading:

> Tom's two years on the first floor are not *because of* Dick's two years on the ground floor, or of Harry's coming then, and Dick's two years on the ground floor are not *because of* Tom's two years on the first floor, or of Harry's coming then, and Harry's coming then is not *because of* Tom's two years on the first floor, or of Dick's two years on the ground floor. (*W*, p. 114)

Rather, all these changes are more simply, yet ineffably, 'because Tom is Tom, and Dick Dick, and Harry Harry, [. . .] of that the wretched Watt was persuaded' (p. 115).

In earlier drafts of *Watt* there was a crucial factor that was almost but not quite a cause for the serial transition of servants, and this was death. In the typescript Arsene and the narrator finish an early, dialogic version of what would become Arsene's 'short statement' (p. 31). Rather than departing hence over the threshold of the kitchen door as he does in the final version of the novel, Arsene dies in the narrator's arms, and this unwilled act inaugurates a new stage of servants 'acting here' at the house. The narrator appears here as poised in 'the series' between two realms; he is much like the humble Watt in ratiocination, but more closely resembles another of the seedy solipsists, Murphy, in his unacknowledged selfishness:

> The man must have been literally exhausted with what he had been through. But we not at all. Not yet. The time would come, and perhaps sooner than we

thought, when we too would be tired, we had not the slightest doubt in our mind about that, but for the moment we were not in the least tired, so the tiredness of our partner could not be expected to interest us particularly. (*Watt* Typescript, p. 173)

Cohn has detailed how the character Watt emerges in the third notebook via a tripartite conceptual apparatus of 'coming, being, and going':

> It is in A3, penned in several places while Beckett eluded the Nazis, that the character Watt moves to the forefront. On the very first page Beckett lists: '1. The Coming; 2. Downstairs; 3. Upstairs. [These are grouped as "The Being."] 4. The Going.' (Cohn 2001, p. 110, Cohn's editorial)[20]

Some of this tripartite structuring is also retained, in refined form, in the final novel where for Watt 'Mr Knott was harbour, Mr Knott was haven, calmly entered, freely ridden, gladly left' (*W*, p. 115). In concert with Mr Knott being the haven that is 'calmly entered, freely ridden, gladly left', Watt's own oscillations around the house map onto these as 'The Coming', 'The Being' and 'The Going'.[21] For Geulincx all his life, all his 'coming hither, acting here, departing hence', is indeed determined entirely by 'the Lord': 'For He who joined us to our body can alone remove us from it' (*Met*, p. 113).[22] Only God generously bestows the causal connections between 'coming hither, acting here, departing hence', making the three stages of life fully congruent (or 'consisting') with one another. However, for Watt there is no such divine harmony between events. As Murphy did, Watt also lives without consolations of the all-powerful.

Yet even though Watt's coming, being and going are shadowed not by comparisons between himself and Christ (such as Estragon's in *Waiting for Godot*), or by a consoling admiration of himself as an 'enduring miracle', they are nevertheless shadowed by a mysterious 'purpose'. Arsene asks Watt the following rhetorical questions, among others, on the matter of servants coming and going:

> is there a coming that is not a coming to, a going that is not a going from, a shadow that is not the shadow of purpose, or not? For what is this shadow of the going in which we come, this shadow of the coming in which we go, this shadow of the coming and the going in which we wait, if not the shadow of purpose, of the purpose that budding withers, that withering buds, whose blooming is a budding withering? I speak well, do I not, for a man in my situation? And what is this coming that was not our coming and this being that is not our being and this going that will not be our going but the coming and being and going in purposelessness? (*W*, pp. 48–9)

Arsene implies with his longing for the alternatives that he had been seeking a kind of purposelessness via his employment as servant, action free from 'the shadow of purpose', and although he admits he might appear to be departing the house in purposelessness, this (as with other causal incongruities) is appearance only, and Watt should not get too carried away with the appearance. The only real difference in Arsene's purpose between now and then, between the coming and the going, again invokes mortality in that 'then it was living and now it is dead' (p. 49). Imagining this coming, being and going in floral metaphors, Arsene subverts any optimistic pastoral connotations by diagnosing waste and ruin in every hope that seeks fulfilment, where every 'budding' and 'blooming' necessitates concomitant withering and dying. He describes a self-annihilating structure that echoes, in a complex weave of Beckett's philosophical analects, Bruno's identified contraries that were outlined in *Dante. . .Bruno.Vico..Joyce*: 'The maximum of corruption and the minimum of generation are identical: in principle, corruption is generation' (*Dis*, p. 21). Every action in such a closed system is shadowed by its contrary: Mr. Endon by Murphy, Mr Knott by Watt, budding by withering, purpose by purposelessness.

Taking Arsene in a sense at his word, it is worth posing questions of this 'shadow of purpose', and the following discussion does so, and reveals that Geulincx provides an enlightening recourse in addressing them. Might it be possible, without psychologizing the literary figment too reductively, to elucidate Watt's motivation, what the 'purpose' of Watt's coming, being and going is, in relation to the house of Mr Knott, if anything? Can a reader infer what this 'shadow of purpose' is that is cast over Watt's tripartite literary life, knowing it is never explicitly stated and knowing the novel to be comprised of many frequently discrete scenes that confound – either by Beckett's pre-established plan, or, more likely, by their very arbitrariness and almost-connectedness – generalized critical appraisal? One possible approach, I want to claim, one way in which the question 'what's Watt' might be asked, resides with a conception of 'need' as underlying the novel's ratiocination which, in order for it to be properly explicated, benefits from recourse to Geulincx.

Watt and Need

While visiting Germany in January 1937 Beckett read Friedrich Stieve's *Abriss der deutschen Geschichte von 1792–1935*, and, as Nixon describes, was disappointed to discover that it 'was not the reference book on German history he was seeking' (Nixon 2011, p. 177). Beckett vented his frustrations in his diary regarding Stieve's impulse to drain 'historical chaos' of its distinctiveness through 'Rationalism':

> I say I am not interested in a "unification" of the historical chaos any more than I am in the "clarification" of the individual chaos, & still less in the anthropomorphisation of the inhuman necessities that provoke the chaos.

What I want is the straws, flotsam, etc., names, dates, births & deaths, because that is all I can know. . . . I say the background & the causes are an inhuman & incomprehensible machinery & venture to wonder what kind of appetite it is that can be appeased by the modern animism that consists in rationalising them. Rationalism is the last form of animism. Whereas the pure incoherence of times & men & places is at least amusing. (German Diary, 15 January 1937, UoR)[23]

Beckett's diary entry gives a clue to his politics, at least to his 'distrust of the political and historical assertions encountered in Nazi Germany', assertions that were of course themselves a unifying appropriation of diverse backgrounds in the service of a soon to be violent appetite. As Nixon argues, the entry also gives an insight into Beckett's aesthetic thinking insofar as it renews his:

> attack on anthropomorphism as a falsification of essential incoherence, and reasserts an emphasis on the 'incomprehensible machinery', which had determined outer reality in *Murphy* and resurfaces as the 'pre-established arbitrary' in *Watt* [. . .]. (Nixon 2011, p. 178)

Certainly, Watt seeks to order the 'essential incoherence' of the world, as well as his knowledge of the world, in such ways as these correspond one to the other. In the case of the pot, for example, 'It resembled a pot, it was almost a pot, but it was not a pot of which one could say, Pot, pot, and be comforted' (*W*, p. 67). Ackerley adds that Beckett was 'particular about this capitalization' (Ackerley 2005a, p. 99) as it stands for the Platonic distinction between idea and instance, between Form ('Pot') and matter ('pot') (a stylistic convention Beckett had also followed when distinguishing 'Kick' from 'kick' in *Murphy*). The extent of Watt's anguish correlates with how far the instance (the lowercase) differs from the idea (the uppercase). But this is not because the pots differ greatly. On the contrary it is because they very nearly coincide, and indeed 'if the approximation had been less close, then Watt would have been less anguished' (*W*, p. 67). Although Watt wants his words and world to correspond, when they are just such a negligible distance apart all analysis and categorization would be easier for Watt if they would just separate fully and have done with it. It is the temptations of partial congruence that taunt his critical faculties. Watt is a consistently, determinedly, unremittingly rationalist protagonist, but I want to leave aside reading *Watt* in terms of its parodying the progressive abstract structures of Cartesian rationalism, with much excellent work already having taken Beckett scholarship down this 'road', and argue instead for a new perspective on Watt's ratiocination: that it is born of something more elemental, that his frustrated *méthode* has roots in the 'incomprehensible machinery' of something far more chaotic than its 'blooming' manifestations above ground. Underlying, nourishing the appetite of this frustrated ultrarationalist's needs for precision is instability, insatiability and an unremitting need that hints at the presence of a more elemental 'kind of appetite'.

Shortly before the composition of *Watt*, in certain of his critical writing Beckett had begun to theorize how ideas of unquenchable need and artistic impetuses might interpenetrate one another. In 'Les Deux Besoins' ['The Two Needs'] (1938), for example, with untypical recourse to a diagram Beckett places 'autology' at the delimiting boundaries of an aesthetic programme structured according to conceptions of 'need'. The diagram illustrates 'l'autologie créatrice' in terms of the hexagon formed at the intersection of a mysterious and uncharacteristically quasi-transcendental hexagram:

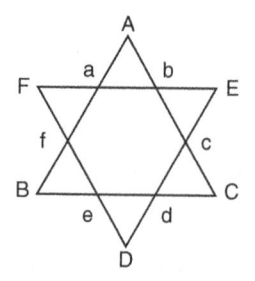

```
          A
       a / \ b
    F ───/───\─── E
       \ f   c /
        \     /
    B ───\───/─── C
       e \ / d
          D
```

> Besoin d'avoir besoin (DEF) et besoin dont on a besoin (ABC), conscience du besoin d'avoir besoin (ab) et conscience du besoin dont on a besoin – dont on *avait* besoin (de), issue du chaos de vouloir voir (Aab) et entrée dans le néant d'avoir vu (Dde), déclenchement et fin de l'autologie créatrice (abcdef). Voilà par exemple une façon comme une autre d'indiquer les limites entre lesquelles l'artiste se met à la question, se met en question, se résout en questions, en questions rhétoriques sans fonction oratoire. (*Dis*, p. 56)

> The need to need (DEF) and the need that one needs (ABC), the awareness of the need to need (ab), and the awareness of the need that one needs – that one *needed* (de), the result of the chaos of wishing to see (Aab) and the way into the nothingness of having seen (Dde), the beginning and end of creative autology (abcdef). That, for example, is one way of indicating the limits within which the artist begins to question, puts himself in question, turns into questions, into rhetorical questions without an oratorical function.[24]

The complex intersecting needs, surprising not least in their emphatic absoluteness, a quality which bears little relation to the shades of grey for which Beckett's aesthetics are more widely known, elaborate a framework set out shortly prior to 'Les Deux Besoins' in a review of Denis Devlin's poems:

> As between these two, the need that in its haste to be abolished cannot pause to be stated and the need that is the absolute predicament of particular

human identity, one does not of course presume to suggest a relation of worth. Yet the distinction is perhaps not idle, for it is from the failure to make it that proceeds the common rejection as 'obscure' of most that is significant in modern music, painting and literature. (*Dis*, p. 91)

The two needs summarized in Beckett's review of Devlin state in embryonic clarity what 'Les Deux Besoins' goes on to elaborate with intersecting layers: an assertion of an 'absolute predicament' of need, rather than the impatient, negating rush to overcome the need, is the goal of worthwhile art. A statement of, and resignation to, the impossibility of achievement is the statement made by 'significant' art.

In German one word for need is *not*, where *die not* is potentially both 'the need' and also 'the emergency'. If we think of Mr Knott's name as compound, as character names in Beckett's oeuvre are frequently thought of,[25] this will help to illustrate how Mr Knott is in some sense a figure, or a figuring, of 'need', while also of something more panicked and less controllable, the 'emergency'. According to the novel's ostensible narrator Sam, the only two surmises Watt makes of Mr Knott of any validity whatsoever concern the issue of Mr Knott not needing:

> For except, one, not to need, and, two, a witness to his not needing, Mr Knott needed nothing, as far as Watt could see.
> If he ate, and he ate well; if he drank, and he drank heartily; if he slept, and he slept sound; if he did other things, and he did other things regularly, it was not from need of food, or drink, or sleep, or other things, no, but from the need never to need, never never to need, food, and drink, and sleep, and other things.
> This was Watt's first surmise of any interest on the subject of Mr Knott.
> And Mr Knott, needing nothing if not, one, not to need, and, two, a witness to his not needing, of himself knew nothing. And so he needed to be witnessed. Not that he might know, no, but that he might not cease.
> This, on the subject of Mr Knott, was Watt's second, and closing, conjecture not entirely gratuitous. (*W*, p. 175)

There is a Berkeleyan impetus of connotation here in Watt's second 'conjecture' concerning Mr Knott's need 'to be witnessed' in order to verify his existence, so that 'he might not cease'. Aligned here too, however, in Watt's 'first surmise' is a conception of need formulated in synchronicity with Geulincx's axiom: in order to properly adhere to Geulincx's ethical axiom *ubi nihil vales, ibi nihil velis*, a person needs not to need. Without finding it possible to set one's desires at naught, to need nothing, that person will never achieve Geulincx's negative ethical consciousness (and it is what might be called today a state of mind) where one's will can as fully as possible be determined by Occasionalist impotence. Freedom from futile desire is just such a freedom from need, and accordingly the statement of Geulincx's 'absolute predicament' is his Occasionalism, neatly encapsulated by the axiom. Beckett insists upon the 'absolute predicament' of need via Watt's non-relations with Mr Knott, Watt's being proximate to but not truly with Mr Knott. He sees Mr Knott fleetingly, and serves him variously, orbiting the fixed point and going away again, and this non-encounter plays out the insatiable nature of need. Watt, as servant, takes the place of Mr Knott's needs – it is thanks to Watt that Mr Knott needs nothing. Yet Watt himself is left always having to need, always requiring some action be done in the world in order to appease another's needs. Watt's entrapment in this paradoxical state of need, wherein he must get rid of all of his own needs if he is to dedicate his service as a servant while at the same time always acting on behalf of need, the needs of someone else, shadows his ultrarationalist *méthode* with a mysterious 'purpose' that is elemental and ineffable.

Important to a reading of *Watt* as concerned with conceptions of 'need', specifically with an inevitability of insatiable need, and freedom from need as a kind of Geulingian nothingness, is Arsene's 'short statement'. Arsene guffaws, in Democritean fashion, at the fleeting transcendent nature of his moment off a ladder, and goes on to describe his reasoning that followed the momentary freedom in terms of constraint and need:

> And yet it is useless not to seek, not to want, for when you cease to seek you start to find, and when you cease to want, then life begins to ram her fish and chips down your gullet until you puke, and then the puke down your gullet until you puke the puke, and then the puked puke until you begin to like it. The glutton castaway, the drunkard in the desert, the lecher in prison, they are the happy ones. To hunger, thirst, lust, every day afresh and every day in vain, after the old prog, the old booze, the old whores, that's the nearest we'll ever get to felicity, the new porch and the very latest garden. I pass on the tip for what it is worth. (*W*, p. 36)

Critics have productively read Arsene's sentiments in terms of both Schopenhauerian will-lessness and Leopardi's extinguishing of desire.[26] However, Arsene's statement also revolves around certain Geulingian conceptions of need. In accord with Geulincx's 'Adminicule of Humility' Arsene describes how 'when you cease to seek you start to find', paralleling Geulincx's cautioning that 'No-one ever attained Happiness by doing something to attain it' (*Et*, p. 353), and that in order to properly attain 'Happiness' one must cease to seek it. This 'Adminicule' – a 'prop' or 'support' – and its relation to seeking and serving, gives a further resonance to the ladder in *Watt*, the support or prop that is temporarily, if metaphorically, removed from Arsene. Arsene implies with his own tale of fleeting freedom that it may be possible for a seeker, such as Watt, to find what they seek; but unfortunately such discovery yields a sickening result. When Arsene fell from (or to) grace, achieving a flawed momentary transcendence, the 'incident' (*W*, p. 35) gave up little more than a passing awareness that he had indeed just experienced 'existence off the ladder' (p. 36). It gave Mr Hackett less than this, with his more literal fall yielding only back problems.[27] Better, Arsene tells Watt, to be in a place where one desires but where one cannot satiate these desires. Such a place, in Geulincx's terminology, would be just here where one is, where one has no power and where one cannot achieve what one nevertheless needs. Arsene's conclusion as a prior servant, going as Watt is coming and passing on 'the tip for what it is worth', is that the best of all is to desire intensely, even slavishly, in a place where precisely that which you desire is what you cannot have. The upshot is that desire, need, is inevitable if one is not to have rammed 'down your gullet' all the puke of 'habit'. Arsene's tip is ethical: such 'need' cannot be wilfully negated, as Murphy tried to do by plugging himself into his chair and his internal depths while yet still subject to the big-world's 'Celia, ginger, and so on'. Nor, Beckett's next novel tells us, can it be substituted with others for very long as Watt in his domestic servitude attempts by serving the needs of Mr Knott. If we cannot prevent desires and the desperate hope of action and fulfilment unless resigned to the banality of satisfaction become habit then, Arsene says, we should embed ourselves in desires precisely where we cannot fulfil them and thereby, in an ironic *fait accompli*, imprisoning them as our own torturers.

Such a conclusion breaks in half Geulincx's well balanced axiom, dispensing entirely with the more ethical part, the possibility of wanting nothing, and leaving only the validity and inevitability of a place where one has no power, where one is worth nothing and where one cannot get what one will inevitably need. It might well be inferred that such a place is the kind of 'domain' Beckett had in mind when he wrote to Duthuit about the all-encompassing importance of Geulincx's axiom imagined as a place, 'a domain where one is worth nothing', the extent of which it is 'scarcely possible to exaggerate'.

Feldman has also traced Arsene's ladder to Geulincx, though this is to a specific metaphorical ladder in *Ethics* that Geulincx employs to describe the pragmatic workaday ways in which humanity must, at God's behest, keep itself alive:

> The virtuous man is always ascending and descending this ladder: he seeks ease that he may be fit for work; he wants to be fit for work that he may work; he want to work that he may have something else to eat; he wants to eat that he may live; he wants to live because God has ordered it, not because it pleases him, and not because life (as it has become popular to say) is so sweet. (*Et*, p. 327)

Feldman argues that 'Arsene's entire statement is powered by an appropriation of Geulingian ineffability', and that compared to the importance of other philosophical texts through which one might read Arsene's ladder, such as Mauthner's *Kritik* or Wittgenstein's *Tractatus*, Arsene's analogy 'would seem to make more sense in the context of Geulingian detachment, or withdrawal into consciousness' (Feldman 2009a, p 50). Time off the ladder, for Feldman, is time away from an everyday world of working and serving and into the inner mind. For Ackerley the ladder represents more a rationalist structure 'by which the soul ascends, as Descartes imagined he might climb, by clear and distinct degrees, to truth and knowledge of God' (Ackerley 2005a, p. 65), a structure which the novel devotes much energy to critiquing.

Yet this ladder carries even more resonances of Geulincx's rationalist philosophy than those of an everyday working world and the Cartesian *adminicule*, the support from which one must, in humility and aware of the futility of seeking satisfaction, jump or fall off (rather than, having ascended, throwing it away as might be the case were the ladder Wittgenstein's). Arsene wistfully tells Watt of his momentary 'slip':

> I felt, that Tuesday afternoon, millions of little things moving all together out of their old place, into a new one nearby, and furtively, as though it were forbidden. And I have little doubt that I was the only person living to discover them. To conclude from this that the incident was internal would, I think, be rash. For my – how shall I say? – my personal system was so distended at the period of which I speak that the distinction between what was inside it and what was outside it was not at all easy to draw. (*W*, p. 35)

This fleeting, unspeakable moment of 'reversed metamorphosis' is Arsene's maximal point of his time at the house, his purposeful climax and, as per Bruno's identified contraries, it was simultaneously his minima, his arbitrary ending. The moment of change that is 'other than a change of degree' is a moment of simultaneous pathos and bathos, of 'budding' that is also a 'withering'. Inevitably shadowing with 'purpose', Arsene repeatedly questions what this event was only to conclude with *a posteriori* exactitude that the reality of the 'slip' was, indeed, 'not an illusion' (p. 37). He can say nothing about it other than that it was and, precisely in being real but unspeakable, Arsene's experience is 'ineffable'.

Watt and the Ineffable

Arsene describes the mystical knowledge that is shared by those initiated into the 'series of servants', where its description also recalls the way Beckett wrote of 'what has ^sometimes^ been called the occasional kind', as 'what has so happily been called the unutterable or ineffable, so that any attempt to utter or eff it is doomed to fail, doomed, doomed to fail' (pp. 52–3). This 'ineffable' was described in more detail earlier in *Watt*'s composition:

> what we know partakes in no small measure of the nature of what has so happily been called the unutterable of [sic] ineffable, so that any attempt to utter or eff it is doomed to fail, the discourse being frequently interrupted by long loud bursts of crying and of laughing, and finally brought to a standstill, without any useful information having been imparted. (*Watt* Typescript, p. 243)[28]

The 'ineffable' is fundamental to Geulincx's Occasionalism. Indeed, it is its primary epistemological criterion. As discussed in Chapter 1, it is the impossibility of being able to know how something happens that forces us to admit we cannot be said to do that thing. When this is the case, when we are left disconnected, ignorant of how things can happen, then how such things happen is said to be 'ineffable'. There is an important distinction to bear in mind here, however, which Beckett clarified in his transcriptions:

> Something is said to be *ineffable* not because we cannot think or speak of it (for this would be *nothing, nothing* and *unthinkable* being the same . . .) but because we cannot think about or encompass with our reason how it is done. And in this sense God is ineffable not only in Himself but in all His works. (*Et*, p. 334)

According to Geulincx, ineffability is the proper domain of God alone, God who 'is ineffable because one can understand *that* He is, but not *how* He is' (*Met*, p. 97).[29] In any reasoned description of experience in the world, this 'ineffable something is always missing' (*Et*, p. 334), necessarily remains unaccounted for and can only properly be known by God. It is primarily via 'the ineffable' that Geulincx integrates his mysticism with his rationalism, and it is along comparable lines that *Watt* is more then a novel of rationalist entropy or Cartesian critique. *Watt* too is shadowed by the 'ineffable' that Arsene speaks of, by the unknowable residual realms of experience that are not exhausted by an otherwise exhaustive enumerative method. Arsene warns the next servant in line that the ineffable will elude and confound the rationalist's capacities for assimilation, and so an underlying need is doomed either way, to dissatisfaction or, worse, to satisfaction.

Ackerley writes of the Geulingian ineffable in *Watt* that 'Despite Arsene's clear warning that the attempt to utter or eff it is doomed to fail, Watt will persist in his attempts to do so, even as his world becomes unspeakable' (Ackerley 2005a, p. 85). Watt's persistence is itself a fairly ineffable thing. His 'purpose' and 'needs' manage to fly by the kinds of rational nets Watt himself uses, and rarely appear over the surface of the text. But bubbling under *Watt*, like the bogland of the early drafts, are darker thoughts and forces. Set against the context, if not quite the backdrop, of the massively violent appetite of World War Two, *Watt* is certainly a multifaceted 'game', but it is also much more than 'only' a game. Even Watt's thoughts about something as clear and distinct as how the door of Mr Knott's house came to be locked indicate something more than rationalist enumeration and can point instead to 'an aesthetic impulse within Watt that is increasingly overcome by the rationalist prurit, or urge to reason' (p. 56). Such an impulse can be variously involved with ideas of beauty (as with the locked door) or need, and it is in these underlying impulses, rather in the novel's more overt applications of a Cartesian *méthode*, that it bears traces of Geulincx. As 'the last form of animism' rationalism in *Watt* is marked by something deeper, darker and difficult to extricate oneself from, and while Geulincx's writings on rationalism itself do not appear to have greatly influenced Beckett's writing *Watt*, certain other impulses have their intertwined, indebted parts to play, even if fleetingly.

Mercier and Camier in Watt's 'Series'

Towards the end of *Mercier and Camier* a bombastic reincarnation of Watt, a very different character bearing the familiar name, appears. The novella's pseudo-couple protagonists meet this new Watt in a street, where Watt describes himself as 'unrecognizable' and 'not widely known, [. . .] but I shall be, one day'. The scene inserts this Watt, as well as the protagonists of the work that Watt has just wandered into, within the broader 'series' of Beckett's oeuvre:

> I knew a poor man named Murphy, said Mercier, who had a look of you, only less battered of course. But he died ten years ago, in rather mysterious circumstances. They never found the body, can you imagine. My dream, said Watt. (*MC*, p. 91)

Inviting Mercier and Camier for 'one on me' in a spirit of camaraderie with those who, like himself, play out their parameters within the unforgiving confines of a Beckett novel, Watt and the pseudocouple collapse in a bar where Watt looks back at his own strange questing past and proffers, for the benefit of the drinking public, the kind of gnomic statements that Arsene had once lent Watt while Watt had comforted himself with the embers of the fire in Mr Knott's kitchen. Among these mysterious statements, Watt announces his author's own future aesthetic horizons as a stage of the 'series'. As Pilling describes the scene, 'it falls to Watt to predict what Beckett will attempt in narrative terms when, as soon, *Mercier et Camier* will be done with' (Pilling 1997, p. 209). Thoroughly inhabiting his bathetic mystical role as drunken prophesizing seer, this second Watt announces the coming of Beckett's masterworks of voice, those first person narrators and their narratives such as Molloy, Malone and the Unnamable that will arise from the ashes of Murphy, Mercier, Camier and Watt:

> Il naîtra, il est né de nous, dit Watt, celui qui n'ayant rien ne voudra rien, sinon qu'on lui laisse le rien qu'il a. (Beckett 1970, p. 198)
>
> One shall be born, said Watt, one is born of us, who having nothing will wish for nothing, except to be left the nothing he hath. (*MC*, p. 93)

In the terms of Geulincx's ethical axiom the new Watt ordains the coming of the next 'one'. He also changes the status of his own previous namesake, altering the Watt of *Watt* post-facto in relation to identities-to-come, turning Beckett's protagonists into a series not unlike that of the servants in *Watt*. In the English version Watt performs his ceremonial invocation with Biblical solemnity in the style of a drunken John the Baptist, 'hath' translating grandly the more colloquial French; Watt is very serious about this being to come. Yet he makes it while causing a fuss in a pub, raging while drunk, to the annoyance of the bar manager. Perhaps, then, Watt's solemn tone is sullied a little by its context, Beckett's tongue a little in his cheek. Why might it fall to Watt, a Watt noticeably different from his prior namesake, to announce this future coming? More vitally, why is such a pronouncement framed in the terms of *ubi nihil vales, ibi nihil velis* borrowed from Geulincx, and what does the tongue in cheek do to the sound of the axiom?

Beckett wrote *Mercier et Camier* between July and October 1946 after completing *Suite* (an early version of *La Fin/The End*) and immediately prior to beginning *Premier amour/First Love*. During this time the manuscript of *Watt* was doing the familiar rounds of being rejected by numerous publishers, continuing the pattern begun over a year earlier by Routledge, who rejected *Watt* despite their previous 'whole-hearted enthusiasm for' (T.M. Ragg to SB, 6 June 1945[30]) the novel that they did accept for publication: *Murphy*. Beckett wrote to Reavey, who had earlier been responsible for placing *Murphy* with Routledge, of the depressing issue:

> My book Watt has been turned down by Routledge. Mr Ragg and Mr Read agreed that it was "wild & unintelligible" and felt very sorry for the author of Murphy. (SB to GR, 21 June 1945: *L2*, p. 16)

Perhaps this chronological overlap of 1945–6 might go some way to explaining the intrusion of a raging, frustrated Watt into the later French novella, with both works current in Beckett's mind and one – *Watt* – the source of some practical frustration and not only for Beckett. But this coincidence does not tell the whole story. A more substantial answer to the question of why Watt reappears in the later novella to proclaim Geulingian ethical and aesthetic prophesies lies in Beckett's conception of the earlier *Watt* as having 'its place in the series'; Beckett invokes this most serial of protagonists to make the point about the by now serial nature of Beckett's literature. Watt might be 'unrecognizable' from his earlier avatar, and 'barely known' because of not yet being (and with little sign of ever being) published, but as Beckett said, his 'place in the series [. . .] will perhaps appear in time', and this is just what Watt bitterly announces in *Mercier and Camier*.

Furthermore, it is clear from the way Watt phrases this important interjection that Geulincx's philosophy of incapacity and humility is to be central to whatever this work 'to come' will be, even if it is not clear yet exactly how. As the following chapter argues, Geulincx is important to a number of Beckett's literary turns at this stage, including that from third to first person, as well as from English to French. With these possibilities in mind, attention turns to *La Fin/The End* and the texts' pre and postpublication versions and variants with specific focus on a paragraph that names Geulincx, in order to explore just how 'one [who] shall be born' can collect on this Geulingian legacy.

Chapter 4

Suite/La Fin/The End:
Continuations and Conclusions

The previous chapter argued that the multifaceted serial nature of *Watt* – its composition processes, final form and content – orchestrates this novel's place within Beckett's oeuvre, and that at the same time it is in this work's very seriality that Geulincx was of most use to Beckett. The chapter ended by arguing from a scene in *Mercier and Camier* that a version of Watt reappears to announce, by borrowing Geulincx's ethical axiom, the coming of Beckett's future narrators. It is at this point in Beckett's 'series' of works, therefore, at the beginnings of the immediately post-war writings, a period that has come to be known as the 'frenzy of writing'[1] with the author under 'siege in the room' (Bair 1978, p. 346) – phrases that imagine the period as a kind of maddened war zone that is also, like the spaces in which many of the works take shape, closed – that Beckett, via Watt, signals a significant turn in his works, a change that is as momentous as a rebirth. This chapter explores the published and unpublished versions of a specific paragraph in the novella *Suite/La Fin/The End* that names both Geulincx and his major work *Ethics*, in order to argue for the important parts the philosopher plays in a new phase of Beckett's texts, a phase characterized most obviously by a turn to writing prose in French, as well as by first person narration. Geulincx's place within this text is *traced* to its origins in the manuscript in order to see just what part he initially plays in these crucial turns, while the contours of the passage in which appears are then *traced* over in a kind of archaeological, or *autospeliological*, analysis of the passage as a palimpsest, a stratified text that bears residues of, and even presages, erasures, effacements and rewritings. *La Fin/The End* has one of the most fascinating and convoluted publication histories in Beckett's entire oeuvre. This chapter's genetic approach to the novella reveals Beckett altering the text, even removing entire characters, as late as 1960, some 14 years after the piece was first drafted. A historicizing approach to the text's versions and variants takes us on a route through Beckett's approaches to translation, both theoretical and practical, as well as through his altering thinking about how knowledge so dearly won years earlier in 1936 might now be set aside in favour of new abilities with a new voice. Importantly, Beckett's altering thinking about this text, and Geulincx's place within it, can be seen altering on the page in decisions, retractions and experimentations that manifest broader shifts of focus with regard to source incorporation and influence. Tracing Geulincx's places in versions of *La Fin/ The End* offers a revealing insight into the ways and moments in which Beckett pushed 'the ends' of Modernist literature in new and unprecedented directions.

'What Follows'[2]

Suite et Fin, the two-part French novella that would become *La Fin* after its first part was published as *Suite*, later to be translated as *The End*, was begun in February 1946. *Suite* was published in Jean-Paul Sartre and Simone de Beauvoir's *Les Temps modernes* in July of that same year, though this truncated publication would lead to acrimony between Beckett and the magazine's editors.[3] Begun in English, partway through its composition *Suite* was morphed into Beckett's first extended foray into writing prose in his adopted French, thereby inaugurating the famously productive stages of his middle period. *Suite* was then translated by Richard Seaver in partial collaboration with Beckett (discussed in detail below) and published as *The End* in *Merlin* 2.3 (1954). Beckett was furious with this version, however, and the translation was thoroughly revised for *Evergreen Review* 4.15 (November–December 1960). *Evergreen*'s now-standard English language version of the novella has been republished a number of times in England and America, with minor textual variants.[4] *La Fin* was first fully published in Éditions de Minuit's *Nouvelles et Textes pour rien* (1955), and again in 1958 in an edition that included illustrations by Avigdor Arikha, and it continues to be reprinted by the Parisian company.

The following discussion focuses first on the standard version of the passage that describes the narrator–protagonist being gifted by a now dead tutor a copy of Geulincx's *Ethics*. The discussion then shifts to the passage's origins in Beckett's 'Suite' notebook before moving forward through divergent published variants up to its final translations. What I will call the 'Geulincx passage' (that is with a nod to the 'passage' of the Geulingian ship on which Molloy imagines his constrained freedom – a move away from enslavement/ enthrallment to freedom/individuality) instances a kind of crucible in which a number of important elements of Beckett's work of this period are forged, alloyed, worked and reworked in a visible struggle for a creative, though constrained, freedom. Beckett makes his hugely important turn from writing prose in English to French at the precise point of this passage. Yet this turn towards untrammelled possibilities is coupled with a backwards glancing at his prior, autodidactic and somewhat autologous education. The resulting tensions manifest as subtle textual choices, altering through different versions of the novella, that speak to Beckett's uses of source materials such as are derived from Geulincx, and to his previously expansive approach to self-education as it might inform his work more broadly.

The End: Vision and the Tutor

The reading of the Geulincx passage that follows depends primarily on the importance in, as well as *to* the passage, of sight and 'seeing'. As a specific moment of sight in Beckett's oeuvre the passage has implications for thinking about sight in the wider oeuvre, while it is itself also contextually informed by these other instances of sight. Seeing, looking, gazing and staring, in various forms both into the self and out at the world, are powerful elements from this point in Beckett's oeuvre. For example, *The Unnamable*'s narrator will gaze straight ahead, eagle eyed and unwavering, complementing the narrative propulsion of a novel deriving from a negated and so paradoxical will to 'go on' (*U*, p. 134). It is thanks to these staring eyes that the fictionalized narrator sees his earlier avatars whirl round him, and it is through them he expels what might be either tears or 'liquefied brain' (p. 3). *Film* (1964) opens with a fullscreen shot of an eye opening, blinking and staring back at the viewer looking at it, before the piece explores, for purposes of merely 'structural and dramatic convenience' as the script states it, Berkeley's *Esse est percipi* [to be is to be perceived]. Comparably, *Rockaby* (written in 1980) draws to its end with the unseen offstage speaker aligning W's being (*esse*), with a capacity to perceive via the eyes (*percipi*), where the implication is that W's *esse* is 'fuck[ed]' at the same moment her perceiving eyes stop seeing:

rock her off
stop her eyes
fuck life
stop her eyes
rock her off
rock her off (*CDW*, p. 442)

Beckett also employed imagery of sight prior to *Suite*. In the very early drafts of *Watt*, for example, a long passage in the first notebook entitled 'The Eyes' details those of Erskine (*Watt* Notebook 1, p. 91). The passage is separated and titled similarly to how categories of Scholasticism had determined from the first page of the notebook the novel's proposed structure and contents ('Who, what, where, by what means, why, in what way, when' (p. 3)). In this sense, 'The Eyes' are as important as the 'where' which would become 'The Nothingness', later the house, and the 'who' which would become Quin, later Mr Knott. Beckett's even earlier descriptions of psychological or imaginative life as proximate to sight include a letter to MacGreevy in 1936 in which he aligns the creative impulses of his mind with where it physically sits 'behind the eyes':

> I have neither written anything nor wanted to, except for a short hour, when the frail sense of beginning life behind the eyes, that is the best of all experiences, came again for the first time since <u>Cascando</u>, and produced 2 lines and a half. (SB to TM, 16 February 1936: *L1*, p. 447)

This fascination with vision and seeing as related to creativity also has roots in an early interest in what Beckett called Rimbaud's 'eye-suicide – <u>pour des visions</u>'. As discussed in Chapter 1, Beckett referred to Rimbaud's sightless seer as falling short of Geulincx's double-sighted abilities, his 'Janus or Telephus eyes'. It has also been noted how Beckett detailed the powerful impressions Geulincx made upon him via other intertextual comparisons based in sight, where he describes Geulincx's eyes as 'very patiently turned outward, and without Schwärmerei turned in-ward'. By 1946, however, Beckett appears to no longer have felt that seeing, either out through the eyes or inward as part of exploring 'life behind the eyes', was any longer 'the best of all experiences', and the Geulincx passage in *La Fin/The End* speaks of precisely this change.

The passage comes immediately after an abrupt change in the narrative. Earlier the narrator had been up to the usual tricks of an expelled, wandering protagonist of Beckett's prose; negotiating the vicissitudes of institutionalized charity and transactions, sleeping in a barn, meeting a man in a cave and wrestling with a cow in a forest, before getting back on a road and half-heartedly attempting to get run over by passing carts. All these before a typical moment of passivity and adjacent steely purpose, when 'the day came when, looking round me, I was in the suburbs, and from there to the old haunts it was not far, beyond the stupid hope of rest or less pain':

> So I covered the lower part of my face with a black rag and went and begged at a sunny corner. For it seemed to me my eyes were not completely spent, thanks perhaps to the dark glasses my tutor had given me. He had given me the *Ethics* of Geulincz [sic]. They were a man's glasses, I was a child. They found him dead, crumpled up in the water closet, his clothes in awful disorder, struck down by an infarctus. Ah what peace. The *Ethics* had his name (Ward) on the fly-leaf, the glasses had belonged to him. The bridge, at the time I am speaking of, was of brass wire, of the kind used to hang pictures and big mirrors, and two long black ribbons served as wings. I wound them round my ears and then down under my chin where I tied them together. The lenses had suffered, from rubbing in my pocket against each other and against the other objects there. I thought Mr. Weir had confiscated all my belongings. But I had no further need of these glasses and used them merely to soften the glare of the sun. I should never have mentioned them. (*E*, p. 49)

Suite/La Fin/The End: *Continuations and Conclusions*

The primary claim I want to make in reading this passage is that there is an important and complex association, an association that is subtly pushed to the point of identification, between 'the *Ethics*' and 'the glasses'. So when the narrator writes that he has 'no further need of these glasses', he is thereby also writing of his having 'no further need of' 'the *Ethics*'. These two objects (treating *Ethics* at this point specifically as a physical object, the book that is 'given' by the tutor and the physicality of which is hinted at by its having a 'fly-leaf', so not yet as something that might be seen *through*) become, in a certain sense, fused as one and the same object, and this is a fusion that is made to take place in the act of reading the passage. Specifically, Beckett's highly attuned syntax makes these two ontologically distinct objects appear inseparable; a lack of the adverb 'also' from the sentence naming Geulincx by its very absence brings about this strange melding, where the missing distinguishing boundary – what would be 'this and *also* this' – allows the two objects to collapse into each other. The sentence in question (third in the passage) is enclosed by sentences on either side of it neither of which make any mention of 'the *Ethics*', with both instead referring explicitly only to 'the glasses'. These are the three sentences (the second, third and fourth) quoted separately:

> For it seemed to me my eyes were not completely spent, thanks perhaps to the dark glasses my tutor had given me. He had given me the *Ethics* of Geulincz. They were a man's glasses, I was a child.

The lack of conjoiner in the middle sentence is obvious, yet its implications are subtle. If the tutor had *also* given the young student Geulincx's *Ethics* then the two objects would be categorically distinguishable from one another. Without this *also*, the echo of 'glasses' that sounds in '*Ethics*', where the two-syllable 'glasses' begins an alliterative pattern in which the word is also almost but not quite rhymed at '*Ethics*', concatenates 'glasses' and '*Ethics*'. A similar concatenation occurs between the 'tutor' and 'Geulincx', two brittle-sounding words that are more connotative of authority and didacticism, in contrast to the softer, enabling ways and means of 'glasses' and '*Ethics*'. The double couple, the two sets of two words, push the objects beyond mere contiguity. Instead, the echoes of the objects and authors in each other's counterparts collude in an implicit, though imperfect, identification.

The identification between the glasses and *Ethics* is not only paradigmatic. It is also, to borrow Roman Jakobson's term, syntagmatic; it is partly through the rhythm of these sentences that Beckett achieves this shading, a greying or *vaguening*,[5] of one realm of existence into another. Leaving out *also* results in an exact repetition of the three words 'had given me', and these instances of 'had given me', separated only by a period and the single word 'He', add to the sense that the objects (and, indeed, people) are identical. When a reader's own eyes scan across these lines, these eyes too become in a sense 'Janus eyes' that see two things at the same time. That is, when we read 'had given me' in the second sentence, the ostensible object of which is only 'the *Ethics*', a residual presence of the object of 'had given me' from the first sentence ('the glasses') becomes present again, is subtly recalled, and this ghostly residuum supervenes upon the object of the second sentence. In fact, the faint recollection is set up even before encountering the alliterative echo. Before a reader's eyes even reach 'the *Ethics*', the repetition of 'had given me' brings with it an expectation, what might even be called a *prejudice*, that the object of the sentence is already going to be 'the glasses'.

There are a number of other stylistic manoeuvres that intensify the impression of objects being fused. For example, the issue is partly one of punctuation when the narrator notes the apparent ownership of the items:

The *Ethics* had his name (Ward) on the fly-leaf, the glasses had belonged to him.

In this sentence not only is there a missing 'also' or 'and'. But if these two objects are to be thought of as separate, then a reader might be entitled to expect that the comma halfway through the sentence would instead be a period. In what becomes thereby *ethical* writing of *Ethics*, Beckett subverts such callow entitlement. Like the alternately frustrated and teary-eyed non-artist Watt when faced with the ineffable and infinite, a critical close reader of this passage can become similarly 'anguished' by 'approximation', between what is almost, but not entirely, one thing and also two. Paul Auster called Beckett 'the master of the comma' (Auster 2003, p. 346), and use of it here instances an ability to manipulate rhythm itself as a carrier of implied meaning. In this sentence about the fly-leaf, 'what follows' after the midway comma reads as if it were a qualification of what came before it, of 'The *Ethics*'. Just like Watt, and Geulincx before him, the reader is obligated to deploy their 'Reason': it follows from the fact of the name on the fly-leaf that the glasses had *therefore* belonged to the tutor, and so that these are one and the same object. Comically (if not especially *funnily*), however, this ownership only literally *follows from* the earlier proposition. It comes after, but it is not therefore *caused by*, what goes before. A reader would do well to bear in mind Arsene's cautioning words about the impressions of cause and effect when all there is in reality are the more Occasionalist and unknowable coincidental congruencies of simultaneity. As in Geulincx's Occasionalism there is no truly 'effable' interconnecting agency. Here with a simple single comma Beckett performs a new incarnation of what Kenner called the 'partially congruent', enabling a particularly Occasionalist-style simultaneity of ownership to more fully appear as the identification of one object with the other, bringing an illusory impression of cause and effect.

If this stylistic reading of the first part of the Geulincx passage is persuasive then the enquiry might be curiously made as to why Beckett orchestrates this fusion of the glasses and *Ethics*. A first step in addressing this invites recollection of the often-cited programmatic statement made in *Dream of Fair to Middling Women*. Importantly, however, it was Belacqua who 'mused' and 'submused' about the possibilities of fiction here. Not, that is, directly Beckett; the elusive 'programme' for fiction is itself fictionalized. Nevertheless, the 'smartness' and 'slickness' outlined by that fictional protagonist of the first novel echo through the rest of Beckett's oeuvre:

> The blown roses of a phrase shall catapult the reader into the tulips of the phrase that follows. The experience of my reader shall be between the phrases, in the silence, communicated by the intervals, not the terms, of the statement, between the flowers that cannot coexist, the antithetical (nothing so simple as antithetical) season of words, his experience shall be the menace, the miracle, the memory, of an unspeakable trajectory. (*Dr*, p. 138)

In the reader's 'experience' of the Geulincx passage's fusion of objects, Beckett has manifested just this 'unspeakable trajectory' that he first described in 1932. The middle period prose, inaugurated by *La Fin/The End*, is certainly less *flowery* than Belacqua's aesthetic epiphanies in *Dream*. *The End*'s narrator, for instance, will instead plant, manure and 'piss on' 'a crocus bulb [. . .] in an old pot' that only manages 'a few chlorotic leaves' (*E*, p. 43). Nevertheless, at moments this prose does achieve something like the being flung between 'roses' and 'tulips', between one object and another like it, where a reader must exist in 'the intervals', 'between the phrases'. The Geulincx passage, then, achieves just what Beckett had wanted for so long, an in-between space for literature that is itself particularly Geulingian. The novella's narrator is indeed 'born' of a number of previous protagonists, but also of Beckett's stamina and tenaciousness, his own long-developing artistic 'Obligations'.

Pockets of Philosophy

A further way to think of the ambiguities and ambivalences in the Geulincx passage is informed by Beckett's changing attitude to the incorporation of potential source material, a topic discussed in previous chapters regarding *Murphy* and *Watt*. In earlier works, with *Dream of Fair to Middling Women* the earliest long prose work and concomitantly the most extensively and explicitly woven from recycled fabrics, from what *Dream* itself refers to as 'the tag and the ready-made' (*Dr*, p. 48), moments of intertextual 'intrusion' were frequently welcomed, and were rarely dismissed as radically within the text itself as they are in *The End*, where the narrator bemoans of his glasses/*Ethics* 'I should never have mentioned them'. Chapter 2 discussed variation among such moments in *Murphy*. The Geulincx passage is a specific instance of what Wood called Beckett's 'uneasiness' about the 'intrusion' of philosophical voices and figures; Geulincx's name is invoked at the same moment as it is dispelled, the gift of

Ethics recalled affectionately at the same time as Beckett kills off the tutor who imparted the knowledge. Perhaps Geulincx is being invited to stand as a metonym for the intellectual fascinations of all Beckett's previous narrators, a paradigm empty of specificity but simultaneously full of force. The barely recognizable, almost-forgotten name that sits in the margins and footnotes of philosophical history is certainly well pitched to evoke the fragmentary and partially lost knowledge that these narrators frequently insist upon as their knowledge. Yet such an evocation also becomes, by dint of naming Geulincx and *Ethics*, a highly specific fragment of knowledge. The Watt in *Mercier and Camier* spoke of a narrator to come 'who having nothing will wish for nothing, except to be left the nothing he hath'. In putting away Geulincx by invoking Geulincx the narrator of *The End* makes a very Geulingian manoeuvre; he indeed wishes for nothing except to be left the nothing he has, yet this negative nothing wished for is necessarily only thinkable in terms derived from the more positive existences of the things he has. Beckett's tutor might well be, to borrow the fragments from Thomas in which Beckett had appraised the quietist impulse in 1936, very sorry to be in his chamber, his body having asserted its agency beyond the control of the mind and killed him, but the residues of what was imparted – Beckett's philosophical education and fascinations – cannot be nullified quite so categorically and Beckett does not pretend to do so.

Instead he produces a particular stylistic 'actualization' of that double manoeuvre that determines so many of his fictional characters, a contradictory impulse to leave coupled (or as it has come to be known pseudo-coupled) with a commitment to stay. The passage enacts a crucial moment of struggle and uneasiness, shot through with Beckett's turning to a philosophical source at a moment of major transition for his work. There are precedents for such recourse, as previous chapters have discussed. The Geulincx passage in *The End* too shows that there is frequently no moving forward in Beckett's oeuvre that is not also a being tied back, no creative freedom even in an ironized and minimal language that is not also constrained by, in some way obligated to, its own history. This constrained freedom is an ethical Geulingian type of freedom, and in this sense it can be argued that Beckett's middle-period stylistics enact what we might productively term, with particular reference to Geulincx, a philosophical ethics of form.

The passage's insistence upon the fragmentary and the residual, rather than on the entirely erased, is made more forceful through its second half, which concerns the contents of the narrator/protagonist's pockets. The glasses/*Ethics* that have been rubbing together while in the narrator's pockets are a highly effective, though (to borrow Uhlmann's use of the word) 'occluded' image of the refining and amalgamating of possible sources of intellectual reference, the various 'adminicules' that are of importance to Beckett's works of the post-*Watt*/post-war period. In the possession of this new first-person narrator/protagonist, fragments of previously strictly delineated, Fach-style systems of knowledge are pushed and scraped together, where they suffer 'from rubbing' such that each element of a system (be it an image or an axiom) becomes so distorted by others that none can be seen, or seen through, clearly and distinctly. Referring to Molloy's pockets of sucking stones, Feldman argues that a consideration of how entries about Protagoras and Zeno in Beckett's 'Philosophy Notes' give rise to partial quotation in later works such as *Endgame* and *Mercier and Camier*, reveals that 'Allusions become like revolving stones to be shifted and manipulated, all the while hidden in pockets of age-old trousers' (Feldman 2006, p. 36). The Geulincx passage foregrounds just such a process of shifting, sifting and manipulating. Yet these glasses are not only an image of fragments of previously visionary knowledge 'rubbing' together, they also connote the flimsy coherences of the very systems of knowledge Beckett had previously adored so much. The 'brass wire', for example, used normally for hanging 'pictures and big mirrors', impersonates a system of connections, representing in makeshift fragments a rough approximation of an original. Both of the more usual uses for the wire imply the gaze, a *despectio* gaze outward at the world in 'pictures' of it, or inward at the self, in 'big mirrors'. Yet the crumpled mess of patched-together copies that is these glasses implies that neither direction can now be distinguished clearly. These degraded and distorted lenses, handed down and fit only for single pragmatic, formalized purpose sit at the border between self and outer world, not quite fully preventing the outside world from getting in and not quite letting the eyes see out. As elements of what would once have been discrete instances of 'notesnatching' are indelibly engraved by one another, so too each is committed to an earth, buried – *en-graved* – in that stratified geological/psychological zoning the investigation of which is the 'auto-speliology' of the *Watt* drafts. Molloy says of burying Lousse's dog that 'I contributed my presence. As if it had been my own burial. And it was' (*Mo*, p. 34). In a sense too the synecdoche that is the burial of Geulincx enacted in *The End* via the killing of the tutor is also the burial of the kinds of narrators who might have been glad of the gift of *Ethics*, and who might therefore have been in thrall to their tutors, their accursed intellectual progenitors. The literary rebirth heralded by the Watt of *Mercier and Camier* will be 'what follows' the sacrificial death of the philosophy tutor, Ward.

This is not to argue, however, that these glasses should be read exclusively as a metaphor for the *Ethics* of Geulincx. It is precarious at this stage of 'the series' to alight on such conveniences of correspondence, neatnesses of identifications. But this does not mean that alighting is therefore to be avoided entirely. Beckett's art of nonrelation that he described in 1937 called forth a 'literature of the unword' (*Dis*, p. 173) that sought to dissolve the 'terrible materiality of the word surface' (p. 172). From the mid- to late 1940s onward, Beckett brings *immateriality* to bear with increasing effectiveness in opposition to an art of 'allegory, that glorious double-entry, with every credit in the said account a debit in the meant, and inversely' (p. 90), as he described it in a 1936 review of Jack B. Yeats. What is crucial in reading works from the middle period is less a locating of what might at first sight be a persuasive singular correspondence, but rather a foregrounding of the blurred, 'occluded' ontological boundaries between the realms of existence that Beckett's imagery occupies. Easy correspondences are the dangerous neatness that can function as a trap for the 'gentle skimmer' mocked in *Murphy*. As Uhlmann and others have argued, it is not the case that during and after World War Two Beckett's writing rejects philosophy outright, but rather that his texts 'continue to interact in important ways with works of philosophy' (Uhlmann 2006a, p. 65). Tracing the accurate contours of these 'important ways' becomes increasingly complex and even, as it follows the routes of increasingly self-lacerating prose, self-undermining. Nevertheless, perseverance pays off in tracking the continuities and discontinuities of Geulincx's influence across the oeuvre.

So, with the above reading of the Geulincx passage as an important instance of irresolvable ambivalence within the oeuvre in mind – a simultaneous rejection via an embrace of Geulincx – I will now turn back to the origins of the passage in its earliest incarnation in the 'Suite' notebook, before looking at further versions including in the English-language *Merlin* and beyond, when it became part of *The End* and *La Fin*. This sub-series of versions of the work complements and complicates the reading of the passage set out above, revealing that Beckett's reshaping and translating the passage plays out certain textual struggles that are resolved in the ambivalent finality of the later version, but through a process that includes intriguing instances of textual error, amendment and experimentation.

Suite in English

The final sentence of *Suite* as published in *Les Temps modernes* ends 'au delà du stupide espoir de repos ou de moindre peine' (Beckett 1946, p. 119), translated later as 'beyond the stupid hope of rest or less pain'. The Geulincx passage, then, would have been the opening section of the second part of *Suite et Fin* had de Beauvoir consented to publish as Beckett thought was agreed (see n. 3). In the 1954 English *Merlin* publication of the novella where it is titled *The End*, a line break, the only one in the work, separates these paragraphs. These two divides give a clue as to the important role the passage plays in the novella's early incarnations, a role that is even more pronounced in the 'Suite' notebook.

As Cohn has detailed following Knowlson's discovery of the notebook (which Cohn describes as 'a manuscript treasure'), it is at the precise point of the Geulincx passage that Beckett turns from English to writing in French:

> Until recently, it was thought that Beckett [. . .] shifted after the war to creation in French. However, the 'Suite' notebook modifies that view of Beckett as a French writer [. . .] On March 13 – often a significant number

for Beckett – he stopped ten lines down on the twenty-eighth page of his manuscript and drew a horizontal line across the page. In his rushed handwriting, he recapitulated in French a passage he had written about the narrator-protagonist's tutor, who had given him dark glasses and *The Ethics of Geulincx*, and who was found dead on the floor of his water closet [. . .]. The death of the tutor was the occasion of Beckett's birth as a major French writer. (Cohn 2001, p. 129)

The passage, therefore, reveals not only the birth-in-death of a first-person narrator (a perspective that Beckett had experimented with in the Ur-*Watt* as first-person plural before reverting to the third person). It was also where Beckett moved to French. The following transcription from the 'Suite' notebook adheres topographically to the text as it appears in the notebook. While this gives the impression of the novella as written with a short-line, poem-like structure, this is a result of Beckett's elongated, right-leaning 'rushed handwriting' and the size of the notebook:

Being now for the moment
virtually decent – far changed –
as far as my face was concerned,
capable of no expression ~~but the~~
other than that of [?][6] gravity
nor of any ~~sound but the formal~~
but the ^most^ formal sound, I [?][7]
to cover its lower part with a black
cloth and to entreat alms on a
sunny corner, a south-western
corner. For ~~it was my belief~~ I suspected that
my eyes were not as yet totally
extinguished, thanks no doubt
to the smoked glasses that my
tutor had given me, together with
the *Ethics* of Geulincx, when I was
13 or 14 ^years old^. ~~He had the foresight
to~~ They were a very fine pair of glasses,
full size, with gold branches. He
was a far seeing man. He was found
~~dead~~ one morning ^on the floor^ in his W.C., his
dress in shocking disorder, ~~xxxx~~
~~A cerebral haemorrhage~~ dead of
an infarct.

_____ ('Suite' notebook, pp. 27–8)[8]

With this horizon line marked right across page 28 of his notebook Beckett decisively separated his oeuvre, with English on one side and French on the other. He then went back to the beginning of the passage and, as Cohn describes, recapitulated it in French before continuing to the end of the novella, now a *nouvelle*, in French. What is immediately most striking about this first version of the passage in relation to the reading of the later version presented above is that Beckett uses a conjoiner in 'my tutor had given me, together with the *Ethics* of Geulincx', where 'together with' categorically separates the book from what are here 'smoked glasses'. Beckett does go on in this version to invest the glasses with an ambiguity, where the tutor is 'a far seeing man', a man perhaps whose capacity for what Beckett referred to as Geulincx's '<u>sub specie aeternitatis</u> [from the perspective of eternity] vision' is his 'only excuse for remaining alive'. Without the perspective, the tutor dies of a heart attack, or what was a '<s>cerebral haemorrhage</s>'. However, the tutor's being 'far seeing' is more than a visionary ability. It is also an inability, his being long-sighted as opposed to short-sighted and so his being in need of the corrective lenses that are handed down to his protégé. Yet the ambiguities in this double meaning are constrained by the narrator being given *Ethics* 'together with' the glasses. We can therefore see in this passage, when compared to the later version, Beckett negotiating ways of instantiating an irresolvable ambivalence about being simultaneously free and constrained. Yet this is not as fully formed as it would become. While there is a tantalizing fragment of how the tutor might have '<s>had the foresight to</s>' do something that is related to the gift of *Ethics* as well as to the age of the young and impressionable recipient, Beckett's curtailing this and turning instead to the glasses as 'very fine' cuts off what may have been resulting in a more obviously dual use of 'sight'.

Suite in French

Something was lacking in this English version, and it was presumably in a somewhat 'pioneering spirit' (that which Molloy lacks), perhaps also one of some frustration, that Beckett struck a blow across the English page and began again in French. While he had written a number of poems and critical pieces in French by 1946, something in English at precisely this point gave Beckett the impetus to shift languages and not return to English as a language of prose composition for some eight years (other than in translation) with the short piece *From an Abandoned Work*, the title of which perhaps calling not only to its status as derived from a larger jettisoned piece but also to the 'work' of being an English author that Beckett had earlier, indeed right here in this passage of his notebook, 'abandoned'. Beckett might have come to similar conclusions to those Belacqua had 'mused' over regarding his own desire to 'write without style': 'Perhaps only the French can do it. Perhaps only the French language can give you the thing you want'. In 1932 Belacqua's earnestness had been rejected by his narrator for its not yet managing to fathom the subtleties of actual, rather than theoretical, creative work: 'Don't be too hard on him, he was studying to be a professor' (*Dr*, p. 48), and the possibility of French prose was shelved for some 14 years. Perhaps too it was the English absolutisms of connections such as 'together with' that Beckett realized constituted in part that frustrating 'imperturbability' (*Dis*, p. 171) of grammar and style imagined in 1937 as the outmoded formal mannerisms of a Victorian gentleman. Seeking then to perturb his own conventions and to trust (a little blindly in darkened glasses) an instinct, in what can surely be characterized at this nascent stage as his *experimental* decision to write prose in French, Beckett took a second, French, swipe at his tutor and killed him off again.

Yet the experiment appears to not have instantaneously yielded 'the thing' he wanted in 1946 either, though at least this time Beckett had the patience and confidence to persevere. The French passage that follows the notebook's language borderline is much closer to its eventual published counterpart than the English, but there are still important similarities to the English notebook version. For the most part Beckett retains in French the absolute demarcations between the objects (and adds the teasing 'occasion'):

Il m'avait
donné, à la même occasion, l'Ethique
de Geulincx.
('Suite' notebook, p. 28)

He had given me
on the same occasion, the *Ethics*
of Geulincx.

This became simply 'Il m'avait donné l'*Ethique* de Geulincz' (Beckett 1955, p. 105) in the published text. Similarly, while this French passage saw the arrival of the signed fly-leaf, the book was still kept separate from the glasses:

L'Ethique
portait son nom sur la page de garde
et xxxx xxxx xxxx les lunettes
lui avaient peut-être appartenu
aussi.
('Suite' notebook, p. 28)

The *Ethics*
bore his name on the fly-leaf
and xxxx xxxx xxxx the glasses
had perhaps belonged to him
too.

These lines were eventually published as 'L'*Ethique* portait son nom (Ward) sur la page de garde, les lunettes lui avaient appartenu' (Beckett 1955, p. 106), which introduces the crucial comma and avoids the fixity and distinctness in the 'Suite' notebook. Beckett also brings over the border from the English the visionary status of the tutor, who is 'un homme du voyant' [a man of vision] ('Suite' notebook, p. 28). The question still abides, however, of if Beckett did not immediately find 'the thing you want' in the turn to French in this passage, when did he?

The End in Merlin

Although he completed the nouvelle as a French text before translating it back into the language in which *Suite* had been started, giving the impression that if this bilingual text might have a primary version it would be the French, thanks to de Beauvoir's strict editorial stance of 1946 it was *The End* that first saw full-length publication. This was in 1954 in the English language Paris-based literary quarterly *Merlin*, edited by Alexander Trocchi and Seaver, dubbed by Beckett the 'Merlin juveniles' (SB to GR, 8 May 1953[9]). The *Merlin* version of *The End* reveals significant variants in the text that bear on reading a fusion of the glasses and the *Ethics* as a product of syntax, and so the corresponding passage is quoted in full:

> So I covered the lower part of my face with a black rag and went and begged at a sunny corner. For it seemed to me my eyes were not yet completely spent, thanks perhaps to the dark glasses my tutor had given me when I was small. He had also given me, on the same occasion, the *Ethics* of Geulinex [sic], I don't know why. They were a man's glasses already, with a gold frame, for he was farsighted. They found him dead one fine morning, crumpled up in the water closet, his clothes in awful disorder, struck down by an infarctus. The *Ethics* had his name (Ward) on the front page, and the glasses had perhaps belonged to him too. The bridge, at the time I am speaking of here, was of brass wire, of the kind used to hang pictures and big mirrors, and two long black ribbons served as wings. I wound them round my ears and then down under my chin where I tied them together. The lens had lost their opacity, doubtless from rubbing so long in my pocket against each other, and against the other objects there. But I had no further need of these glasses and used them merely to soften the glare of the sun. If I speak of them, it is for the sole reason of explaining why my sight lagged behind my other senses. (Beckett 1954, pp. 153–4)

It is clear that the missing conjoiners hypothesized above, and which manifest as 'together with', 'à la même occasion' and 'aussi' in the 'Suite' notebook,

Suite/La Fin/The End: *Continuations and Conclusions*

make a similarly explicit appearance in this published version. The tutor 'had also' given the student, 'on the same occasion, the *Ethics* of Geulinex [. . .] and the glasses had perhaps belonged to him too'; there is no confusing the two objects whatsoever. Not even the man's being 'farsighted' appears to imply anything about his *Ethics*. How might this be accounted for, and what, if anything, does this version illuminate about Beckett's intended uses of Geulincx?

Importantly, Beckett did not approve this version, either before or after its publication. Despite being credited as 'translated from the French by Richard Seaver in collaboration with the author' in *Merlin*, Seaver apparently did most of the translating on his own, and vitally Beckett never saw proofs before publication. Given how angry Beckett was when he saw the publication, his not being involved at proof stage might well imply that he never saw a complete translation at all, something that would have been expected well before proofs. Seaver told his side of the story in a preface to a 1976 Grove Press reader, where he wrote that *Merlin*'s *The End* was 'my translation. Well, sort of my translation' (Seaver 1976, p. xiv). According to Seaver, Beckett had suggested that the editor attempt the translation, and the two met to discuss Seaver's first draft in Paris at Le Dôme, Montparnasse:

> Beckett began to read. After a few minutes of perusing first my translation, then the original, his wire-framed glasses pushed up into the thick shock of hair above – the better to see, no doubt – he shook his head. My heart sank. Clearly, the translation was inadequate. 'You can't translate that', he said, fingering the original with utter disdain. 'It makes no sense.' (p. xxiii)

Beckett went on to point out places in Seaver's translation where 'you're literally right', but where Seaver should make such moments what Beckett called 'a bit tighter' (p. xxiv). For instance, according to Seaver the opening lines changed through these collaborative sessions from the following:

> They dressed me and gave me money. I knew what the money was to be used for, it was for my travelling expenses. When it was gone, they said, I would have to get some more, if I wanted to go on travelling.' (p. xxiii)

The passage became less explicit, partly as a result of importing the famed Beckettian notion of going 'on' by trimming the final sentence:

> They clothed me and gave me money. I knew what the money was for, it was to get me started. When it was gone I would have to get more, if I wanted to go on. (p. xxiv)

However, the collaborative process Seaver describes comes under some strain when we take into account how furious Beckett was when he saw the published version. The passage that *Merlin* actually published was the first of the above quotations, the one that, as Seaver tells it, Beckett had advised Seaver on explicitly. Beckett vented his frustrations to *Merlin*'s editor-in-chief, Trocchi:

> I have received, not from you, a copy of the latest issue of Merlin.
> My text is full of errors. Why did you not send me proofs? If, in this instance, circumstances had prevented me from correcting them, and they would not have, at least you would have done what it was incumbent on you to do. Are you too forgetting, in the fuss of editing, the needs of writers?
> I am still waiting for you to begin payment of royalties you owe me.
> I begin to weary of your treatment of me.
> If we cannot have ordinarily correct relations, it is better we should have none at all. (SB to AT, 27 August 1954: *L2*, pp. 498–9)[10]

It is unfortunate that there is no detailed description of what Beckett considered the specific errors to be, even if Trocchi's reply might be taken to indicate the existence of such details: 'That you were able to get so many recriminations on one small page does credit to your literary ability but says little for what I believed was our friendship' (AT to SB, 30 August 1954[11]). Consequently, it cannot be asserted with certainty that the differences between the two English versions of the passage were indeed some of those 'ridiculous mistakes' Beckett found in *Merlin*. However, given Beckett's desire to make the text 'a bit tighter' and his apparent balking at Seaver's initial literalism, the inference is perhaps justified. According to a letter Beckett sent to Seaver on 12 November 1953, there had been a meeting planned between the two of them to discuss translation of *L'Expulsé*, but Beckett had to cancel having realized he had scheduled a meeting to discuss the French translation of *Watt* with Daniel Mauroc that clashed. No further letters between Beckett and Seaver from 1953–7 survive, so whatever happened to a rescheduling cannot be known. What seems possible, however, is that *The End* slipped through the cracks of Beckett's increasingly busy schedule, and so he was unable to check a final version of the translation, while at the same time Seaver submitted the wrong, earlier draft for publication.[12]

Something interesting also results from a comparison of *Merlin*'s version with the French passages of the 'Suite' notebook. Seaver's 1954 rendering of 'on the same occasion' would appear highly speculative, were it not for 'aussi, à la même occasion' in the French part of the 'Suite' notebook. Whichever French text Seaver was working from, it seems unlikely that it was the final French version as later published by Éditions de Minuit, but was rather a further version somewhere between the French as it was in the 'Suite' notebook and as it appeared in Minuit's 1955 edition; something closer to a full version of *Suite et Fin* as Beckett had planned it for *Les Temps modernes*. The fifth *Watt* notebook

Suite/La Fin/The End: *Continuations and Conclusions* 113

at HRHRC bears the title 'Samuel Beckett *Watt* V / Suite ~~et fin~~ / 18.2.45 / 5 Paris / Et debut de L'Absent / *Malone meurt* / Novembre–Janvier 47/48'.[13] However, as Ann Beer and J. M. Coetzee have both pointed out, there is no sign of *Suite* in the notebook, and as Beer describes it, 'presumably Beckett wrote this [title on the cover] when he did not expect to need more than five notebooks, and returned to correct "Suite et fin" to "Suite" when he found a sixth was required' (Beer 1985, p. 60). Ackerley points out that the opening pages are torn out of this notebook.[14]

That mysterious missing version from which Seaver worked as the basis of *Merlin*'s translation has in fact only very recently appeared. Tucked away inside an envelope in folder JEK A/2/296 (a folder otherwise mostly dedicated to material directly involving the van Veldes) in the recently acquired Knowlson collection at Reading, is a typescript of the second, concluding part of 'Suite', which begins as expected just where *Les Temps modernes* left off, and echoes 'la même occasion' and 'aussi' of the notebook. Here what is the 'tuteur' gave the glasses to this narrator 'quand j'étais petit', to a more diligent young student than later incarnations, who manages when older and writing as he claims 'à présent' to spell Geulincx's name correctly, an indication that the later misspelled 'Geulincz' is likely a wilful misremembering. Taken together with the truncated half in *Les Temps modernes*, this newly discovered half of *Suite* not only helps explain (and goes some way to redeeming) Seaver's translation (if not the decision to print it), and underscores the arguments of the current chapter about stages of ambiguity and Geulincx's importance in these. More importantly, a full *Suite* is now available for consultation, a text that is vital to an understanding of Beckett's changing aesthetics in the 1940s. It is scheduled to appear fully documented as part of a forthcoming *Beckett Digital Manuscript Project* online module and publication on the nouvelles.

Why *The End* did not End There

The publication and translation history of this short text after the *Merlin* version becomes quite complex. In summary, it runs as follows: Beckett wrote to Seaver in a letter of 5 March 1958 describing how he remembered their collaborations, and proposed a system according to which they would share the workload with a view to publishing *Stories and Texts for Nothing* via Grove:

> If you have not succeeded in getting hold of a copy of <u>Nouvelles et Textes pour Rien</u> let me know and I'll send you one. The first edition is out of print and the second one due any day, with drawings by Avigdor Arikha. There are only three stories – those you mention. A fourth, <u>Premier Amour</u>, written at the same time, never appeared anywhere, and I have scrapped it. I thought we had gone through pretty carefully together your translations of

all three, but you must be right and it was only The End. [. . .] I think I shall try and translate the Textes pour Rien myself, they being in the idiom more or less of L'Innommable which I have just finished translating. My idea was for the book to appear with you figuring as translator of the stories and me as translator of the Textes. I should be very pleased if you would agree to this arrangement. (SB to RS, 5 March 1958)

Seaver agreed to this arrangement, and the two then went on to discuss titles for the *Stories*, and tried to settle various confusions deriving from misremembering the earlier stages of translation. However, the planned edition did not appear until 1967, Beckett's many other commitments conspiring to slow it down.

Beckett amended an English typescript of the story in 1959 in advance of *Evergreen*'s publication. He sent it back to Seaver with the following note appended:

Herewith The End with my corrections. Your translation is excellent and they are for the most part just fussiness and contrariness and author's licence. If there are any you disagree with let me have a note of them and we'll find something else or revert to your text. I can't remember if we worked on the other two together, perhaps only one, L'Expulsé it seems to me. I have finished the first Texte pour Rien and sent it to Barney. "Esquire" wants it, of all improbable ducks. (SB to RS, 6 March 1959)

The *Evergreen* version is almost identical to the above-cited Faber version and so is not quoted in full here. The only variant in the passage distinguishing it from Faber's is that the tutor's name appears on *Ethics*' 'front page' (Beckett 1960, p. 33) instead of on the 'fly-leaf'. This is an interesting variant in itself, in that the subsequent change from *Evergreen*'s generalized vocabulary ('front page') to a more technical literary one ('fly-leaf'), a change Beckett made to the galley proofs of Grove's 1967 *Stories and Texts for Nothing* (now at HRHRC), gives a phrase that intimates more closely the forgotten learning of the young student, exhibiting a fragmentary synecdoche of this learning. The amendment mitigates against a conception of 'the series' as entirely one of reductions from specifics to the general and abstract, with this alteration of 'front page' to 'fly-leaf' inserting specialist specificity.

After Seaver published *The End* in *Evergreen Review*, he republished that same version in a collection he coedited with Trocchi and Terry Southern, entitled *Writers in Revolt* (1963). In 1967, when the story appeared in both Calder's *No's Knife* and finally in Grove's *Stories and Texts for Nothing*, Beckett made further alterations, excising entirely a character that had first appeared in the 'Suite' notebook. His brief existence in the text had been just prior to the Geulincx passage:

The town planner with the red beard, they removed his gall-bladder, a gross mistake, and three days later he died, in the prime of life. (Beckett 1960, p. 33)

Suite/La Fin/The End: *Continuations and Conclusions*

Beckett also finally amended the inaccurate spelling of 'Geulincz' to 'Geulincx' in the galley proofs of the 1967 Grove *Stories and Texts for Nothing*, a change that did not make it across the Atlantic in time for Calder's 1984 *Collected Shorter Prose*.

In the meantime *La Fin* was published with Minuit in 1955 and again in 1958. Comparable to the now standard English version, and in contrast with that botched by *Merlin*, this French text also carries the ambivalence regarding the ontological status of these two objects:

> Je me couvris donc le bas du visage d'un chiffon noir et allai demander l'aumône à un coin ensoleillé. Car il me semblait que mes yeux n'étaient pas tout à fait éteints, grâce peut-être aux lunettes noires que mon précepteur m'avait données. Il m'avait donné l'*Ethique* de Geulincz [sic]. C'étaient des lunettes d'homme, j'étais un enfant. On le trouva mort, écroulé dans les W.-C., les vêtements dans un désordre terrible, foudroyé par un infarctus. Ah quel calme. L'*Ethique* portait son nom (Ward) sur la page de garde, les lunettes lui avaient appartenu. Le pont, à l'époque dont je parle, était en fil de laiton, de la sorte qu'on emploie pour accrocher les tableaux et les grandes glaces, et deux longs rubans noirs me servaient de branches. Je les enroulais autour des oreilles et les ramenais sous le menton, où je les nouais ensemble. Les verres avaient souffert, à force de se frotter dans ma poche l'un contre l'autre et contre les autres objets qui s'y trouvaient. Je croyais que Monsieur Weir m'avait tout pris. Mais je n'avais plus besoin de ces lunettes et ne les mettais plus que pour adoucir l'éclat di soleil. J'aurais mieux fait de ne pas en parler. (Beckett 1955, pp. 105–6)

Beckett had apparently found the French to be 'the thing' he wanted. But the first part of *Suite* that de Beauvoir published in 1946, along with the recently unearthed second part, is so extensively different from Minuit's 1955 version, even while Minuit's does still include the 'town-planner' (here 'L'urbaniste à la barbe rouge' (p. 105)), that it is clear Beckett undertook an extensive redraft of the French. It seems likely that he did this at least in part as a consequence of the problems of translating the early French version back into English with Seaver. This means that *La Fin*, a nouvelle frequently dated as 1946 and thereby attributed to the very beginnings of Beckett's middle period in accord with its extant manuscript stages, should probably more accurately be thought of as a text that derives from a period in which Beckett was both a much more experienced writer of French and translator. *La Fin* was given its final form(s) years after Beckett had completed, and then translated, the novels of the trilogy. Both the English and French versions that are widely published today, therefore, are not texts that come unmediated from Beckett the nascent French writer, however much we might wish onto the shorter texts the status of preliminaries prior to the longer novels. Even the French, from which later English translations are derived, owes its surviving form to intervening years of intra-language translation. That Geulincx played a part at many important and self-reflexive moments of this text's transition, moments that are later repeatedly revised, is yet another facet of this philosopher's importance for Beckett's oeuvre.

Sailing and Sinking

In what might come to be seen as a flawed but nevertheless pioneering historicizing study of Beckett, Pascale Casanova wrote that *La Fin/The End* 'can be read as one of Beckett's most exhaustive attempts to describe all the "practical" implications of Geulincx's principles'.[15] This is because, according to Casanova, '"The End" is the story of a quest for immobility and serenity, the story of someone "becoming Belacqua" in order to attain freedom' (Casanova 2006, p. 66). As previous chapters have argued, however, theorizing Beckett's incorporations of and recourses to Geulincx as entirely determined by a Geulincx of the little world not only sells the philosopher's system short, it also disavows the relevance of a significant proportion of Beckett's notes on Geulincx that took into account precisely the '"practical" implications' of Occasionalist impotence, the everyday consequences of the fact that we cannot act but we must nevertheless act; we cannot 'go on' but we must 'go on'. As Feldman points out too, although for this narrator:

> to 'know I had a being, however faint and false, outside of me, had once had the power to stir my heart' [. . .] this is not enough to keep him from retreating to a boat, ostensibly committing very un-Geulingian suicide. (Feldman 2009a, p. 45)

The interior into which the perpetually expelled narrator climbs and shuts himself at the end of the novella, full of regret for lacking 'the courage to end or the strength to go on' (*E*, p. 57), is the coffin for the last of Beckett's protagonists who will categorically, wilfully, die. First Belacqua (in 'Yellow'), then Murphy, Arsene in the Ur-*Watt* and now this nameless narrator. As Chapter 2 discussed, for Geulincx suicide is impossible because:

> it is quite clear from our inspection of the human condition that men move neither their own nor other bodies, and consequently, it is as impossible for us to choose death as to cut short life and bring forward death.

More than this, however, suicide also conflicts entirely with the second ethical obligation according to which one must 'labour' under the requirement 'not to depart this life unless God has summoned you' (*Et*, p. 339). Similarly, for Beckett too from this point onward, 'un-Geulingian' suicide is also just not

Suite/La Fin/The End: *Continuations and Conclusions*

good enough. But it is not good enough in a literary, creative sense; death is just too simple and easy an option for one so thoroughly concerned with, and committed to, the detail of desolation. Better, Beckett was discovering during the middle period, to stifle the urge to stop, even while needing to stop.[16] While there would be brutal and bloody murders committed by Molloy and Malone's Lemuel, for example, and there will be torture and cruelty in *How It Is* and *What Where*, peaceful, willed death will just not suffice any longer.

While Geulincx is at the heart of *La Fin/The End*, specifically at a kind of literal textual centre of the piece, so as the old philosophy tutor dies from a heart attack the presence of Geulincx is short circuited, exited and ushered away. The very passage in which his name appears enacts this process of his being ushered out, in redrafting, translation and republication. It is the birthing process of the yet to be fully fledged new 'one' of whom Watt spoke that can be seen taking place through the text's variant versions. So what will happen when this tutor is dead, rather than in the process of being killed? What will happen to Beckett's philosophical analects, engraved and en-graved, scraped together in mutual erasure and buried in ancient rock, when he writes arguably his greatest achievements in prose, the trilogy *Molloy, Malone meurt/Malone Dies* and *L'Innommable/The Unnamable*? The following chapter asks these questions and finds surprising answers to be found in a number of textual residues, fragmenting allusions and echoes of philosophy in the narrative performativity of these great works.

Chapter 5

The Trilogy: Imagery and Axioms

This chapter provides a critical reading of the importance of Geulincx for the trilogy of novels of Beckett's middle period *Molloy*, *Malone meurt/Malone Dies* and *L'Innommable/The Unnamable*, with particular focus on *The Unnamable*. It first takes a visual approach, enumerating these novels' imagistic allusions to Geulincx, the first of which explicitly names the philosopher, before focusing a similar genealogical approach linguistically by explicating the partial quotations of Geulincx's ethical axiom as it is variously manifested throughout the novels. This dual analysis frames Beckett's developing uses of borrowed imagery and quotation within a conceptual impetus to 'vaguen'[1]. As recorded by Rosemary Poutney as well as by S. E. Gontarski, Beckett's marginalia in a *Happy Days* manuscript stated that when revising the draft he should 'vaguen' the description of the stage set, instancing an impetus Cohn describes as 'a despecifying process that would become habitual in the composition of his drama' (Cohn 2001, p. 263). It would also be put to effective use in prose, and the lineages of imagery and fragmented quotation derived from Geulincx that can be traced through the trilogy is a paradigm of Beckett's 'fantasia' in microcosm; much as the trilogy is a 'series' of works within Beckett's broader 'series', so the ways in which Geulincx is employed within these three novels manifests, but on a smaller scale, the ways in which he is used across the oeuvre. As the project to trace the importance and viability of Geulincx for Beckett's oeuvre begins with an analysis of explicit citations in *Murphy* and moves towards barely-there fleeting presences in the fragmented and minimalist texts of the late period, so too within the trilogy the progression of a *vaguening*, a transition from the explicit to the implicit, can be tracked. It is a movement that is also one from intertextuality to intratextuality, whereby later allusions to Geulincx call not only to Geulincx's own texts, but they also reach out to the already refracted references to Geulincx that exist within Beckett's texts.

Following these discussions the chapter argues that the 'one [who] shall be born [. . .] who having nothing will wish for nothing, except to be left the nothing he hath' heralded by the Watt of *Mercier and Camier* is an identity manifested and achieved (for it was an aspiration as much as a matter-of-fact description) in discrete moments by the self-asserting, self-negating, first-person narrative voice of *The Unnamable*. To this end I test Uhlmann's provocative suggestion that *The Unnamable* manifests less a Cartesian than a Geulingian form of *cogito*, and argue that Beckett manages with *The Unnamable* to achieve something entirely new in the 'series' that can be traced to Geulincx. In Weller's terminology, Beckett achieves an 'actualization' of principles fundamental to Geulincx's ethics in narrative, aligning the seeking and turning away from self that is inherent to Geulincx's *humilitas* with *The Unnamable*'s paradoxical non-self-assertion. Geulincx's axiom, therefore, can be central to a reading of the climax of Beckett's middle period works.

Molloy Sets Sail

The only explicit naming of Geulincx in the trilogy occurs in the following passage from the first section of the first novel, where Molloy has recently left Lousse's house. The narrator–protagonist questions his capacity for choice and action, and in this context wistfully, a touch sentimentally, reveals his affection for Geulincx:

> Now as to telling you why I stayed a good while with Lousse, no, I cannot. That is to say I could I suppose, if I took the trouble. But why should I? In order to establish beyond all question that I could not do otherwise? For that is the conclusion I would come to, fatally. I who had loved the image of old Geulincx, dead young, who left me free, on the black boat of Ulysses, to crawl towards the East, along the deck. That is a great measure of freedom, for him who has not the pioneering spirit. And from the poop, poring upon the wave, a sadly rejoicing slave, I follow with my eyes the proud and futile wake. Which, as it bears me from no fatherland away, bears me onward to no shipwreck. (*Mo*, pp. 49–50)

Molloy refuses to face the fact of his own impotence, which would be fatal. As Moran will also do, Molloy gilds his impotence, adorning it with admiration of the philosopher of freedom-in-slavery, the by now 'old' Geulincx. The valiant, because certain to fail, effort of an oxymoronic, Janus-eyed 'sadly rejoicing' slave destined to wish for a shipwreck that will not come is, Molloy opines, the benchmark of freedom if you are not much of a freedom fighter.

In 1999 Uhlmann brought to public view a letter written by Beckett to *Molloy*'s German translator Erich Franzen in 1954, in which Beckett was unusually expansive in his explications of the allusions in the passage that mentions Geulincx, tying it to the passage from *Ethics*:

> This passage is suggested (a) by a passage in the Ethics of Geulincx where he compares human freedom to that of a man, on board a boat carrying him irresistibly westward, free to move eastward within the limits of the boat itself, as far as the stern; and (b) by Ulysses' relation in Dante (Inf. 26) of his

second voyage (a medieval tradition) to and beyond the Pillars of Hercules, his shipwreck and death. . . I imagine a member of the crew who does not share the adventurous spirit of Ulysses and is at least at liberty to crawl homewards. . . along the brief deck. (SB to EF, 17 February 1954)[2]

Beckett neglects to mention Homer to Franzen in this connexion, though perhaps merely because it is too obvious. The blackness of the boat is less obvious, but can be explained. Entry no. 714 in the 'Dream' notebook reads 'black cruiser of Ulysses', which Pilling annotates in relation to Victor Bérard's translation of the *Odyssey*:

> Bérard, 175; *Odyssey*, X, 501–502. CF. 'Draff' ('black as Ulysses's cruiser'; *More Pricks Than Kicks*, 198), the 'black ferry' of the poem 'Text', and 'the black boat of Ulysses', (*Molloy*, 'trilogy' 51). (Beckett 1999a, p.103)

Dante does not mention the colour of the boat in the *Inferno*'s canto XXVI, but following Pilling's work on the 'Dream' notebook we can see how the boat being 'black' reveals the *Molloy* passage to be even more expansively allusive than Beckett indicates. A particularly striking parallel between the episode as related by Dante and the context of the ship's passenger in *Ethics* lies in how both narratives rely on a dualist distinction between an inner and outer world. In the *Inferno* Ulysses exhorts his crew onward on the perilous journey 'beyond the Pillars of Hercules' through flattery of their inner lives as well as their heritage and heroism in the 'big' physical world:

> Consider what you came from: you are Greeks!
>   You were not born to live like mindless brutes
>   but to follow paths of excellence and knowledge. (Dante 2003, p. 309
>   (Inf. XXVI 118–20))

The path of an inner world of 'knowledge' supervenes upon the exploratory and dangerous journey in the physical world. Both are journeys of 'excellence', and as in *Ethics*, the proper way to live in the social world is dependent upon an inspection of the private inner world.

As might be expected, the passage in *Molloy* has been cited many times in discussions of Beckett's interests in Geulincx. Feldman describes it, for example, as one that 'perfectly corresponds to a sentence in Beckett's transcriptions of the *Ethics*' (Feldman 2009a, p. 45), a sentence in which Geulincx attempts to find a space within all-encompassing impotence for a Christian-like free will. It is the passage Beckett directed Franzen to:

> Just as a ship carrying a passenger with all speed towards the west in no way prevents the passenger from walking towards the east, so the will of God,

carrying all things, impelling all things with inexorable force, in no way prevents us from resisting his will (as much as is in our power) with complete freedom. (*Et*, p. 317)

The passage from *Ethics* appears in an annotation to Treatise 1, Chapter 1, § 2, Reason.[3] The section in the main body of the Treatise that Geulincx annotates, however, is worthy of further investigation, as it speaks to Beckett's fascination with Geulingian thought as embodying – manifesting as well as describing – an ethics of failure. Fundamental to Geulincx's conception of the authority of God is that it is metaphysically impossible to resist. For Geulincx it is pointless to think of resisting, because there is no real agency with which to resist. Yet, to again paraphrase *Ohio Impromtu,* 'even were it in [our] power' it would be morally wrong to resist what is God's perfect will anyway. This thoroughgoing submission that is both metaphysical and ethical (and is thereby captured in the axiom) endangers the viability of both actual free will and freedom to intend, despite the fact that Geulincx stakes his entire ethics on intentionality. Geulincx's theorizing the omnipotence of God's capacity for causation and humanity's incapacity to resist this in any way might be read as invoking a ruthless, unmovable and authoritarian God, a God whose pre-established synchronicity is singularly tyrannical. Geulincx sees the dangers and buttresses against them, detailing what can appear as his ethical fatalism:

To wish to obey the absolute, true and strict will of God in some matter, is to wish what has already been done; whether you like it or not, you will obey, just as all things will necessarily obey. (But here is not the place to speak of why this does not make God the author of Sin, and of how it is consistent with our freedom of will). (p. 16)

The correct place to 'speak of why [. . .] freedom of will' is unaffected by this 'strict' inevitability that looks suspiciously like determinism is, according to Geulincx, in his annotations. Annotation 9, describing the passenger on the ship, is then appended to this paragraph in order to reconcile a sense of God as ultra authoritarian with human free will. Surely, it must be concluded, Geulincx's ship analogy fails his self-imposed test. The image of a ship-hand crawling in the opposite direction to the vessel's forward motion fails because it does not capture the internalized intentionality that Geulincx argues is the only measure of ethical worth. Beckett transcribed, for example, Geulincx's intentionalist statement, '*Whatever men do, they are all judged by their intention*' (p. 349). The failure in the analogy is a similar failure, though one here left unexplained, to that which Geulincx admits in the cradle analogy. What the ship analogy does achieve, however, given its failure on these terms, is an image of futility that, it might well be supposed, would have greatly appealed to Beckett. It is in an unintended sense of the image – as an image of thorough futility and failure – as well as (as Geulincx intended) an image of affirmative freedom, that Beckett was struck so forcefully that he would incorporate it into his work 20 years after he read it, as a paradigm of the possibility of freedom 'for him who has not the pioneering spirit'.

In an article entitled 'The Shipwreck of Belief', van Ruler discusses another of Geulincx's ship analogies to illustrate how the 'different ways in which the analogy operates in [Herman] Witsius and [Ruardas] Andala on the one hand and Geulincx on the other, are indicative of their conflicting theological views' (van Ruler 2003, p. 127). In the other analogy Geulincx describes how a ship could be 'made ready, fitted-out' in all good preparation, yet such planning would not (and could not) prevent circumstances from conspiring against the ship, where it might be 'plunged into a storm, or captured by pirates' (*Et*, p. 143). Geulincx deploys this further ship analogy in the context of his theorizing sin and divine punishment, where it illustrates arguments for the impotence of the will (according to 'the unhappy man's' philosophy misfortune is inevitable and cannot be willed away). Similarly, he writes of a merchant on a ship that is indeed 'plunged into a storm' to again illustrate Occasionalist freedom. Describing what he calls freedom to '*do as thou pleasest; or. . .do as thou art minded*' (p. 323), Geulincx uses a case study of 'the merchant who when a storm blows up flings his merchandise into the sea [and who therefore] does *not* enjoy this kind of freedom'. Rather, this merchant 'does not do what pleases him, but on the contrary acts against how he is minded, and would by no means do it if he were not forced to do it' (p. 205). That images of ships and storms are so ingrained in Geulincx's texts is of little surprise. He was after all 'born within a mile of the ships that visited Antwerp's harbour, and [. . .] knew about sea-trade' (van Ruler 2003, p. 126). Geulincx even uses a shipping analogy to define propositional content: 'as there is no shipwreck without a ship, neither is there a negation without an affirmation'.[4]

This ship on which Molloy imagines himself is the only appearance of Geulincx's ethical and metaphysical vessel in the first novel of the trilogy. Uhlmann writes that 'The ship image recurs on three occasions in *The Unnamable*' (Uhlmann 2006a, p. 78), and with citations keyed to the first Grove Press publication of 1958, lists these as 'pp. 68, 72, 148' (p. 165). This list is arguably a little incomplete, however. The image recurs a further time in *The Unnamable*, its appearance even more refracted and abstracted from its origin, more *vaguened*. In missing this fourth, fleeting appearance, Uhlmann misses something that is integral to the lineage – its instancing a micro-'series' of imagistic *vaguening*, Beckett reducing the memorialized residues of what once were sources to what he called the 'fundamental sounds' (SB to Alan Schneider, 29 December 1957[5]) of his middle period works. Uhlmann is surely right to see a bigger picture of Beckett's evolving art as one that moves from direct relation, from more readily identifiable influence and allusions (despite their obscurity), to a more complex art of non-relation, and to point out that

Geulincx has a part to play in this transition. Yet in seeing Beckett's uses of Geulincx, as many scholars have done, in terms of an incorporation of images that remain fairly intact even if 'occluded', the analysis cannot see those fleeting reappearances of the philosopher that show a different pattern, one that locates Beckett's uses of philosophy as synchronized with his will to 'vaguen' the 'series' overall. When we come to read Geulincx in the trilogy, it is, I argue, the transitional, changeable nature of the series of imagery that chiefly characterizes it.

Geulingian Imagery in *The Unnamable*

The Unnamable is so continuously ingrained with the 'aporia' (*U*, p. 1) foregrounded in its very first paragraph that any attempt to write generalized critical commentary on this self-negating novel, so exhaustively characterized by what *Texts for Nothing* 13 calls 'the screaming silence of no's knife in yes's wound' (*TN*, p. 53), is bound to be undone; nothing can ever be asserted of the novel without taking account of such an assertion's necessary concomitant negation. So, at least, runs one viable opinion on the critic's relationship to this work. It is the perception of such undermining oppositional structures that is in part responsible for what Bruno Clément, while stopping short of calling it a ventriloquizing of the critical response, describes as a 'duality of narrative authorities [in] the Beckettian text':

> The not-very-attentive reader (indeed, as experience proves, even the more battle-hardened reader) only belatedly becomes aware (if indeed he or she becomes aware at all) that there is in the work, in the text that he or she reads, a voice resembling, to the point of their being mistaken for one another, the critical voice. (Clément 2006, p. 119)

Clément describes a broad category of 'a' critical voice already embedded in, indelibly bound into, 'the' work. Yet these words of caution, of Clément's and of mine ventriloquizing the extreme sceptic above, must themselves be cautioned, as they themselves already assert generalized critical statements. It is incumbent to note how the option of 'aporia', for example, proposed by the novel's narrating voice as he introduces himself, is itself asserted without anything like a total commitment to its implications. It is framed in a question: 'how proceed? By aporia pure and simple? Or by affirmations and negations invalidated as uttered, or sooner or later? Generally speaking' (*U*, p. 1). Not even this assertion of a framing structure for the novel-in-embryo is without its own particular element of ironic self-reflexive doubt and specificity. Following this precedent, the doubts and hesitancies that permeate this novel are of course not all 'pure and simple'. Rarely can *The Unnamable* be found 'Generally speaking'. This most uneasy of novels doubts and hesitates in specific instances, in individual moments, and some of these hesitancies and doubts are more assertive than others. Still others are discarded, undermined, directly opposed, left partially unresolved, or ignored, all in multifarious, combinatory ways. The critic should be wary of voicing anything too broad and general about the novel, because such an approach is indeed likely to be undermined by specific textual moments that work against generalizations. But this does not mean that one should refrain entirely from critical commentary on the novel for fear that one's critical voice is always already embedded in the text, where the voice of commentary can only be the sound of oneself being second-guessed. It is possible to speak of this novel without being engulfed by its voracious appetite for all comers, but the safest way to do so, I argue (if one is wary of 'pioneering' too soon becoming blundering), is by attending to the specificities of individual textual moments, always aware that consequent generalizing is the riskier strategy. Admittedly, there is little reason to assume that 'safety' is the thing to be aimed for when engaging with *The Unnamable*, but perhaps it can at least caution too clumsy steps at the outset.

These general comments about general comments are important for two reasons. They seek to underwrite an approach to Geulincx's relevance to *The Unnamable* as one comprised in the first analysis of specific textual moments, though ones that function within broader frameworks. Second, they frame the first strongly made assertion of self-identity in the novel. For this is an assertion that is not, at least not immediately, 'invalidated as uttered'. Just as claims about the novel can be made more confidently when focused on specific moments, some assertions in the novel are made more forcefully and categorically than others. There is only one instance in this novel of selfhood where the first person pronoun constitutes an entire sentence. It is, as so many of the other instances of 'I' in the novel are, asserted in the context of a questioning, but it also instances a rare and strongly asserted self-identity, and it occurs as a continuation of the lineage of ship imagery derived from Dante and Geulincx:

> I. Who might that be? The galley-man, bound for the Pillars of Hercules, who drops his sweep under cover of night and crawls between the thwarts, towards the rising sun, unseen by the guard, praying for storm. Except that I've stopped praying for anything. No no, I'm still a suppliant. I'll get over it, between now and the last voyage, on this leaden sea. (*U*, p. 50)

The narrator does not retract, or even otherwise object to, his identification here with the slave making his first moves for freedom, dropping the broom and crawling towards the east. A simple question mark after 'storm' would have pointed towards such scepticism. Instead, what is qualified in this passage, in the 'Except that I've stopped praying for anything. No, no, I'm still a suppliant' of the fourth and fifth sentences, is not the narrator's identity as the 'galley-man', but only the actions of this identity. That is, it is striking that the opening 'I' of this passage is left open, remaining asserted as the 'galley-man' of Geulincx and Dante's ships. One would not want to say that the narrator consistently throughout the novel aligns himself with Geulincx's singular galley-man, but at this point they do, while other possibilities are indeed 'invalidated'; the question of whether or not the 'galley-man' still prays, for example, is first asserted and then denied, before finally being left, suitably *vaguened*, as implied.

Beckett's intriguing pun here is 'thwarts'. While these 'thwarts' are literally the slats across a boat as seats for rowers (the seats athwart/across), 'thwarts' also connotes being hindered or stopped. Crawling 'between the thwarts' is then a movement of freedom through extrication that, in virtue of its nautical resonances, recalls Stephen Dedalus's Icarian aspiration to 'fly by those nets' of 'nationality, language, religion' (Joyce 1992a, p. 220) where his aesthetics will parallel his self-exile in distant lands in *A Portrait of the Artist as a Young Man*. Beckett's Geulingian protagonist crawling across the deck, heading in the opposite direction to that in which the ship is travelling and so only free to get as far as the bounds of the ship, in contrast to Stephen's heroic flight into open-ended air, serves as a useful summary image of the contrasting visions of freedom and constraint the two protagonists pursue. While Stephen would be determiner of his own 'uncreated conscience', even that of his entire 'race' (p. 276), Beckett's 'galley-man' is 'still a suppliant' who cannot even properly achieve freedom for himself.

Both Molloy and *The Unnamable*'s narrator imagine a ship being wrecked by a storm. Molloy remembers with fondness, with his 'love' for Geulincx, how he thought of himself carried by the vessel 'onward to no shipwreck'. *The Unnamable*'s narrator brings the image into his perpetual present tense, wherein he is impotently 'praying for storm'. The wish for shipwreck that is almost present in *Molloy* is made forcefully in *The Unnamable*, which thereby develops the Dantean impetus in these images, alluding to Ulysses's ship that met a storm five days after passing through the Pillars of Hercules:

Our celebrations soon turned to grief:
   and from the new land there rose a whirling wind
   that beat against the forepart of the ship

and whirled us round three times in churning waters;
   the fourth blast raised the stern up high, and sent
   the bow down deep, as pleased Another's will.

And then the sea was closed again, above us. (Dante 2003, p. 309 (Inf. XXVI 136–42))

Even in the allusion to storm and wreck so closely allied to Dante, however, Geulincx is also present. Ulysses describes the fatal storm as having 'pleased Another's will', and in this ascription of the storm deriving from God, as only possible as deriving from God, it is also fatalistic, and therein the two tales come together in a shipwreck caused directly by the only possible agency of God.

In a sense this 'galley-man' ('galérien' in *L'Innommable*) is also a figure of the writer. Just as Malone has his pages taken away each day, pages he fills with words he does not understand, so *The Unnamable*'s narrator is an author, a self-fashioner, who corrects and writes on the galleys that are the final stage before a book is printed. This 'galley-man' secretly throws away the tools of his trade in order to crawl to freedom, much as Beckett seeks in this climactic novel to do away with the gentilities of outmoded styles and syntax that he had been aspiring to leave behind for so long.

A few pages after its first mention in *The Unnamable* the narrator returns to this ship and his identification with the 'galley-man', abstracting the imagery from what it was previously to something more *vaguened*, less obviously tied to either Dante or Geulincx:

> I am he who will never be caught, never delivered, who crawls between the thwarts, towards the new day that promises to be glorious, festooned with lifebelts, praying for rack and ruin. (*U*, p. 52)

Similarly to the image's first appearance in the novel, here it also frames a self-identity asserted with a commitment force that is often absent, in complex and multivalent ways, from so many other assertions of self in the novel. Beckett appears to have obtained from Geulincx an analogy for a sense of identity that, even under the violent attacks of *The Unnamable*'s narrator repeatedly and variously stabbing 'no's knife in yes's wound', is not yet annihilated. However, even though such a sense of identity is not entirely discarded or disregarded, images of this galley-man are progressively and steadily fragmented through the novel. The pastoral but ominous 'rising sun' of earlier appears in this second image as 'the day that promises to be glorious', marking a vaguened shift from objects to atmospherics, from a specific thing to an intimation of mood, as the 'storm' of the first image becomes the consequences of that storm, the less specific 'rack and ruin'. A transition from relation to non-relation was traced through an analysis of the Geulincx passage in *Suite/The End/La Fin* in Chapter 4. A similar transition is enacted within *The Unnamable*, but here the alterations and refinements take place within the sinews of the final published text, viewable within the novel itself.

In the third appearance of this ship, possibilities of real physical escape become limited to mere visual glances of prospective freedom, of the new sunnier day:

> What a joy it is, to turn and look astern, between two visits to the depths, scan in vain the horizon for a sail, it's a real pleasure, upon my word it is, to be unable to drown, under such conditions. (*U*, p. 109)

This is the version of the image Uhlmann's account misses out.[6] Perhaps this is because Uhlmann considers that it does not qualify as a part of the lineage. Certainly it differs from the other images. It is, for example, the only instance not to mention 'thwarts'. Yet it does give the direction of looking as the same as earlier ('astern', which is the rear of the ship, as Molloy described looking out from the 'poop' deck, which is the top rear of the ship). These locations and directions bear comparison with Beckett's description to Franzen of a man 'on board a boat carrying him irresistibly westward', who nevertheless resists and travels 'eastward within the limits of the boat itself, as far as the stern'. This third image also marks an important moment in a progression characteristic of Beckett's prose and drama of the late-middle period as one from movement to stasis. The turning to 'look astern', while the ship travels forward, is the stilled and contemplative version of the physical crawling 'towards the east' and 'the rising sun'. Continuing the pattern of this ship imagery instantiating in microcosm broader shifts within Beckett's 'series', at this crucial point the balance tips, and Beckett's attention is ostensibly no longer on searching and seeking, on trying to find a physical space of freedom on the limited deck of the ship, and instead it shifts to the possibilities of standing still, looking, contemplating and waiting.

The final of the four images appears shortly after the third (as did the second from the first), a few pages from the end of the novel. There has been a further change on board this mysterious ship carrying ghosts of Beckett's past, and the galley-man with his hope of impossible freedom has, if not quite mutinied, taken some kind of charge:

> Now it's I the orator, the beleaguerers have departed, I am master on board, after the rats, I no longer crawl between the thwarts, under the moon, in the shadow of the lash. (*U*, p. 110)

Whatever nameless authority was keeping the deckhand subjugated and dreaming of a freedom in drowning has 'departed'. The narrator is now second in command 'after the rats', those elemental and often violent creatures that reappear throughout Beckett's texts, confounding enumerative rationalism or a possibility of transcendence as they do so. This new type of freedom in stasis, in no longer crawling towards a freedom to be found elsewhere, no longer even standing still and observing the possibility of freedom, asserts the central paradox of Beckett's middle period. As Alice and Kenneth Hamilton argue of Beckett's twinning of Geulincx with Democritus, the conclusions reached by Beckett in navigating between these two reside in a resignation to irresolvable paradox:

> Beckett's people appear to be given two choices: either stasis (the immobility to which bodily weakness eventually reduces everyone, in any event) or circular motion. Both amount to the same thing in the end, namely, getting nowhere. The wise accept the necessity for the absence of any goal to their wanderings, and react with Democritan laughter; while the less wise – as in *Waiting for Godot* – say, 'Let's go,' and do not move. Molloy is a good example of the wise man who has learned the lesson which his creator has drawn from Democritus and Geulincx. [. . .] He ends his narrative with the words, 'I longed to go back into the forest. Oh not a real longing. Molloy could stay, where he happened to be'[. . .]. (Hamilton and Hamilton 1976, p. 73)

The comparable culmination in *The Unnamable* inheres in that most climactic of Beckett's lines – 'I can't go on, I'll go on' (*U*, p. 134). Still subject to the movement of the boat, the stillness of stasis within movement is the fleeting best that can be hoped for, and that is what the narrator asserts they achieve. In a more recent assessment of how these two philosophers operate together for Beckett, Weller argues that the two 'points of departure' Beckett offered to Kennedy in 1967, both of whom establish different versions of a nothingness – Democritus's of the void between atoms, Geulincx's of being unworthy and incapable – indicate 'an antinomy at the ontological level and a distinction between the ontological and the ethical in his [Beckett's] own literary treatment of the nothing' (Weller 2010, p. 108). Might Geulincx's axiom and the ship that conveys a comparable binary movement be one place where Beckett brings the two sides of such a distinction closer together?

The ship from Geulincx, described by Beckett as deriving from *Ethics*, also has a near relative in a much earlier image. In *Dream of Fair to Middling Women* Beckett described a ship on which Belacqua 'is alone on the deck of steerage-class' travelling round the south coast of England at night. In almost cruel complicity with the reader and foreshadowing Pozzo's order to Lucky in *Waiting for Godot* to 'Think!' (*CDW*, p. 41), the narrator asks of his fictional puppet 'what would be the correct thing for him to think for us'. He decides on Belacqua's stilled pause looking out from the boat, mirroring the narrator's own self-conscious hiatus:

> To begin with, of course, he moves forward, like the Cartesian earthball, with the moving ship, and then on his own account to the windy prow. He can go no further with security. He leans out to starboard, if that means landward when land is to the right of the ship's motion, and scans the waste of waters, the distant beacons. Was it Beachy Head or the Isle of Wight, was it Land's End or tragic lightboats standing afar out about the shallows of

the sea, or lightbuoys moored over the shoals? They were red and green and they lancinated his heart, they brought down his lips and head over the froth of water. If I were in, he thought richly, and it up to me to swim to one of those lights that I can see from here – how would I know that land was there, I would see no light from the level of the sea, I would certainly drown in a panic. (*Dr*, pp. 134–5)

As Pilling and Ackerley have pointed out of this scene, Beckett derives the 'Cartesian earthball' from specific readings in Descartes.[7] In *Principles of Philosophy* Descartes seeks to define 'What external place is' via an analogy of a person on a moving ship. He argues that 'the names "space" and "place" do not signify a thing different from the body which is said to be in the place', and so 'external place' must be thought in relative terms:

> Thus, when a ship is heading out to sea, a person seated in the stern always remains in one place as far as the parts of the ship are concerned, for he maintains the same situation in relation to them. But this same person is constantly changing his place as far as the shores are concerned, since he is constantly moving away from some and toward others. Furthermore, if we think that the earth moves {and is rotating on its axis}, and travels from the West toward the East exactly as far as the ship progresses from the East toward the West; we shall once again say that the person seated in the stern does not change his place: because of course we shall determine his place by certain supposedly motionless points in the heavens. (Descartes 1984, p. 45)

Descartes's 'earthball' moves 'on its axis' just as Belacqua moves in relation to the land and in relation to the ship. Belacqua, that is, is very rarely stilled in relation to what he experiences as a particularly boisterous environment. He is buffeted by the constantly changing world around him more often than he is able to resist it. Such concern with freedom conceived as stasis in relation to movement on board a ship, traceable through *Dream* to Descartes, then later through *The Unnamable* via Geulincx, evinces Beckett's altering foci on particularly Cartesian and post-Cartesian strains of freedom. Beckett himself made journeys by ship around the coast of England a number of times,[8] and as will be shown in the following chapter sea voyages also appear again refracted through the Geulingian ship in *Comment c'est/How It Is*. Before that, however, one other appearance of the troubled ship in the trilogy should be addressed.

The Ship in *Malone Dies*

The appearance of the troubled ship in *Malone Dies* is itself somewhat troubled. Malone, sick of the 'Mortal tedium' (*MD*, p. 44) of his embedded fictional narratives, describes instead certain of his earlier faltering attentions. These include incidents and characters that recall moments from Beckett's previous novels, such as Murphy's encounter with Mr. Endon ('With the insane too I failed, by a hair's-breadth'). Malone continues:

> Bawling babies are what dumbfound me now. The house is full of them finally. Suave mari magno, especially for the old salt. What tedium. And I thought I had it all thought out. (p. 45)

'Suave mari magno' derives from Lucretius's *De Rerum Natura* [*On the Nature of Things*], in which the first century BC Roman poet expounds an atomist philosophy that includes a number of axioms. But Malone's allusion is also one among the lineage of ship imagery. The subject of the opening two lines of the second book of *De Rerum Natura*, subtitled 'The Dance of Atoms', is markedly similar to Beckett's storm-battered ship from Geulincx as it appears in *Molloy* and *The Unnamable*:

> Suave, mari magno turbantibus aequora ventis
> e terra magnum alterius spectare laborem (Lucretius 1821 (Book II.1), p. 96)
>
> How sweet it is to watch from dry land when the storm-winds roil
> a mighty ocean's waters, and see another's bitter toil (Lucretius 2007, p. 36)[9]

Again Beckett is drawn to a dichotomy between watching or wishing for a storm to wreck a ship and the actual events surrounding the person watching or wishing, who is either safely on 'dry land' or crawling 'along the deck'. Malone watches from the shore, immune from disasters befalling another, just as the 'galley-man' will watch for catastrophe knowing he too is safe from it. The partial quotation is thereby also a voice of *Malone Dies*' self-reflexivity, if not quite of the critical voice Clément describes embedded in Beckett's texts: Malone himself, safe and dry but dying in bed, narrates a story in the third person of a troubled sea trip, a story that brings his own novel to a disintegrating finality. Eventually exhausted at the end of his narrative, Malone – via the 'vice-exister' Lemuel – rapidly hatchets to death most of his protagonists before corralling the last of them into his boat. Lemuel then sets them sailing and the middle of the three novels ends upon a final image of Lemuel's hatchet raised in the boat, the oars lolling in the sea, the scene frozen but fading in Malone's collapsing telling of it. Malone himself, however, dying and eventually dead, is safe from all this 'roil' and 'toil' in his bed just as if watching the scenes unfold from the 'dry land' of the shore. He is the 'old salt' in both its senses – as the adventuring seafarer imagined on board, and as the storyteller returned safe from the voyage.

The Axiom

Around two-thirds into Molloy's narrative the narrator–protagonist leaves Lousse's house, having gilded his Geulingian impotence to do otherwise, and wanders the town. He ensconces himself on the stairs of a 'mean lodging-house' before again wandering off 'in search of a familiar monument' by which he might identify the town as his. Molloy describes the scene around him, which comprises 'a narrow alley [. . .] Little windows [. . .] Lavatory lights I suppose [. . .] a blind alley [. . .] two recesses', and nesting incongruously amongst this semi-realist depiction is Molloy's statement on axioms:

> There are things from time to time, in spite of everything, that impose themselves on the understanding with the force of axioms, for unknown reasons. (*Mo*, p. 60)

Molloy aligns his impressions of the physical world around him, those inevitable elemental fragments of being in the world (as *The Unnamable*'s narrator says, 'I have few illusions, things are to be expected' (*U*, p. 2)), with acts of intellection. The 'windows', 'lights' and the 'alley' 'impose themselves' clearly and distinctly on Molloy's sense of himself in the world. Nevertheless, for Molloy it is 'axioms' that remain the paragon of visceral fact and forcefulness, the more unquestionable and absolute verifier. Bearing in mind this reference to the power of axioms to 'impose themselves on the understanding', the following analysis traces the versions of Geulincx's famous ethical axiom (*ubi nihil vales, ibi nihil velis*) as it reappears in various guises across *Malone meurt/Malone Dies* and *L'Innommable/The Unnamable*. This sets up arguments that follow about just how forcefully the epistemological boundaries established by that axiom determine acts of intellection that are given narrative form in *L'Innommable/The Unnamable*.

The one appearance of a version of Geulincx's axiom in *Malone Dies* is notable for how it diverges from the French *Malone meurt*. The passage containing it occurs in Malone's story of Macmann:

> Et il allait de plus en plus du côté de la muraille, sans toutefois trop s'en approcher car elle était gardée, cherchant une issue vers la désolation de n'avoir personne ni rien, vers la terre au pain rare, aux abris rares, des terrifiés, vers la noire joie de passer seul et vide, ne rien pouvant, ne rien voulant, à travers le savoir, la beauté, les amours. (Beckett 1951, p. 197)

> And he clung closer and closer to the wall, but not too close, for it was guarded, seeking a way out into the desolation of having nobody and nothing, the wilds of the hunted, the scant bread and the scant shelter and the black joy of the solitary way, in helplessness and will-lessness, through all the beauty, the knowing and the loving. (*MD*, p. 108)

In the English version any allusion to Geulincx is barely noticeable. However, a more literal translation of the French 'ne rien pouvant, ne rien voulant' would be 'able to do nothing, wanting nothing' or 'without being able, without wanting'. Such a translation would more overtly echo, as the French passage in *Malone meurt* does, Geulincx's axiom. With an emphasis on capacity rather than on value, on being able rather than on being worth, Beckett reproduces the metaphysically slanted Latin axiom in a sparse French. In contrast, 'in helplessness and will-lessness' lacks any Geulingian syntactic inflection at all. If one were inclined to posit a potential source for this English phrase with its explicit 'will-lessness' a much more likely candidate than Geulincx would probably be Schopenhauer. The two advocates of philosophical will-lessness, Geulincx and Schopenhauer, might then be shown here, in the sort of analysis Harold Bloom dismisses as typical 'source hunting' (Bloom 1997, p. 31), as separate sources for Beckett, for the passages in *Malone meurt* and *Malone Dies* respectively. When these passages from both are placed side by side, however, they reveal themselves as instances of just the sort of intertwined, mutually engraved fragments of prior learning that rattled round the pockets of *The End*'s narrator. When Adorno called for recognition that *Fin de Partie/Endgame* presents 'mind itself' as the 'reified residue of education' (Adorno 1982, p. 121), he was locating just this stratum of Beckett's middle period work where, in the second and third novels of the trilogy, presence itself is put radically into question in a continuous present. Beckett's translation of this fragment from *Malone meurt*, produced sometime between mid-1954 and October 1955,[10] is not a simple case of jettisoning the presence of one referent (Geulincx) for a better (Schopenhauer), just as on a broader scale Beckett's acts of translation are not a matter of jettisoning one language for a newly favoured better. Rather, the translation refines, and in the process 'reifies', the more overt 'residue' of Geulincx in the French to become one more fundamentally reduced to its sounds, a wispy sound ('will-lessness') that might at first read as straightforwardly Schopenhauerian, but which can instead be seen, having noted the Geulingian axiomatic inflection in *Malone meurt*, as part of a more complex dynamic.

In contrast to the axiom's translation from *Malone meurt* into the version in *Malone Dies*, translations from *L'Innommable* to *The Unnamable* tend to retain the Geulingian inflections of their originals. The axiom appears clearly twice in *The Unnamable*, yet there are also a number of other instances where it is partially quoted or alluded to. In a phrase complementing Beckett's intriguing use of the language of puppetry to describe Geulincx's ontology – the 'fascinating guignol world' – the narrating voice dismisses the work of previous narrators; previous works were 'clumsily done, you could see the ventriloquist'. In contrast, the narrator hopes, the real work is 'about to begin'. Such work will happen in a place, a closed place that is the spatialized development of earlier mathematically closed systems (such as those Watt attempts to fill out with his

The Trilogy: Imagery and Axioms 133

rationalizing), and the real work happening in this closed place owes its possibility to the forcefulness of Geulincx's axiom:

> Quick, a place. With no way in, no way out, a safe place. Not like Eden. And Worm inside. Feeling nothing, knowing nothing, capable of nothing, wanting nothing. (*U*, p. 63)

This closed place with 'no way in, no way out', and that in being hermetically sealed is thus 'safe', where there would be no more 'puppets', is the place where Worm exists. The strange single syllable, upended 'M' named Worm who in Geulingian terms would be 'capable of nothing, wanting nothing'. Such sealed safe places that delimit impotence and nothingness, the narrator says a little later, are 'blessed':

> the place to be, where you suffer, rejoice, at being bereft of speech, bereft of thought, and feel nothing, hear nothing, know nothing, say nothing, are nothing, that would be a blessed place to be, where you are. (*U*, pp. 90–1)

This and the previous quotation form stages of the axiom's extension into domains of nothingness other than those directly derived from Geulincx, ones sensory and ontological. As Weller describes Beckett's interest in 'nothingness' as conveyed in the languages of philosophy:

> Just as the Democritean affirmation of the ontological nothing is part of a more general economy within Beckett's works, the other pole of which is the Permenidean/Geulincxian denial of that nothing, so Geulincx's ethical nothing is part of a more general economy, the other pole of which is a desire for company (that is, for the world) that finds expression in the line from André Malraux's novel *La Condition humaine* (1933), which was to become the epigraph to chapter 9 of *Murphy*. (Weller 2010, p. 117)

At specific moments of *The Unnamable* Beckett collides these other nothings, putting these 'other pole[s]' into contact with one another, the 'positive' and 'negative' – as he described Geulincx and Malraux as they pertain to Murphy's own 'poles' – together in a rewiring of the circuitry of his own previous systematization. Such revolving and rewiring is the climax of what might be termed Beckett's 'literary fantasia' conducted with Geulincx. The many poles, positive and negative, are recombined and result variously in short circuits, unforeseen surges, or circularity, imparting various problematic propulsions to the narrative. Furthermore, the 'place to be, where you are' as a place in which one is subject to Geulingian impotence, situates the narrator squarely within that domain Beckett described to Duthuit of which 'There is little risk of anyone's exaggerating its extent'. You are inevitably there, and only need to agree on (or resign yourself to) the extent of the 'domaine'. While Geulincx's axiom is embedded within a series of fractured part repetitions in the first quotation here, disguised and perhaps therefore appearing somewhat throwaway, it in fact conveys much more 'force', as Molloy describes the power of axioms, in its intratextual echoes. It underscores the idea of a freedom inhering in stasis, that of Belacqua on the ship and the 'galley-man' of *The Unnamable* turning to look astern, where the solace or conclusion of a 'place to be' is achieved precisely by, as the second Watt hinted at, being just 'where you are'. Beckett even keeps this idea of Geulingian impotence as possible in a 'place to be, where you are' in mind after completion of *The Unnamable*. Its reappearance in the final of the *Texts for Nothing* is slightly altered again, and the possibility of refuge within a close space is no longer so certain: 'What a joy to know where one is, and where one will stay, without being there' (*TN*, p. 51).

The second appearance of the axiom in *The Unnamable* repeats some of these same nothings, while it also locates them within a broader context of Occasionalist metaphysics:

> I can't say anything, I've tried, I'm trying, he knows nothing, knows of nothing, neither what it is to speak, nor what it is to hear, to know nothing, to be capable of nothing, and to have to try (*U*, p. 120)

The futility of physical action (being 'capable of nothing'), its being tied with such immediacy to an epistemological incapacity ('he knows nothing'), combined with the obligation to act anyway ('to have to try'), is a remarkably resonant point in Beckett's 'fantasia'. The moment reproduces the very transition Geulincx stages in *Ethics* between a theoretical and a practical ethics. As de Vleeschauwer has argued, defending against claims that Geulingian Occasionalism implies the thoroughgoing quietism or solipsism it is often mistaken for, *Ethics* defers to neither of these.[11] There are indeed discrete moments where Geulincx is carried by tendencies towards both, tempting as they must have been to a thinker so concerned to shut out the external world, even if just for a while. Yet as has been discussed, there is also an important transition in *Ethics* that shifts the focus from a theoretical ethics of self-immersion and resignation to incapacity, into the very practical everyday ethics that advocates – indeed depends upon and is directed entirely towards – a thorough engagement with a world of pragmatic decisions. The impetus for this comes about precisely because of a need Geulincx recognizes 'to have to try' irrespective of the fact that one cannot actually do anything. One must act, despite apparent futility; one must 'go on', despite not actually being able. Geulincx readily admits that *Ethics* cannot provide the novitiate with answers to the multitude of specific ethical decisions made throughout a life, and nor does his Occasionalist project opt for an elegant Kantian categorical solution to the problem, despite its concision with neatly balanced axioms. But what *Ethics* does seek to do is provide structured mediation between the abstracted realms of *humilitas, inspectio-sui* and everyday and divergent ethical decisions encountered all the time. That is, Geulincx advises on hypothetical imperatives, though he gives them the name *obligatione* [obligations], of which, as discussed in Chapter 1, he enumerates seven. For instance, the fourth obligation stresses the need to find oneself a job or career and to commit to it with determination. Yet such determination should only last, as the fifth obligation in turn makes clear, only and until this choice becomes too much to bear. That is, Geulincx directs, if a chosen 'mode of life' (*Et*, p. 346) becomes too awful then one should act pragmatically and take up something else, '*redirecting the course of my pilgrimage elsewhere, if need be*' (p. 348). Geulincx's pragmatic yet open-ended, systematically interwoven obligations, that he argues all flow naturally from the axiom, show his strict rationalist thought yielding to the possibility of the unforeseen and unknown. What is certain is that you cannot, in fact, really do anything. Geulincx concedes, however, as does *The Unnamable*'s narrator, that you 'have to try'.

This combination of impotence and obligation also resonates with Beckett's critical writings of the period as regards his thinking about an art of failure. For example, in the *Three Dialogues* in a rare clarion call Beckett wrote the following frequently cited assessments of the artist:

> to be an artist is to fail, as no other dare fail [. . .] failure is his world and the shrink from it desertion, art and craft, good housekeeping, living. (*Pr*, p. 125)

According to the dramatized Beckett (B) who nominally attempts to convince a version of Duthuit (D), it is feeble for an artist to attempt what B calls mere disturbances of things 'on the plane of the feasible'. Asked what other plane is possible B admits 'Logically none', but this should not prevent one turning in disgust from such feasibility, such graspable possibility and achievability, 'weary of puny exploits, weary of pretending to be able, of being able, of doing a little better the same old thing, of going a little further along a dreary road'. B prefers instead:

> The expression that there is nothing to express, nothing with which to express, nothing from which to express, no power to express, no desire to express, together with the obligation to express. (p. 103)

D points out that this is a 'violently extreme and personal point of view'. But precisely in being 'extreme and personal', B's 'point of view' reflects the deeply integrated philosophical aesthetics that Beckett had to hand when he was writing the middle period prose. Weary of a 'dreary road' – that Cartesian progressive méthode upon which Watt and before him Descartes stumbled, beside which Estragon and Vladimir wait, and in which the narrator of *The End* hopes to get run over – the 'puny exploits' of 'being able' should be refused, and one should turn instead to an 'obligation'. Just as in Geulincx's ethics, the consolations of believing that one does indeed do something are not worth the price; it is better to accept ultimate incapacity. Thus, with all due self-aware irony B's paradoxically confident expression of the futility and failure of expression effectively ends the first of the dialogues.

It would surely be claiming too much to assert a direct influence on Beckett's theorizing artistic failure and obligation as derived from Geulincx. Nevertheless it is striking that at the culmination of Beckett's 'series', at the climax of the final novel of the trilogy, assertions of knowing nothing and being capable of nothing borrow Geulincx's axiom. There are further striking resonances in the criticism. B's proposed 'fidelity to failure' (p. 125) is, B asserts, 'a new occasion', the word 'occasion' repeated three times in the final dialogue. It is Bram van Velde who might 'make painting independent of its occasion', who is the first to make painting that is 'bereft', or 'rid if you prefer, of occasion in every shape or form, ideal as well as material, and the first whose hands have not been tied by the certitude that expression is an impossible act' (p. 121). The 'fantastic theory', as D describes it, draws important parts of its vocabulary from Beckett's Geulingian 'fantasia': the 'occasion' of the gesture achieved, communication made, is no good because it is an illusion. Van Velde 'is the first to accept a certain situation and to consent to a certain act' (p. 119). This acceptance of and consent to, with all apparent humility, incapacity and consequent 'obligation', parallels Beckett's knowledge of Geulingian Occasionalism, and finds its own obligated expressions in the taut and torn prose of *The Unnamable*.

The final appearance of the axiom is only a few pages from that novel's end. Asking once again who exactly all this torrent of words has been 'about', the narrator continues:

> I don't know who it's all about, that's all I know, no, I must know something else, they must have taught me something, it's about him who knows nothing, wants nothing, can do nothing, if it's possible you can do nothing when you want nothing, who cannot hear, cannot speak, who is I, who cannot be I, of whom I can't speak, of whom I must speak. (*U*, p. 123)

Here, closing in on the non-closure of the end of *The Unnamable*, Geulincx can still be found embedded in Beckett's contorted prose. Yet it is interesting that at this relatively late stage in 'the series' the philosopher is not discarded, as a matter now resolved or a question now answered, as he was at certain stages in *Murphy*. Instead, the years of familiarity with Geulincx and his axioms have deepened Beckett's sympathies for the intractable nature of Occasionalist impotence, in proximity to which *The Unnamable*'s narrator chooses repeatedly to define his 'I'. Geulincx appears here in a question that is left unanswered:

'if it's possible you can do nothing when you want nothing'. Working against the idea that Beckett's oeuvre is one that seeks to wholeheartedly reject uneasy intrusions of philosophy or philosophers, consistently resisting them as a kind of infringement on sovereignty, the fragmentary incorporation of Geulincx's axiom as a question reveals here a different development in Beckett's thinking about allusion and philosophy; he is still willing to set himself philosophical problems he had once rendered as solved. To borrow Gontarski's phrase, Beckett's *intent of undoing*[12] works to unravel the neatness of his earlier thinking, undoing what had been done earlier in sympathy with a deeper thinking about the aesthetic possibilities of Geulingian impotence that also found its way into the theory–drama of the *Three Dialogues*.

'Fundamental Sounds': Pre-Established Harmony

A brief background of Beckett's 'Philosophy Notes' is helpful to contextualize a discussion of the ways in which Beckett utilizes pre-established harmony in *Molloy* and *The Unnamable*. As these Windelband-derived notes have it, Geulincx's *Ethics* is where the Occasionalist conception of God as the ultimate arbiter between will and action is 'furthest developed'. Beckett noted what Windelband referred to as the '*anthropological* rationale' of Geulincx: 'Illustration of the 2 Clocks which having once been synchronised by same artificer continue to move in perfect harmony', before noting how 'Leibniz illustrated with same analogy his doctrine of "preestablished harmony"'. He then goes on to record the following distinction as made by Leibniz between a more typically Cartesian and a post-Cartesian Occasionalist conception of pre-established harmony:

> [Leibniz] characterised Cartesian conception by immediate and permanent interdependence of 2 clocks, and Occasionalist by constantly renewed regulation of clocks by clock master. (TCD MS 10967/89r)

The distinction is intriguing. Going back to Windelband's philosophical history reveals that the division is in fact not quite so sharply delineated. For example, Windelband argues that compared to those of Leibniz, Geulincx's texts are particularly ambivalent about just how interventionist God is in Geulincx's rendering of pre-established harmony:

> in the latter author [Geulincx] doubt is not entirely excluded as to whether God's causality in this connection is regarded as a special intervention in each individual case, or as a general and permanent arrangement. In some passages, indeed, the former is the case, but the spirit of the doctrine, taken as a whole, doubtless involves the latter. (Windelband 1901, p. 415)[13]

This unintended doubt, Windelband argues, is particularly prevalent in the analogy of the baby in the cradle, but according to Windelband it is in the analogy of the two clocks where Geulincx is at his clearest.

Uhlmann suggests that an occluded instance of this clock used to illustrate pre-established harmony appears in *Molloy*, where it is 'a gong, which Molloy hears at the end of his narrative and which calls Moran to his dinner' (Uhlmann 2006a, p. 78). This gong might, however, also be seen as part of the lineage of objects that includes the bell which 'rings piercingly' in *Happy Days* waking Winnie to 'another heavenly day' (*CDW*, p. 138), connoting little of simultaneities but instead bringing something of the interrogating authority that is found in other instances of intrusion and subjugation; in the beams of spotlight projected in *Play* and *Not I*, for example, or the switch that goes on and off in *What Where* marking the passing of offstage interrogations. There are, however, explicit appearances of pre-established harmony in the trilogy. Molloy, trying to find the right tense in which to speak of his life ('now I speak of it as something over, now as of a joke which still goes on, and is there any tense for that'), describes what we might read as alluding to Occasionalism's 'regulation of clocks by clock master':

> Watch wound and buried by the watchmaker, before he died, whose ruined works will one day speak of God, to the worms. (*Mo*, p. 34)

Paul Davies has described Molloy's statement of burial, made just prior to the actual burial of Louse's dog Teddy, that burial which was also 'my own', as 'echoing Leibniz' (Davies 1994, p. 61), which is surely accurate. Yet the ascription is perhaps not exhaustive. The imagery is also 'echoing' Geulincx; Beckett's 'Philosophy Notes' indicate that Geulincx's version of pre-established harmony was imagined as a clock 'having once been synchronised by same artificer', similarly to how Molloy's has been 'wound and buried by the watchmaker'.

Beckett delved further into Geulincx's clock analogy in the transcriptions from *Ethica*:

> It is the same as if two clocks agree precisely with each other and with the daily course of the Sun: when one chimes and tells the hours, the other also chimes and likewise indicates the hour; and all that without any causality in the sense of one having a causal effect on the other, but rather on account of mere dependence, inasmuch as both of them have been construed with the same art and similar industry. (*Et*, p. 332)

Geulincx uses the analogy to illustrate the incongruous non-relation of will to action. Just as 'motion of the tongue accompanies our will to speak' (pp. 332–3), for example, so two clocks tell the same time, though with neither clock *causing* the time as told by the other.[14] Later in the novel Molloy again refers to pre-established harmony when describing his new direction of wandering:

> I am no longer with Lousse, but out in the heart again of the pre-established harmony, which makes so sweet a music, which is so sweet a music, for one who has an ear for music. (*Mo*, p. 62)

As Davies also informatively points out, Beckett is 'echoing [. . .] Plotinus and Pythagoras, whose doctrines of music in the forces of the universe entered Europe through the Florentine court of Marsilio Ficino' (Davies 1994, p. 61). There is, however, very little that is harmonic about this world outside the strange and temporary sanctuary of Lousse's house. Molloy is 'out in the heart again' of a much more chaotic universe than Pythagoras's, and any 'sweet [. . .] music' Molloy hears in concert with this 'pre-established harmony' is surely a sound somewhat of chaos. Beckett's version of pre-established harmony, taking a lead from Geulincx as well as from these others cited by Davies, is established as an elemental world of ruinous entropy. Molloy does not actually hear this music of the spheres; at least he does not describe it if he can hear it. He has no 'ear for music'. What he does have an ear for is fractured memory, for having once heard this music. Molloy's world, that is, might be a pre-established world, a world in which he can do nothing to alter the course of events, where he 'could not do otherwise', but it is not therefore one of 'harmony'.

Such inability to interact with clockwork events in the world also informs other parts of the novel. Still in his house erratically plotting the search for his nemesis, Moran admits to self-delusion when he wonders why he accepted 'this commission'. He proposes that it might be his 'Honour', though admits 'It did not take me long to gild my impotence' (*Mo*, p. 109). Moran's inability to alter the course of events that are at the behest of an unknown (except by name) authoritarian entity, even despite his own determined sense of property and propriety when it comes to the immediate domestic surrounds of his son, maid and house, pits him too against something that is pre-established, but that is also far from harmonic.

Nescio

In a 2008 review of *Ethics*, Ackerley describes how he is impressed by a claim made by Uhlmann in the introduction to *Ethics*. Uhlmann had made the claim previously, in 2006, but Ackerley points out that situated 'in the more immediate surrounding of Geulincx' actual writings, it resonates more meaningfully' (Ackerley 2008, p. 207). Ackerley describes the claim as not only fundamental to a philosophical reading of *The Unnamable*, but to Beckett and philosophy more broadly:

> I should like to consider briefly the implications of what I believe to be one of the more stunning and important statements about Beckett and philosophy that I have yet encountered; indeed, something that might well shake the foundations of a lot of current scholarship.

The ambitious claim is contextualized by briefly summarizing the 'long established and indeed incontrovertible' foundations potentially shaken that hold to the following:

> just as *Murphy* deals with the Cartesian dualism of body and mind, and *Watt* constitutes an assault upon the Cartesian *méthode*, Beckett's *Trilogy* and especially *The Unnamable* comprise some sort of critique of the *cogito*. (p. 206)

As Feldman also did in Beckett's centenary year of 2006, Uhlmann strove to shift the long-standing critical focus away from Descartes. While Feldman's empirical basis for his attack was in part the lack of manuscript material substantiating, or proportionally corresponding to, emphasis on Descartes, Uhlmann's proposed shift of emphasis derives instead primarily from time spent reading Geulincx:

> I argue that the 'cogito' which is described in *The Unnamable* (and which inheres in later works) is a Geulingian cogito, rather than a Cartesian cogito: that it emerges through an inspection of the self which leads to the understanding that one knows nothing (as in Geulincx) rather than to a point of foundation upon which one might build up an accurate knowledge of the world (as in Descartes). To my mind Geulincx and Beckett have in common the core affirmation that we are ultimately ignorant: while Beckett has stated that the key word to his works is 'perhaps', Bernard Rousset has claimed that 'nescio' (I do not know) is the key word to Geulincx'. (*Et*, p. 306)

This 'insight', as Ackerley describes it

> at a stroke [. . .] defines the incontrovertible truth that *The Unnamable*, arguably the key-stone to Beckett's entire Temple of Wisdom (or should that now be the Folly of Nescience?), is a Geulingian work, and that the philosophical position assumed within it can be understood only in these terms (for the moment I am content with 'only'). (Ackerley 2008, p. 207)[15]

Uhlmann's arguments are more detailed in the '*cogito nescio*' chapter of his 2006 *Samuel Beckett and the Philosophical Image*, where he argues for Beckett's use of an 'image of thought' (Uhlmann 2006a, p. 61) derived from Geulincx's insistence on ignorance and impotence, which in turn determines the epistemological boundaries in *The Unnamable*. Images of thought, according to Uhlmann (whose definition is derived from Deleuze's conception of them), are primary, underlying systematized relations between coordinates of knowledge that delimit epistemological borders. They determine what can be known before any secondary categories that might appear to play this determining role are invoked. These secondary categories are dependent on that first category of the image, even masquerading as the first category. Such patterned relations constitute, according to Deleuze, 'a prephilosophical understanding' (Deleuze 1995, p. 148[16]) upon which philosophical understanding is based, without that philosophical understanding necessarily acknowledging, or even being aware of, its basis. Uhlmann's claim is that Beckett 'borrows an image of thought (a way of imagining what it means to think) from Arnold Geulincx' (Uhlmann 2006a, p. 87), one derived from Geulincx's repeated insistences on the nature of human ignorance. Uhlmann argues that 'following Geulincx, he [Beckett] identifies the cogito (the "I think") with a nescio (an "I do not know")' (p. 90), an epistemological alignment resonant with the many instances in Beckett's works of 'one confronted by ignorance, suffering that ignorance' (p. 92). However, although Uhlmann makes the provocative assertion that impresses Ackerley, it is not investigated in detail, and thus its viability has not really been exhaustively tested. While there is not the requisite space to offer a full reading of *The Unnamable* here that might take account of its diversity in specificity, its multitude of individual textual moments, the following interpretation of one short passage is intended to go some way towards a future, complete, exhaustive analysis of this novel's Geulingian impetuses.

As noted in Chapter 1, Beckett transcribed the word *nescio* from *Metaphysica Vera*:

> Secundo S. Varios habeo cogitandi modos in infinitum.
>
> Cogito ergo, et infinitis modis cogito; sed illae res quas cogito num sic sint ut cogito, adhuc nescio. (TCD MS 10971/6/2r)
>
> Proposition 2. I have innumerable modes of thought. [. . .]
>
> Therefore I think, and think in innumerable modes. But whether the things that I think really are exactly as I think of them, I still do not know. (*Met*, p. 32)

Beckett also transcribed the word as part of a passage from *Ethica*, and underlined it:

> Haereo, nescio, nec habeo quod dicam aliud, nisi <u>nescio</u>. Nescio modum, quo sum in hac condicione..; tantum abest ut sciam, quomodo ad illam condicionem devenerim. (TCD MS 10971/6/23)

But I cannot get beyond I do not know, there is nothing I can add to this I do not know. I do not know how I came to this condition... What is lacking is the knowledge of how I came to this condition. (*Et*, p. 334)

He later deployed it in *The Unnamable* where it appears in a passage that can be read as a critique of Cartesian clear and distinct foundations of perception. The narrator describes Worm:

> Feeling nothing, knowing nothing, he exists nevertheless, but not for himself, for others, others conceive him and say, Worm is, since we conceive him, as if there could be no being but being conceived, if only by the beer. Others. One alone, then others. One alone turned towards the all-impotent, all-nescient, that haunts him, then others. (*U*, p. 60)

The passage produces a critique that aligns a Cartesian conception of self with thinking itself. That is where these 'others' constitute an ontology conjured, as if magically, from within an epistemology. Worm is brought into existence through an act of intellection, where his being 'conceived' is a pun on this birth precisely as a product of his being thought. In that there is no real possibility of conjuring anything real from thinking alone – other than the fictional avatars 'turned towards' their 'all-impotent, all-nescient' creator, there being no real possibility of asserting the self at the same moment as being that self – the *ergo* of Cartesian cogitation is collapsed, 'shrunk to nothing' like Murphy's linking conarium. While the cogito was also a foundational axiomatic first principle for Geulincx, his immediate problematizing of it in his second metaphysical proposition paves the way for his critique of causation more broadly. Beckett produces a critique that appears to conclude even more radically in a parodic version of the cogito that amounts to no more than 'I think, therefore I think'. While it is difficult to assert a generalized viability of '*the* philosophical position assumed within'[17] *The Unnamable*, much as it was difficult to go along with Wood's 'general uneasiness', nevertheless at certain moments there are fragmentary critiques that course through the text and which bring to light the possibilities of a fully textually based reading of a Geulingian critique of Cartesianism in the novel that pays due attention to the multifarious, individualized ways in which this is enacted.

Beckett transcribed Geulincx on the subject of naming what might be considered unnameable, or just unnamed: 'Things do not depend on names, and if there are not names for newly-discovered things, let some be devised' (*Et*, p. 324). In the same annotation Geulincx quotes Horace on the topic, which Beckett also transcribed:

It has been right, and always will
To give a name to what has none (p. 325)

The Trilogy: Imagery and Axioms

In contrast to the Cartesian inheritance of clarity that is to the benefit of Geulincx's thoughts on thoughts, even though the philosopher concludes that he 'cannot get beyond *I do not know*', *The Unnamable*'s narrator cannot even confidently name his own thoughts as thoughts: 'I only think, if that is the name for this vertiginous panic as of hornets smoked out of their nest' (*U*, p. 64). The narrator then later sums up self-inspection as an operation of naming:

> it's the fault of the pronouns, there is no name for me, no pronoun for me, all the trouble comes from that, that, it's a kind of pronoun too, it isn't that either, I'm not that either. (p. 123)

Such parallels between Beckett's narrator and Geulincx's philosophical entrapment within ignorance, however, should also be resisted, even while Geulincx writes that '*I*, as one who escapes all the senses, and who himself can neither be seen, heard, or touched, am by no means a part of the world' (*Et*, p. 330). *The Unnamable* certainly exhibits a number of sympathies with Geulincx. Yet such sympathies cannot reduce the entirety of this broad novel to one predominantly driven by a singular Geulingian focus. The 'name for' *The Unnamable*'s narrator is not 'Geulingian', even if the devising critic might be tempted, Watt-like, to resolve partial congruency.

Chapter 6

Late Works

Who, what, where, by what means, why, in what way, when
(*Watt* Notebook 1, p. 3)

What is it to approach the possibility of the presence of Geulincx in Beckett's late works, in anything beyond the *Textes pour rien/Texts for Nothing* of 1951/1952? To be clear from the start, there are no longer any obvious references to Geulincx to be found. There is little in the way of a Geulingian lineage of imagery comparable to that running through *L'Innommable/The Unnamable*, and certainly nothing like *Murphy*'s invocation of the beauty of Geulincx's axiom can be expected. If a valid discourse is to be had about the presence of Geulincx in the late works it must simultaneously somehow address itself to his apparent absence.

Are there any reasons to suppose Geulincx's relevance to a reading of late works whatsoever? One straightforward reason is that as late as June 1967 Beckett told Kennedy that Geulincx would be one of his 'points of departure' should he be in the unfortunate position the critic found herself in, studying his work. Such a departure point, however, might be thought to be relevant solely to the early works, works composed when Beckett was himself at a point 'of departure' beginning his 'series'. After all, Kennedy was writing a monograph focused on *Murphy* when she contacted Beckett with the questions to which he responded by quoting Geulincx. When Beckett wrote 'my work' in this 1967 letter perhaps he only meant *Murphy*, despite his also saying that Geulincx was 'already' in that early novel.

This might be an unlikely appraisal of Beckett's intention, given his similar description to Montgomery of 'The heart of the matter'. Even so, better reasons than this single fragment of correspondence are needed for exploring Geulincx and the late works. If possible these reasons would engage with important reservations about the validity of any project tracing influence upon Beckett *per se*, because general reservations along these lines can often find most purchase in the context of the later works, where reduction and abstraction make more typical comparative study increasingly difficult. O'Hara, for example, put forward reservations to such a project in 1981 and in so doing spoke for more general objections potentially raised in regard to anything like influence and the late works:

> any discussion of the influence of [. . .] Mr. X on Beckett is likely to be either simpleminded, if it implies that X's influence has reached Beckett and shaped his work purely and without adulteration, or exasperatingly modified, temporized, complicated, and footnoted to death if it admits that Mr. X must be understood in the light of J, S, and R, with √2 always to be considered. (O'Hara 1981, p. 253)

A number of critical approaches in Beckett studies since 1996, some 15 years after O'Hara's statements, have indeed become extensively 'temporized', if by this O'Hara means subjected to the accurate dating of Beckett's reading, the content of his correspondence, his note-taking and manuscript composition. It is what might be termed empirical temporizing, for example, that cautions against reading an extensive influence of Geulincx in either *Dream of Fair to Middling Women* or *More Pricks Than Kicks* that would posit this influence as beholden to anything more than serendipity, thematic congruence or a part of Beckett's broader interests in philosophical history. This is because, quite plainly, Beckett did not read Geulincx in the original until after these works were completed. Such an approach might indeed become 'complicated' and 'modified', given that the potential exists to find, in these earlier works, themes, imagery and various approaches to the incorporation of philosophy that in specific ways correlate with how Beckett also treated his later research. Such arguments about parallels, fascination and coincidence might convince or they might not. But is the fact that scholarship might become 'temporized' a convincing objection in itself? O'Hara's argument is surely one of taste, and though his analysis might be 'exasperated' with the approaches *Tracing 'a literary fantasia'* takes, that analysis does not demolish the validity of studying influences upon Beckett *per se*. Interestingly, O'Hara makes this broad statement in the context of one of his own studies of influence, in an article on Beckett and Schopenhauer, in which no clear alternative for how a study of influence on Beckett should proceed is offered, the argument progressing to a somewhat 'modified' Schopenhauerian reading itself. For example, certain Schopenhaurian qualities of Beckett's texts are 'modified' via Berkeley:

> The topic of not being able to escape one's self recurs often in Beckett's postwar writings, usually with some reference to Bishop Berkeley. But it derives much of its importance and many of its characteristics from Schopenhauer. (p. 258)

Similarly, when discussing the extensively Schopenhauer-inflected *Proust* O'Hara writes: 'Proust offered Beckett a way of representing in art what

Schopenhauer had emphasized, the primacy of the individual consciousness' (p. 264). All of which is assessed insofar as it leads us towards or away from what O'Hara terms 'Beckett's world' (p. 257), whereby it is enough to validate the comparisons that 'Beckettians will recognize ideas and topics echoed in Beckett's work' (p. 254). Nevertheless, O'Hara's reservations should still be met with answers, even if his own comparative procedures, at least in this article, do not appear to offer thorough alternative solutions. When O'Hara argues that one cannot write of influence upon Beckett because such writing must, if it is not to be simpleminded, be too complex (that is 'modified' and 'temporized'), he shuts off one of the ways in which complexity itself in Beckett's art might be grasped, an art that is so frequently and deeply characterized by complexity even in its moments of stark minimalism. Beckett's own creative impetuses are themselves 'modified' and 'temporized', indeed his works frequently even make use of these both as stylistic performances. Ignoring what is 'modified' or 'temporized' in Beckett's works can be to ignore fundamental aspects of these works.

The scholastic categories of inquiry that inaugurated the composition process of *Watt* ('Who, what, where, by what means, why, in what way, when') might indeed strike one as valid terms in which to ask intertextual questions of Beckett's late works. For example, 'who' is the Geulincx of this period for Beckett? 'What' is he doing to/for/in Beckett's texts? 'Where' exactly is he in these texts? 'By what means' does his presence interact with the text or can we be certain that this is indeed Geulincx? 'Why' invoke or utilize him at all? 'In what way' does recognizing this presence alter our reading? 'When' should we be able to verifiably say this presence is Geulingian? Such questions have served an analysis of Geulincx's various appearances in Beckett's oeuvre well until this point. They have revealed, for example, 'when' in relation to *Murphy* Geulincx becomes important, 'where' he becomes useful for the composition of *Watt,* 'why' he is central to versions of *Suite/La Fin/The End,* and even 'by what means' in *The Unnamable* he provides Beckett with a lineage of imagery and elements of a narrative voice. Such questions will also serve to reveal the necessity of an empirically 'temporized' and 'qualified' presence in certain aspects of the later works. But importantly these forms of question also fall short of recognizing, at least of offering a vocabulary in which to speak of, the even more radical ambivalences and ambiguities operating in the later works. Without finding a way of addressing this shortfall any discussion of Geulincx in the later works runs the risk of being no less constricted than O'Hara's reading of Beckett's Schopenhauer.

One thing that such quantitative questions fail to accord validity to is the more qualitative open-ended possibility of 'perhaps'. As Beckett told Tom Driver in 1961 while discussing dramatic structure as mirroring the presence of 'both light and dark', knowledge and ignorance, as present simultaneously in human lives, 'The key word in my plays is "perhaps"'.[1] Yet this dramatic 'perhaps' is not invoked here in order to excuse the unarguable; variously focusing on Geulincx as 'perhaps' present in the late prose, dramatic and televisual works is not only to focus on a minor or unlikely facet of the works. It is also a way in which that central 'key word' to the late works, the 'perhaps' itself, might be approached.

I have argued in the preceding chapters that traceable through Beckett's work from the time of his Geulincx research in 1936, up until the English publication of *The Unnamable* in 1958, a 'fantasia' persists that with the benefit of hindsight can be seen as chiefly characterized by progression towards its own negation, before it is re-invoked as a still unresolved set of questions, images and syntactic parameters. Allusion and citation in *Murphy* become fragmented in *Watt*, jumbled with other single-use objects in *Suite/La Fin/The End*, and are further abstracted, refined and glossed – Adorno's 'reified' – through the trilogy, most intensively in *The Unnamable*, until they are fully severed from any directly identifiable connection to an origin, an original. In order to be seen in the texts at this severed point Geulincx must be traced indirectly, through that process of fragmentation and combination in what might be summarized as a transition from the intertextual to the intratextual. There is in this trajectory less Geulincx's sliding away from Beckett's sight than an active, purposeful putting away. Geulincx does not simply disappear. He is disappeared, intentionally forgotten, even brutally attacked and en-graved, as per the tutor in *La Fin/The End*. Yet this is not the end of his story.

If we further recall the *Watt* notebooks and the striking Dantean metaphor that imagines various voices of a psyche buried in layers of rock, the archaeological investigation of which is the so-called 'auto-speliology', the metaphor can be used to see more clearly how Beckett's purposeful killing off and burying of Geulincx is not necessarily an act of finality, and why, therefore, its posthumous consequences should be explored. The solidity of this rock, in the context of *Watt* a layered coherence of self, might also function as a metaphor to describe Beckett's forms of source incorporation in the earlier stages of the oeuvre. That is, one might say that Beckett's 'notesnatching' and its concomitant textual incorporations once manifest as an investigable and parsable layering, where the identification of, the Bloomian *hunt for* a source was a matter of digging up the particularities of a discrete stratum, a moment of voice, of quotation, allusion, intact and fossil like. One voice, partial quotation etc. could be separated from another in a relatively clear and critical 'speliology'.

Yet in progressing towards its own negation Beckett's self-devouring 'series' complicates this process. It negates one source with another, just as in the narrator's pocket in *La Fin/The End* each object indelibly etches itself into another, each marking and burying, en-graving, another like itself. Beckett's own layers of rock, his various strata of sources and influences, become themselves folded and reburied inside yet other layers. The memory of Geulincx, for example, engraves those of Dante, Homer and Joyce via the lineage of galley slave imagery. One allusion etches itself into the other to make something entirely new, yet made of old things. As the narrator of *From an Abandoned Work* puts it, 'So in some way even olden things each time are first things, no two breaths the same, all a going over and over and all once and never more' (*TN*, p. 63). All four of these important figures are folded into one another in this imagery. Beckett's intention appears to be not an almighty overcoming of the authority of these previous writers in a Bloomian act of sabotage, making those previous weak in order that he might be strong. Rather, it is his determined reduction of aspects of these authors to certain of their 'fundamental sounds', wherein they are 'reified' as memories of voices.

Daniela Caselli points out in a study of Beckett's uses of Dante, one that argues these uses should not be considered as singular but rather as producing multiple Dantes, that by 1960 Beckett had hoped to entirely dispel even his long-standing company of Belacqua. Beckett wrote to Kay Boyle:

> Belacqua for me is no more than a kind of fetish. In the work I have finished he appears 'basculé sur le côté las d'attendre oublié des cœurs où vit la grâce endormi' (cor che in grazia vive) ['fallen over on his side tired of waiting forgotten of the hearts where grace abides asleep' (heart that lives in grace)], and I hope that's the end of him. (SB to Kay Boyle, 29 August 1960)[2]

Yet the graceful sleeping stillness that Beckett quotes from part one of *Comment c'est* was, as Caselli points out, 'not the end of Belacqua, however: he is also referred to in part two of *How It Is/Comment c'est*, and "the old lutist" is still able to wrench a "wan smile" from Dante in *The Lost Ones/Le dépeupleur* and *Company/Compagnie*' (Caselli 2005, p. 151).

While the recurrences of Dante that Caselli cites following Beckett's hoped for 'end of' Belacqua are still empirically verifiable, still stand out as relatively discrete, this example of Dante shows that even though buried, when we are in the later stages of Beckett's oeuvre, its most ghostly stages, buried identities have the capacity to return. Indeed, Beckett's frequent killing off of a character often serves to revivify later on, the self-cannibalizing serial protagonists drawing their ever less energy from the incorporation of previous avatars or 'vice-exister[s]'. Such literary self-cannibalizing was arguably begun with a pragmatic response to circumstance in Beckett's turning the rejected *Dream of Fair to Middling Women* to various new good uses in stories for *More Pricks Than Kicks*, a kind of recycling that was in turn later imagined figuratively when *The Unnamable*'s narrator observes his previous avatars wheel around him, where 'Malone passes' (*U*, p. 4) though it might be 'Molloy, wearing Malone's hat' (p. 2) along with what resembles 'the pseudocouple Mercier-Camier' (p. 7). More so than with Belacqua, however, Beckett does successfully see to the end of Geulincx. Yet it might nevertheless be expected, given the example of

Dante, that such would not in fact be the final end of Geulincx. How might a ghostly presence or voice of Geulincx, once buried, reassert itself?

In seeking to address these issues this chapter focuses first on a work entirely lacking strata of rock. *Comment c'est/How It Is* takes place in the messy and fluid 'warmth of primeval mud' (*HII*, p. 7). In what was a difficult but breakthrough work for Beckett, one that manifests fluidity in a number of original and important ways, 'old Geulincx' is indeed buried, yet only in a rather shallow grave, and he returns to haunt certain scenes, assertions and stylistic manoeuvres.

Geulincx and Quotation in *Comment c'est/How It Is*

In the muddy world of *Comment c'est/How It Is* the frequent dominant impetus when scraps of old voices that might sound like quotation rear themselves is to quickly suppress them. For example, when *Hamlet* is allowed to break momentarily to the surface the narrator/narrated[3] becomes benign and reassuring, recalled to his duty to 'on and end part one' without recourse to what Edouard Morot-Sir has called Beckett's sometime 'easy magic' (Morot-Sir 1976, p. 63) of allusion:

> a little less of to be present past future and conditional of to be and not to be come come enough of that on and end part one before Pim (*HII*, p. 31)

Yet the narrative does not always recognize its sources in literary or philosophical history, or even the fact that it might have specific sources. Predominantly it recognizes such scraps of quotation when they are as obvious as one from Shakespeare. That is, only when these are most in danger of being uncovered, when the narrator might be ousted as having borrowed rather than stolen the allusion (though the narrative is also of course commenting on its own tenses of grammar). For the reader familiar with Geulincx in Beckett's oeuvre, however, infrequent indirect references still bubble through the mud unremarked upon by the self-lacerating narrative. For example, the multiple nothings of *The Unnamable* return to bring a similar invocation of wide-ranging impotence:

> in the dark the mud hearing nothing saying nothing capable of nothing nothing (p. 53)

The assertion of impotence is phrased similarly to how it was in *The Unnamable*, via Geulincx's axiom; the narrator/narrated's being 'capable of nothing' continues the fragmentation of the axiom that was begun with Murphy's dissatisfaction at its unrealistic though nevertheless enticing beauty, something that progresses across 'the series'.

A second residue of earlier inter- and intratextual references that might surprise in persisting, or recurring again, at this late stage involves the Geulingian galley-man. This final and ghost-like reappearance brings a newly nuanced perspective to this lineage of imagery, one that speaks to Beckett's struggles as a writer of dual cultural origin. Typifying the self-contradictory shifting temporal emphases in *Comment c'est/How It Is*, in part one the narrator/narrated asserts that there is no more ship:

> old dream I'm not deceived or I am it all depends on what is not said on the day it all depends on the day farewell rats the ship is sunk a little less is all one begs (p. 31)

The narrator/narrated is here back in that 'old dream' of the question of whether one is being deceived or not, recalling the to and fro of Malone's 'old aporetics' (*MD*, p. 5) and that 'screaming silence of no's knife in yes's wound', bidding 'farewell' to the rats that have featured so frequently in the series and that in *L'Innommable/The Unnamable* took charge on this very ship. However, just as the last of Belacqua had not quite been seen despite Beckett's hopes to the contrary, the ship too is not yet entirely 'sunk' and it returns in *Comment c'est/How It Is* towards the end of part two. Shortly after the narrator/narrated describes his text as 'little private book these secret things little book all my own the heart's outpourings' (*HII*, p. 72), this heart pours out a further recollection of 'life above in the light'. There are a number of autobiographical recollections filtered through the unpunctuated prose of *Comment c'est/How It Is*, and 'perhaps' this scene too describes one such fragmented memory, of Beckett returning to Ireland[4]:

> home to native land to die in my twenties iron constitution above in the light my life my living made my living tried everything building mostly it was booming all branches plaster mostly met Pam I think (p. 73)[5]

The whole love story between the narrator/narrated and Pam, here set on 'native land', is then told hilariously from start to finish in a single verset that ends bathetically in 'forgiveness', before 'silence falls again'. From this silence rises a scene of what is 'perhaps' Beckett leaving 'native land' from the port at Dun Laoghaire or Cobh, heading for a measure of relief in Europe, in a scene that brings together the pre Geulincx research description of Belacqua musing astern in *Dream of Fair to Middling Women* with the galley-man of the trilogy:

> sea beneath the moon harbour-mouth after the sun the moon always light day and night little heap in the stern it's me all those I see are me all ages the current carries me out the awaited ebb I'm looking for an isle home at last drop never move again a little turn at evening to the sea-shore seawards

> then back drop sleep wake in the silence eyes that dare open stay open live old dream on crabs kelp
>
> astern receding land of brothers dimming lights mountain if I turn water roughening he falls I fall on my knees crawl forward clink of chains perhaps it's not me perhaps it's another perhaps it's another voyage confusion with another what isle what moon you say the thing you see the thoughts sometimes that go with it it disappears the voice goes on a few words it can stop it can go on depending on what it's not known it's not said (p. 74)

While this water 'roughening' at the stern of the ship is that ship's own wake and not so much the gathering storm of *The Unnamable*, the 'clink of chains' of the 'little heap in the stern' situates this recollection as a further (and final) stage in the lineage of ship imagery. The narrator/narrated hears the clink of the chains that he is bound in as he imagines himself once again as the galley-man, though here wondering if he might be confusing himself with someone else. If indeed this 'land of brothers' is the 'native land' of Beckett's Ireland then such a reappearance of the enslaved galley-man travelling the Irish Sea reveals an intriguing and distinctive aspect to the lineage. The ship is travelling in one direction (east towards Europe) but the enslaved narrator/narrated moves in the other (back home to Ireland), similarly to the earlier images in *L'Innommable/The Unnamable* where the slave rebels against inevitable progression. In those earlier images this movement towards the boundary of the boat indexed Molloy's 'great measure of freedom'. Transposing the slave's freedom of movement in stasis to the Irish Sea instantiates one of very few images to be found in Beckett's oeuvre of his culturally divided, mutually committed, literary homelands. Cohn describes Beckett as a 'French-writing Irishman' (Cohn 2001, p. 256) belonging and committed to both places, and writing from a cultural vantage point of navigation between the two. Yet as the narrator/narrated of *How It Is* will describe such voyages, there is little relief to be had in travelling 'west to east':

> we can drag ourselves thus by the mere grace of our united net sufferings from west to east towards an inexistent peace we are invited kindly to consider (*HII*, p. 125)

One should certainly be cautious retrofitting the geographical specificity of this final incarnation of the galley-man onto the earlier appearances. Nevertheless, the fleeting and enfolded presence of Geulincx here brings with it a residue of the earlier imagining of the galley-man as a repository of freedom in constraint. The past-presence of Geulincx brings a particular context to the ghostly imagery of the narrator/narrated leaving 'native land', or 'perhaps' Beckett leaving Ireland, instancing a fractured memory carrying within it and enabling a further fractured memory.

Caselli points to William Colerick's reading of this scene 'as a reference to the episode of Ulysses's voyage as represented in the *Comedy*', and argues that although it is possible to accept, along with Colerick, that imagistic specificities such as the ship, the mountain, dimming light and the roughening water 'refer to Ulysses's tale in the *Comedy*, we can nevertheless read the passage differently'. The passage, Caselli argues, can also be read according to

> an intertextual perspective, in which the 'above mentioned' is not only textual but also intertextual. This example shows how a number of scenes are not precise allusions but rather a 'familiar' murmur, as what has already been said. (Caselli 2005, p. 160)

Such an 'intertextual perspective' might also take into its consideration the galley slave from Geulincx, who also constitutes one of the multifarious strands of the 'familiar' identity here that has 'already been said', already been murmured. Not only does the scene's Geulingian imagery recall that of earlier texts, but the epistemological ending 'it's not known it's not said' echoes the Geulingian epistemological criterion of knowledge: what cannot be said cannot be known.

In moving further away from what Bloom might call mere 'allusion-counting' (Bloom 1997, p. 31) in regard to Geulincx in *Comment c'est/How It Is*, particular moments of the text come to the fore in their being in different ways almost but not quite traceable to Geulincx. At such moments the absence of Geulincx itself becomes a presence, at least for the reader familiar with the Geulingian traces running through the oeuvre.

Geulincx is not named at any point in *Comment c'est/How It Is*, which is in contrast to his fellow (and more famous) Occasionalist Malebranche, who is named among what must rank as some of the most beautiful writing of Beckett's entire oeuvre. The lengthy scene rendered as another semi-autobiographical memory deriving from the Dublin Leopardstown racecourse rises mistily out of the mud before dissipating back into it, disintegrating and fading, the recollection of shared moments between the protagonist and his partner sharing sandwiches and affection enlivened briefly in its telling before it disappears again. Though as the narrator/narrated points out, the recollection is faulty; it might be 'very pretty only not like that it doesn't happen like that' (*HII*, p. 26). Knowlson and Pilling describe the scene as just 'too picaresque and euphoric to be confused with real life' (Knowlson and Pilling 1979, p. 67):

> suddenly yip left right off we go chins up arms swinging the dog follows head sunk tail on balls no reference to us it had the same notion at the same instant Malebranche less the rosy hue the humanities I had if it stops to piss it will piss without stopping I shout no sound plant her there and run cut your throat (*HII*, p. 24)

Malebranche has a dual presence here. He is regarded by the narrator/narrated on the one hand as merely 'the humanities I had', previous learning now useless along with that also listed at other points in the text, 'notions of mathematics astronomy and even physics' (p. 33), 'and with that flashes of geography' (p. 35). All of these 'humanities' and sciences are described by the narrator/narrated as being now nothing but the 'scraps' (p. 3) introduced on the text's first page. Yet Malebranche is also specifically named. Out of an amorphous 'humanities' comes this momentary flash of precision, his name even spelled correctly unlike the mention of Geulincx in numerous versions of *La Fin/The End*. This dual presence of Malebranche, vague yet also specific, reflects certain of Beckett's own experiences of the Occasionalist. Specifically, Malebranche's lack of 'rosy hue', his death, was quite probably something with which Beckett was indeed familiar. Beckett's tutor while he had been studying humanities at TCD, A. A. Luce, was an expert on Berkeley and Malebranche.[6] Luce's influential *Berkeley and Malebranche: A Study in the Origins of Berkeley's Thought* (published in 1934, only two years after Beckett resigned from teaching at TCD) sets itself out clearly: 'My aim is to show that the way to the heart of Berkeleianism lies through Malebranche' (Luce 1934, p. 43). It traces this specific influence upon Berkeley via notebooks and correspondence, particularly those leading up to *Theory of Vision*, the work Beckett annotated with 'Against Geulincx?' and which is in his Paris library. In *Berkeley and Malebranche* Luce describes an 'alleged meeting' between the two philosophers held in Malebranche's Paris monastery, 'when Malebranche raised his voice and lost his temper, and according to the *bon mot*, Berkeley became unwittingly "the occasional cause of his death"' (p. 89). This death of an Occasionalist, the tale of a loss of 'rosy hue' relayed via a tutor, has resonances with a similar death from great excitement, that of the narrator's philosophy tutor in *La Fin/The End*.

Further evidence for Malebranche's importance as a component of any humanities once 'had', by Beckett as per his narrator, resides with Geulincx's first fleeting appearances in the early 'Philosophy Notes', where Beckett summarized some of Descartes's thoughts about 'space' and 'place' that found their way into Belacqua's sea journey in *Dream of Fair to Middling Women*. Beckett noted that there was no such thing as 'empty space', this being because 'Bodies are parts of space, limitations of the universal extension' (TCD MS 10967/187v). He then compares Descartes's ideas on space to Malebranche's epistemology: 'Similar view of mental world by Malebranche' (TCD MS 10967/187v), and also noted the lineage accounting for the more famous Occasionalist in terms of his views on what Tad Schmaltz calls Malebranche's 'Vision in God [. . .] the doctrine that we see all things (that is, bodies) in (that is, through ideas in) God' (Schmaltz 2000, p. 59).[7] The notes go on to cite Malebranche as a parallel to the Spinozan original of *Murphy*'s Chapter 6 epigraph: '(amor intellectualis quo deus se ipsum amat = raison universelle of Malebranche)'

(TCD MS 10967/188r). They also name Malebranche on further occasions, as interchangeable with Geulincx and where he is aligned more closely with La Forge. When Beckett describes Occasionalist conceptions of Divine causation, for example, he conflates Geulincx and Malebranche's views as distinct from Spinoza's:

> According to Geulincx & Malebranche God creates world & us of will, according to Spinoza the world is necessary consequence of nature of God. Causal relation understood in two quite different ways. (TCD MS 10967/190v)

Malebranche also enters the notes at other moments, such as during a summary of Descartes's ideas on error:

> Error is an act of free-will parallel to act of sin; it is the guilt of self-deception. (This thought elaborated by Malebranche). (TCD MS 10967/184r)

The claim deserves to be made that such notes of Beckett's from the early 1930s are part of what, 30 years later, constitute the ghostly 'humanities I had', the learned all-too 'reified' repositories that now only exist as 'scraps'. Similarly to how scenes from Beckett's own life find their refracted and redacted ways into the text, so too do instances of early autodidactic 'notesnatching' such as manifested in the 'Philosophy Notes' and a likely familiarity with Luce's work. By 1960, however, such 'humanities I had' are as fragmented as are the autobiographical images, and similarly are seen only darkly.

There were good reasons for Beckett to name Malebranche rather than Geulincx as one of these 'scraps' in *Comment c'est/How It Is*, other than just Malebranche's eligibility in the context as an Occasionalist. Not the least important of these is that Geulincx could not function in the text in the way Malebranche does; Geulincx's name has been too prevalent through prior works to warrant mention in *Comment c'est/How It Is*. This late text requires 'the humanities I had' to be even further removed from any that were voiced or named in previous works. Had Beckett named Geulincx here minus a rosy hue he would thereby have given the name in three works (*Murphy, Molloy* and *Comment c'est/How It Is*). At the very least such repetition would have constituted Beckett overplaying his hand, over-relying on Geulincx as a name that would span the entire 'series' and beyond. Beckett needed an Occasionalist for *Comment c'est/How It Is* but he had made Geulincx unavailable. That is to say, Geulincx cannot any more function as a simple token of Occasionalism, which is one of Malebranche's functions in this text. In this sense, then, Malebranche serves in part as Geulincx's Occasionalist understudy allowed fleeting limelight. But Malebranche also operates specifically – 'less the rosy hue' – and in the allusion to his death he not only recalls the tutor of *La Fin/The End* but he also exhibits a fragment, a multifarious scrap of Beckett's own 'humanities' deriving from both his early 'notesnatching' and his TCD tutor that is not pointed up at any other place in the oeuvre. In these ways, the non-presence of Geulincx, the presence that is instead allowed to be Malebranche's, is as important for consideration of philosophical relevance to this text as is the overt presence of Malebranche.

Much as in *Murphy*, the important thing was less the resolution of Occasionalist discrepancy but 'the manner in which it might be exploited', the narrator/narrated of *How It Is* admitting of the scraps of humanities that, despite the fragmentary nature of the scraps as recalled, 'they have marked me that's the main thing' (*HII*, p. 33). Perhaps not with the violence with which characters attack and mark each other – with tin openers and their names etched into each other's bodies with fingernails – but such 'notions' have indeed 'marked' the narrator/narrated and his text in deep yet subtle ways.

There are a number of further points in *Comment c'est/How It Is* where this being 'marked' reveals what might 'perhaps' be a residual presence of Geulincx alongside other figures. For example, the novel's elemental mud has frequently been compared to that of Dante's muddier sections of Hell. In 1978 Michael Robinson claimed the novel's narrator 'exists in a landscape which is composed of a number of details from different circles of the Inferno' (Robinson 1979, p.79). Specifically, the mud recalls the fifth circle of the banks of the river Styx to which the wrathful are condemned:

> And I, intent on looking as we passed,
>   saw muddy people moving in that marsh,
>   all naked, with their faces scarred by rage. (Dante 2003, p. 132 (Inf. VII, 109–11))

This mud 'gurgle[s] in their throats' (p. 133 (Inf. VII, 125)) as those who claw their way through the mud inflict attacks on each other with a malice comparable to *Comment c'est/How It Is*:

> They fought each other, not with hands alone,
>   but struck with head and chest and feet as well,
>   with teeth they tore each other limb from limb. (p. 133 (Inf. VII, 112–14))

More recently Daniel Albright has argued of such a comparison that in sections of *Comment c'est/How It Is* the text 'looks like Dante but is in fact quite up to date – a parody of Dante based on modern technology'. According to Albright, Beckett parodies the obligation to express via the medium of radio, whereby 'Each mud-crawler with his can opener treats the man in front of him as if he were a radio, making him speak or sing out through a system of learned responses' (Albright 2003, p. 120). In the study on Beckett and Dante with perhaps the most subtlety and authority, one that takes its theoretical contours from the multivalent concept of 'authority' itself, Caselli correlates the mud of the text with speech:

> *Inferno* VII is reconstructed in *How It Is/Comment c'est*'s painfully detailed exploration of the materiality of speech and its investigation of how repetition and reproduction confer the status of reality upon invisibility. (Caselli 2005, p. 156)

For Caselli, *Inferno* is less a *source* for this text than something which 'participates in the intractable economy of the text by being an "unthinkable beginning", an already said/written which constitutes itself as the transcription of an already said' (p. 157).

In contrast to the number of studies citing Dante's relations to this novel, Geulincx's name has never been invoked in relation to the mud of *Comment c'est/How It Is*. Yet while he offers nothing like the images of violent resourcefulness shown by Dante's unrelenting damned, Geulincx describes a geographically based zone of existence that bears comparison with the novel. Geulincx describes himself staring out at the world from his Occasionalist, disconnected vantage point. He asks what good his eyes are if he will only ever see ill, if he can never know for sure that the world is as he believes it to be. Then with sadness, because in ignorance, he enumerates an ontology comprising 'regions' of the earth as he – admitting quite probably faultily – sees it. Beckett transcribed a summary of Geulincx's regions, which in their mixtures of specificity and generality also have similarities with the zones of 'The Sky' and 'The Nothingness' in which *Watt* would initially take place:

> We see then that the world as it affects our senses can be conveniently divided into regions, and the inhabitants of those regions. The first region is that vast *sky*. . .and the inhabitants of this region are the stars. . .The second region is the air [. . .] its inhabitants are clouds, and the phenomena they produce. . .The third region is the sea, whose inhabitants are fish. . . The fourth region is the land, of which there are two sub-regions: the upper, whose inhabitants are plants and animals. . .and the lower sub-region, whose inhabitants are metals, stones, and every kind of mineral. (*Et*, p. 329)

It is the fourth of these regions, the 'lower sub-region', that gives a Geulingian aspect to the mud of *Comment c'est/How It Is*. This is not only because Geulincx offers an evocative image of a Dantean environment with which Beckett was also familiar, or even because it foregrounds the elemental ontology of 'stones' and 'metals' that constitute so much of Beckett's own literary environments. Primarily it is because of how Geulincx writes of his own body as subject to this fourth region:

My body is a part of the world, an inhabitant of the fourth region, and claims a place among the species who walk over it. (pp. 329–30)

As much would of course be expected of Geulincx's place in the world, that is unless he might want to claim to be something other than a human who would 'walk over' the surface of the Earth. However, Geulincx's walking 'over it' reads in at least two ways, once we have in mind *Comment c'est/How It Is*. Not only is 'it' the earth that is walked over, putting Geulincx safely in the upper fourth region, 'it' is also Geulincx's own body, a body that is itself walked over in an image of cruelty more at home in a murky lower region. Just as he claims a place among the species that walk over the earth, he claims a place among the species that also walk over his body. It is something he does in many other places where he describes his being subject to, in a different metaphorical zone, that 'boundless ocean of miseries, on which I presently toss' (p. 350). As earlier chapters discussed, the sometimes painful facts of Geulincx's own life can creep to the surface of *Ethics*, where he refers to the cruelties and hindrances inflicted upon him, his family and his hopes. Placing himself in this zone reads as though Geulincx is in a series of those who might 'walk over' one another, a series similar to those who repeatedly brutalize one another in turn in *Comment c'est/How It Is*.

In this 'fourth region', as Geulincx describes the world in which humanity lives, any 'I' is subject to the authority of God, of another existing elsewhere, living their 'life the other above in the light' (*HII*, p. 4) as *How It Is* renders its vision of dependency. The narrator of the text is simultaneously produced as the novel's narrated by virtue of the narrator's hearing and recording, 'when the panting stops', this other, this other who is a narrator telling of his own life: 'my life last state last version ill-said ill-heard ill-recaptured ill-murmured in the mud' (p. 3). The fractured narrative that is 'ill-heard ill-recaptured', then, is also an I-heard, an I-recaptured. The narrator's self is both murmuring in the present, and recuperating 'I' from the past, from elsewhere. Such an interweaving of identity and its relations to an ultimately inaccessible other also has its Geulingian precedent. The Occasionalist divide that becomes tangible to humanity, though still limited by a lack of access to the 'ineffable', becomes for Geulincx as tangible as it can be in the fourth region of elemental walking over. Exhibiting both the impressionableness of Descartes's piece of wax[8] and a proto-existentialist sense of being-in-the-world within a theological framework, Geulincx describes humanity being subject to the authority of one who must resemble us and on whom we depend, even though we are not given real access either to our world or to theirs:

Hence also, there must be someone else who can by His own power impress on me the likeness of the world; just as He impresses my action on small parts of the world; and in each case in an ineffable manner, which perpetually eludes me when I try to grasp it.

Just as the world is only 'ill-seen' and 'ill-recaptured' by the narrator of *Comment c'est/How It Is*, for Geulincx there is also only an unverifiable 'likeness' impressed upon him by another, by an authority to which he must defer. He must defer to this other, just as Beckett's narrator requires a narrated, because there is no such thing as direct knowledge or unmediated experience, no event in the present or memory of the past that does not elude one as one tries 'to grasp it'. Such is illustrated in *How It Is*, for example, by the 'very pretty only not like that' cooing of the couple at the racecourse. Geulincx writes that:

> things placed outside us cannot impress their likeness on me; nor can I myself capture that likeness of my own accord; for such things impinge upon or affect at most my body, and this is as much to say that it does nothing of itself towards perceiving them. (*Et*, p. 328)

This is as much to say that a body is not sufficient, much as a narrator is not sufficient. The narrated is required to enliven, to enable narrative, just as Geulincx requires the agency of God to enliven the body, to connect it with the experiencing consciousness of the mind.

Coming, Being, Going II

As well as these fragmentary shards of Geulincx and not-Geulincx in *Comment c'est/How It Is* there are also broader approaches Geulincx takes to ethics that resonate with the structure of that novel. As Chapter 3 discussed regarding Watt's movements in relation to Mr Knott's house, Beckett transcribed Geulincx's formulation that 'I have my whole being (in coming hither, acting here, and departing hence)', the tripartite structure setting clear boundaries that also map onto the tripartite structure of *Comment c'est/How It Is*. Cohn describes this number three, along with the novel's mud, as Beckett's 'debt to Dante'. According to Cohn 'The number three is emphasized – sacred to the Florentine, but arbitrarily chosen by the French-writing Irishman' (Cohn 2001, p. 256). But 'perhaps' this choice is not as arbitrary as it might appear. Just as the mud can be seen to also owe something to Geulincx along with Dante, revealing a similarly intertwined allusiveness to that of the galley slave, so too this 'triune plot' (p. 257) traces similar contours to the triune life that Geulincx describes in *Ethics* and *Metaphysics*, continuing the trend among these earlier images of combining 'scraps' derived from both Dante and Geulincx.

As Beckett transcribed in the penultimate paragraph of his typed notes, Geulincx's seven ethical obligations are bounded by this tripartite structure, mirroring how Geulincx conceives of the structure of life itself:

> I introduce a division of the Obligations into those concerned with death (such as the first two Obligations), those concerned with life (such as the

third, fourth, fifth and sixth), and those concerned with birth (such as the Seventh Obligation). For every Obligation of man is concerned with either coming hither, being here, or departing hence; in short, with *hither, here,* or *hence*. (*Et*, p. 350)

There is, then, an intriguing structural parallel between Geulincx's emphasis on how life is and the sections of *Comment c'est/How It Is*, the three parts of which are announced in the novel's very first words with 'how it was I quote before Pim with Pim after Pim how it is three parts I say it as I hear it' (*HII*, p. 3). However, when it comes to later stages of the novel Beckett frequently confounds such strictly demarcated divisions. The three sections are indeed predominantly bound by the narrator/narrated's coming '*hither*' to Pim, his being '*here*' with Pim, and his having gone '*hence*' from Pim. Yet the struggle to avoid a continual restatement of these categorical differences manifests as the narrator/narrated asserting them out of order, or simultaneously, or as one against the other. It must therefore be acknowledged too that while Geulincx might be seen to operate in such boundaries and borders of the text, his legacy is also, in the text's pushing and rebelling against these boundaries and borders, resisted.

Guignol Worlds

Even in the ontologically minimal and cruel world of *Comment c'est/How It Is* there is occasional and Occasionalist wonder at the body and its apparent miraculous abilities, even if such abilities might only be misplaced impressions of agency. Such wonder appears, for example, at the climax of the novel, where the act that concretizes part two's being 'here' with Pim is the laying on of a hand. The event is mediated via a remarkably Occasionalist perspective:

> Smartly as from a block of ice or white-hot my hand recoils hangs a moment it's vague in mid air then slowly sinks again and settles firm and even with a touch of ownership already on the miraculous flesh (p. 43)

In this taut verset there is little sign of a will motivating this hand. There is not even any 'I' merely congruent with the occurrences observed. The hand feels as though either freezing cold or blazing hot, but the narrator cannot say which. The sensation stops at the hand, and does not reach the experiencing consciousness of the narrator. There is figurative description, but not wilful action. All is 'as from' or 'with a touch of'. All is observed and recorded, but little of the hand's movement is described in terms of an interaction between it and the rest of the narrator/narrated. While it might be 'my' hand that 'recoils' and 'hangs', 'sinks' and 'settles', and so there is ownership, it is as much a cruel ownership of the other, of Pim and not of the self. Molloy had suffered similar fissures and mediated perceptions of his hands. When crouched by the rock like Belacqua at the beginning of his narrative, he gazed 'towards my hand also, which my knee felt tremble and of which my eyes saw the wrist only' (*Mo*, p. 7). As Cornelis Verhoeven describes Geulincx's accounts of movement, 'we become the astonished spectators even of our own activities at the very moment we perform them'.[9]

It is in part the fact that Beckett focuses specifically on the movement of a hand, as Geulincx does in *Ethics*, which leads to the suggestion such moments reflect Beckett's Geulingian Occasionalist interests. Yet 'perhaps' it is as much Malebranche as Geulincx who informs such passages. For the disconnected hand or arm that lays onto and into Pim was also Malebranche's metaphor of choice for illustrating Occasionalist incapacity and disconnection. For example, in *The Search After Truth* Malebranche writes 'I move my arm because of the *union* God has established between my mind and my body' (Malebranche 1997, pp. 669–70). In his study of Malebranche and Berkeley, Luce cites an extract from one of Berkeley's notebooks that, as Luce reads it, pokes fun at Malebranche's argument about limbs: 'We move our legs ourselves. 'Tis we that will their movement. Herein I differ from Malbranch'.[10]

Beckett's emphasis in his transcriptions on the movement of a hand, arm or body follows that of Geulincx's examples. The transcriptions from *Metaphysica Vera*, for example, include the following:

> But my hand is moved not at the command of my will, but by consent to it. (*Met*, p. 42)

The wonder expressed at Occasionalist movement of the hand in *How It Is* is given a deistic aspect when, for example, movement appears to be 'impossible', reliant on a 'miracle' for its achievement of 'the impossible':

> huge cymbals giant arms outspread two hundred degrees and clang clang miracle miracle the impossible do the impossible suffer the impossible (*HII*, p. 55)

For Geulincx, as has been seen, movement in a physical world is entirely dependent upon God's willing such action, who 'in an ineffable manner conjoins certain motions' (*Et*, p. 231) with my own intentions. A human body, according to Geulincx, has no more capacity for being influenced by my own will than any other element of the external world. I am conjoined to all only when God wills it, or 'because of the *union* God has established' as Malebranche describes it. As we have seen too, suicide is discussed by Geulincx as a specific example of how someone cannot control their own body, a particular mind/body divide that also resonates with parts of *Comment c'est/How It Is*, such as 'I am not going to kill myself demanding something beyond his powers that he stand on his head for example or on his feet or kneel most certainly not' (*HII*, p. 55).

Movements of a hand or arm without apparent agency such as appears in *Comment c'est/How It Is* can be seen as even more closely allied with Beckett's ideas on Occasionalism, and Geulincx in particular, when recalling Beckett's description of Geulincx's 'fascinating guignol world'. This is a world where, as Beckett described it, all is puppetry, where people and everything in the world are puppets at the mercy of God the all-powerful puppet-master. The body that lays its hand upon Pim at the climax of *Comment c'est/How It Is* indeed goes on to treat Pim as if he were a puppet. Just like a puppet Pim is an empty vessel until he is mistreated into action, until another will 'walk over' him:

> Pim never be but for me anything but a dumb limp lump flat for ever in the mud but I'll quicken him you wait and see and how I can efface myself behind my creature when the fit takes me (p. 44)

Pim as 'a dumb limp lump' waiting to be quickened by the violent hand of the narrator/narrated serves as a sharp reminder of the authority in Geulincx's authoritarian world. The violent 'fit' that forces Pim into action, and behind which the narrator/narrated can 'efface' himself, recalls us to the dominion of God in Geulincx's world where, as Beckett described it, all is puppetry, where there is no sight of God who is ineffably effaced behind His own actions. Where He is, as Stephen Dedalus describes the artist, 'refined out of existence, indifferent, paring his fingernails' (Joyce 1992a, p. 233), or 'now my nails' (*HII*, p. 44), as Beckett ends the verset on Pim the 'dumb limp lump'.

Tropes of puppetry appear throughout Beckett's oeuvre from his earliest works written before the 1936 Geulincx research. In 'Love and Lethe', for example, the courting couple are likened to puppets not fully in control of their actions, who appear to the narrator, and therefore also to the reader, as not especially authentic:

> Like fantoccini controlled by a single wire they flung themselves down on the western slope of heath. From now on till the end there is something very *secco* and Punch and Judy about their proceedings. (*MPTK*, p. 87)[11]

This critique of Belacqua and his lover Ruby Tough is, perhaps, just as much a self-deprecating comment on the abilities of the narrator as it is a personal judgement about the characters' 'character'. The narrator of *Murphy* insists along similar lines that their star protagonist is distinguished from the other characters in the novel precisely in being the only character in the novel properly free from constraint:

> All the puppets in this book whinge sooner or later, except Murphy, who is not a puppet. (*Mu*, p. 78)

Yet Murphy's self-determination, manifested in his rejection of Suk's horoscope, his refusal to search out a job or to explain himself to curious onlookers such as Ticklepenny, comes with its own problems that undermine the distinction conferred. In July 1936, shortly after finishing writing the novel, Beckett described Murphy's apartness to McGreevy, this time admitting its flaw:

> There seemed to me always the risk of taking him too seriously and separating him too sharply from the others. As it is I do not think the mistake (Aliohsa mistake) has been altogether avoided. (SB to TM, 7 July 1936: *L1*, p. 350)[12]

Murphy's freedom, the thing that Murphy takes most seriously, separates him from the other puppets of the novel a little too baldly, and he thereby becomes a different kind of puppet. Similarly, the narrator of *The Unnamable* describes being 'in my Punch and Judy box' (*U*, p. 53) and promises to finish telling their stories once 'a few puppets' (p. 2) contrived for 'company' (p. 1) have been scattered. When using tropes of puppetry, then, Beckett is frequently concerned with how they might function as framing imagery for a fictional character and for that character's dependence on the controlling, behind-the-scenes puppet master that is their author.

Moreover, such puppetry of Beckett's early and middle periods, specifically the puppetry of a 'guignol world' that owes a debt to Beckett's 1936 fascinations with Geulincx, finds a reinvigorated and particularly focused manifestation in certain of the later works. Indeed, there are specific and identifiable reasons for the early concerns being reinvigorated. In introducing these arguments, I will take a slight chronological detour, going back two years before Beckett's starting to write *Comment c'est/How It Is*, to the short mime *Act Without Words 1*, a play that can benefit from being rethought as a 'guignol world' which thereby sets important precedents for Beckett's later treatment of puppet-style impotence, before I go on to look at how these precedents are reinvigorated and developed in later works 'Still', *Ghost Trio* and *Nacht und Träume*.

Staging 'the happy ones': *Act Without Words 1*

Beckett had guignol worlds – worlds in which humanity depends upon an anonymous and invisible puppet master – very much in mind in 1956. The 28 November letter to Hutchinson in which he described Geulincx's 'fascinating guignol world' was written around the time he was working on the short drama he nicknamed in a letter to Alan Schneider 'the desert mime' (SB to Alan Schneider, 15 October 1956).[13] *Act Without Words 1* presents a man taunted in a desert, a man whom Beckett described as 'human meat – or bones'.[14] The nameless figure is pushed and pulled around by an offstage authority that manipulates and tortures him for no identifiable reason. A number of scholars including Ackerley, Feldman and Weller argue that at least in part (to quote Feldman), 'Beckett's source for *Act Without Words 1* is [. . .] Köhler via Woodworth' (Feldman 2006, p. 106). This reading refers back to Beckett's psychology notes of 1935, in which he transcribed a passage from Robert Woodworth's *Contemporary Schools of Psychology* that describes Wolfgang Köhler's experiments recorded in *The Mentality of Apes*. Beckett noted to himself that he should read Köhler's book (though there are no extant records that he went on to do so), and he recorded Woodworth's summary of Köhler's experiments conducted in Tenerife of 1913–17. Many of these experiments involved chimpanzees and monkeys trying to reach food suspended from above in baskets and as single items by climbing trees or standing on boxes. Sometimes such boxes were stacked, precariously, one on top of the other. The imagery evoked, diagrammed and reproduced in nine photographs in Köhler's study is certainly suggestive of 'the action and setting' (Ackerley 2004a, p. 37) of *Act Without Words 1*. Not only in the movement of the nameless figure with boxes, reaching skywards, but also the heated confines of a cage in Tenerife might go some way to accounting for why Beckett chose a 'desert' as the untypical setting for his mime.

Referring specifically to a female chimpanzee observed by Köhler who would wrap her arms around herself when she wanted to be held, Weller argues the following:

> the movement in his [Beckett's] later dramatic works towards a purely bodily language is arguably a movement towards the language of an animal, not as what the *Oxford English Dictionary* terms a being 'endowed with life, sensation, and voluntary motion,' but as a suffering being, defined by lack not in Descartes's, Kant's, or Heidegger's sense, but because this being 'experiences' lack and 'expresses' that lack by making of her own body both a stage and a substitute. (Weller 2008, p. 218)

Weller's incorporation of Beckett's much earlier reading about Köhler under a broader banner of 'suffering' reconciles the very differently shaped ideas with which Beckett was himself experimenting in *Act Without Words 1*. But if Köhler is important as some kind of direct 'source' for this mime, then *why* this might be so is as important a question as the comparative *how*. The congruity between the imagery in *The Mentality of Apes* and *Act Without Words 1* is both striking and surprising; it is unusual that Beckett would take such imagery as so straightforward and thoroughgoing a 'source' for an entire work, albeit a short work, particularly when there is a gap of some 20 years between his reading Woodworth and writing *Act Without Words 1*. The unknown quantity in a direct extrapolation from Köhler to this mime is this intervening 20 years, and whether or not Beckett ever made good on his instruction to read *The*

Mentality of Apes (the book is not in Beckett's Paris library, though that proves little). As I want to argue, multifaceted dynamics of suffering operate within both *Act Without Words 1* and the later 'Still', an understanding of which can be deepened by thinking beyond Köhler and the apes, and into the more abstract territory of puppetry.[15]

Act Without Words 1 can also be read through the ideas of insatiable need that are manifested in *Watt* in an implicit fracturing of Geulincx's ethical axiom. In summary, in *Act Without Words 1* Beckett puts in play one of Arsene's 'happy ones', one of those who will always need in precisely the place where they cannot satisfy that need, and the visual vocabulary through which he stages this is that of puppetry, where the man onstage is treated by an offstage taunting authority as if he were a puppet of that authority's cruel whims. Seen in the context of Arsene's statement in *Watt*, according to which 'The glutton castaway, the drunkard in the desert, the lecher in prison, they are the happy ones', *Act Without Words 1* might then be seen as more than a self-contained work of 'obvious allegory' (Ackerley and Gontarski 2006, p. 3), or as 'too obvious and pat', as Ihab Hassan wrote (Hassan 1967, p. 192). Cohn has similarly described the piece as instantiating 'slapstick comedy at the cosmological level, and the meaning is almost too explicit' (Cohn 1962, p. 247), with Gontarski summarizing how critics are frequently somewhat embarrassed by the mime's apparent 'directness' (Gontarski 1993, p. 29). Situating the play in a lineage of imagery that takes a cue from Arsene's statement, from an aesthetic of impotence and desperation traceable to Beckett's fracturing of Geulincx's ethical axiom in *Watt*, makes this play somewhat less 'direct'. Given such an inflection, this unnamed man in the desert can be seen as less a straightforward image of generalized humanity, what Beckett's own description of him as 'human meat – or bones' might be taken to mean. Not even an all-too-neat allegory of Existentialism (as Gontarski argues as a way of redeeming the play's torture-farce elements and its theme of freedom and enslavement), the mime can be seen, in light of Geulincx's importance for *Watt*, as a fragmentary shard of the complications and complicities inherent in Beckett's analects of philosophical imagery; a limited work, certainly, but also one that is richer than its clear and distinct clown-like actions can at first appear.

The man enters the stage of *Act Without Words 1* 'flung backwards'. He is whistled back offstage and is flung back on again twice before he 'hesitates, thinks better of it, halts, turns aside, reflects' (*CDW*, p. 203). The whistle continues to direct the man's action, calling his attention to objects and locations on stage; the palm tree, a carafe of relieving water, scissors with which he attempts to sever the rope and of which he wonders how they might also sever his neck, and the cubes with which, like Köhler's apes, he builds makeshift platforms. But it is perhaps the ropes of the play that most forcefully visualize his being tethered as a puppet in a 'guignol world'. The text does not specify how any of the objects should be lowered, only stating a rope when one is dropped for the man to climb up (the 'umbilical rope' (Gontarski 1993, p. 31) as Gontarski describes it), which he then cuts with the scissors. Yet the practicalities of performance dictate that objects need to be lowered either by rope or some other kind of thread, amenable to being hoisted slower or more quickly as the text specifies. Such ties are akin to those of a puppet, and as the man reaches up to the water, bundles cubes on each other and falls off them trying to reach skywards, his movements appear as those of a marionette. Though, importantly, a marionette separated from his puppeteer. As the water is lowered so the man raises his hands, and as the cubes are deposited so he goes to them; he is brought '*hither*' to act '*here*' just as, for Geulincx, God brings humanity into the world to act here, connected invisibly to and conducted entirely at the mercy of this unknowable, unspeakable, 'ineffable' authority.

Yet there is self-consciousness to this puppet, an awareness of his impotence. The puppet-like man is continually preoccupied with his own hands; he looks at them at the beginning of the play, cuts his fingernails part way through the play, and in his final gesture prior to the curtain 'He looks at his hands' (*CDW*, p. 206) again. This is a man decidedly in a world where his own instruments of capacity are no use. They cannot prevent his being tortured, however much he might rebel, and as the play progresses his frustration turns to disillusion. As he stares at his own impotent hands while the curtain falls the effect is one of witnessing his implicitly, silently in mime, asking similar questions to those asked by Geulincx of his 'guignol world':

> Why do so many and such great calamities conspire against me? Have I offended God in some way? [. . .] Thrust into a body as if into a prison, am I paying the penalties that I have deserved, and among others this grave one, that I am oblivious of the offence that I am expiating? (*Et*, p. 351)

This 1956 mime and Geulincx's sideways relevance to it mean that Beckett's later focus on puppetry and the grace of movement in the physicality of characters on page, stage and screen can be thought as a reinvigoration of the puppetry that inhered in earlier work such as *Act Without Words 1*. As will be shown, there are specific and intriguing ways in which this reinvigoration comes about. In order to best consider these, however, the arguments would do well to first assess a later work that also involves a version of puppetry, 'Still'.

'Still'

Written between 17 June and the end of July 1972, 'Still' has a multivalent relationship to Beckett's work thought as a 'series'. Standing apart as an individual piece, the only one of the *Foirades/Fizzles* initially written in English (before

Beckett's self-translation, something he undertook with most of his texts), 'Still' constituted some of the final work in that series. It was also the first text of the tripartite collection that includes 'Sounds' (1972–3) and 'Still 3' (1973). Both these later pieces received their first publication alongside an essay by Pilling in *Essays in Criticism* (1978) in which Pilling praises 'Still' as an achievement of Beckett's 'syntax of weakness', a phrase Beckett used in correspondence with Bray in 1959 and again in an interview with Harvey in 1962.[16] 'Still' also conveys a tripartite series that is internal to the text – a before, during, and after a specific event; its first and third sections are comprised predominantly of strong declarative sentences describing a scene of stilled energy that is unsettled, in the piece's middle section, by the physical movement of the narrated protagonist's hand and head.

Even in this tripartite structure, 'Still' retains traces of Beckett's fascination with Geulincx, with life as 'coming hither, acting here, and departing hence'. Yet 'Still' reflects a Geulingian impetus in much more than its tripartite structure of the hand and head coming 'hither' towards each other, being 'here' if only for a moment with each other, before departing 'hence' from each other. Ackerley and Gontarski suggest that the nature of the middle section of 'Still', the movement of the protagonist's arm rising up to meet his head and his head lowering down to meet his arm, action around which the work centres and which disturbs the surface of the first part's declarative stasis, 'constitutes a return to the concerns of Geulincx and the Occasionalists' (Ackerley and Gontarski 2006, p. 543). These Occasionalist 'concerns' are primarily metaphysical in nature, and refer to the metaphysical axiom 'Quod nescis quomodo fiat, id non facis' (*Op*, vol. 2, p. 150 & vol. 3, p. 207)[17] ['What you do not know how to do, is not your action' (*Met*, p. 35)]. The axiom summarizes the unusual epistemological criterion of Geulincx's Occasionalism, described above, which concludes that no one can be said to actually do anything at all, even something as simple as lifting an arm, because they do not how (that is cannot say fully and with reason) how they could possibly do it.

'Still' indeed describes physical movement as an occurrence that is separate from the protagonist thinking about this movement, let alone willing that movement. As the narrative pace is quickened in the transition from the first to the second section of the text, the nameless man's body seemingly moves of its own, or of someone else's, accord; 'this movement impossible to follow let alone describe':

> The right hand slowly opening leaves the armrest taking with it the whole forearm complete with elbow and slowly rises opening further as it goes and turning a little deasil till midway to the head it hesitates and hangs half open trembling in mid air. Hangs there as if half inclined to return that is sink back slowly closing as it goes and turning the other way till as and where it began clenched lightly on end of rest. (*TN*, p. 156)

The man's right hand here takes 'with it' the entire forearm. This right hand has the ability to hesitate, and it can seemingly choose to hang there, deciding on its own to return to the armrest. It is a steady and graceful movement that disturbs the declarative stasis of the text's first part, and in this steadiness the movement contrasts with the body's un-still-able 'trembling all over' (p. 155) of the first part, constituting an opposition of stasis to movement, as well as one of movement to stasis. The arm's graceful movement is described not unlike a budding plant, its 'opening leaves' not only the arm's leaving behind the armrest, but like 'slowly opening' and 'opening further' also do, imparting a pastoral impetus to the movement that echoes both Arsene's contrarian diagnosis in *Watt* – that any budding will inevitably wither – as well as the big world of nature's sun and valley seen through the windows by the protagonist in 'Still''s first part. The scene also carries an echo of a Celtic past in 'deasil', a Scottish (perhaps surprisingly not Irish) Celtic word which the OED defines as meaning 'Righthandwise, towards the right; motion with continuous turning to the right'. The word brings connotations of magic, and of rituals involving people moving clockwise round a sacred stone or a significant building.[18]

The movement of this hand, then, read as a 'return to the concerns of Geulincx and the Occasionalists', can indeed appear to illustrate Occasionalist incapacity. The narrator does not substitute for God, 'the Bastard, he [who] doesn't exist',[19] a farcical astrological backdrop such as Suk's Horoscope of *Murphy*, but with the Celtic interjection (of a word that also appears repeatedly in 'All Strange Away' (1964)) nevertheless brings a hint of otherworldly magic, ritual and witchery to this familiar and realist movement, yet one that 'Still' makes strange.

The fact that Beckett focuses specifically on the movement of a hand, as Geulincx does in *Ethics*, adds further weight to the suggestion that such movement draws upon Beckett's Geulingian interests. As has been seen, Beckett's emphasis on the movement of a hand, arm or body follows examples given in Geulincx's works. Transcriptions from *Metaphysica Vera*, for example, contain the following on the movement of a hand: 'But my hand is moved not at the command of my will, but by consent to it' (*Met*, p. 42). Movement only takes place by a miracle of divine coordination. Thus, one is conjoined to all only when God wills it. This is, of course, what underlies Beckett's description of Geulincx's 'guignol world'.

Intriguingly, however, there is a gulf of difference between the guignol worlds of *Act Without Words 1* and 'Still'. The unfamiliar setting and slapstick music hall knockabout of *Act Without Words 1* – which takes place under the bright light of a blazing sun, using comic props, the man's action directed by sudden and startling whistles – makes way for an interior in 'Still' that resembles Beckett's own old family house at Cooldrinagh, as well as Molloy's destination; his mother's room. The puppet-like movements themselves also differ;

there is slow and steady movement in place of what was rapid and jerky. Pilling notes how in the context of Beckett's developing aesthetics the stasis of 'Still' enacts a simultaneous achievement and reconciliation with earlier authorial aspirations:

> Nothing better illustrates how far Beckett has travelled in forty years of writing than the way he has 'enlivened the last phase of his solipsism' not, as his 'sometime friend' Belacqua did (in *More Pricks than Kicks*, 1934), 'with the belief that the best thing he had to do was to move constantly from place to place', but rather with the belief that the best thing he can do is to keep still. (Pilling 1978, p. 143)

How might such a transition in Beckett's guignol worlds, summarized broadly as one from movement to stasis, from Arsene's tortured 'happy ones' to one alone in a room, be thought of? What can be said about the nature of Beckett's 'return to the concerns' of Occasionalist philosophy in his late work, beyond its echoes of earlier Geulingian themes and allusions? One possible, 'perhaps' answer to these questions reveals an important instance of Beckett's ability to combine different philosophical ideas into a new, entirely coherent aesthetic idiom, and it is an answer that itself recalls Geulincx's multifaceted approach to philosophy.

As discussed above, a musical fantasia can be improvised or semi-improvised, it can continue in a particular vein but it is free to incorporate new elements. A fantasia is unpredictable and foregrounds itself as a malleable and changeable thing. It can encounter something apparently wholly other that itself yet does not need therefore to turn away to continue being itself; it can incorporate what is other as a new version, a changed version, of itself. William Drabkin describes how Beethoven's fantasias would 'both maintain and break with tradition', and points out that certain of these fantasias could incorporate elements previously anathema to them:

> It was in the Fantasia for piano, chorus and orchestra op. 80 (1808) [...] that Beethoven broke most strikingly with tradition by introducing a chorus into a form that had been instrumentally conceived for some 300 years.[20]

The comparison worth making here is between this history of instrument-only composition, and Beckett's own works until the early 1970s. That is, the 'fantasia' involving Geulincx, having laid implicit and dormant at various times up until now, will be reinvigorated by coming into contact with ideas that might seem entirely alien and other, but which in fact turn out to be quite close to Beckett's earlier ideas on Geulincx, and cohere with them to form something new, yet nevertheless something that is also a continuation of a lineage.

What is intriguing in the movement of 'Still''s narrated, what fits the nameless seated man into a 'series' of protagonists that includes the narrator/narrated of *Comment c'est/How It Is* before him, is that similarly to how Pim was a 'dumb limp lump' waiting (even if unwittingly) to be animated into something resembling life, the arm of this narrated too is that of a puppet. If this assertion is accepted, that the arm of 'Still' is in a sense the arm of a puppet, can it be said that this description is wholly accounted for by describing it as 'a return to the concerns of Geulincx and the Occasionalists', even when Beckett's description of Geulincx's 'guignol world' is invoked? Why 'return' to anything like Geulincx or the Occasionalists at all? The answer to these questions, I want to argue, lies with Beckett's 'fantasia' having encountered, only shortly before Beckett wrote 'Still', something that would further modify and temporize it, that was at first sight other than itself. While this other might not be as seemingly alien as Beethoven's chorus was to the previously exclusively instrumental form, it nevertheless altered any further manifestations of a Geulingian 'fantasia' in the remainder of Beckett's oeuvre. Again, it is useful to recall *From an Abandoned Work*'s 'So in some way even olden things each time are first things, no two breaths the same, all a going over and over and all once and never more.' In 'Still' Beckett does just this, combining an 'olden' thing with a new 'first' thing, in order to make something that is at once 'a going over and over' old concerns and that is also 'once and never more'. I want to suggest that it was Beckett's reading Heinrich von Kleist around this time that prompted a 'return' to the concerns of Occasionalism as a concern with puppetry. At least in part, Kleist accounts for the huge differences between the 'guignol world' of an earlier work such as *Act Without Words 1* and that of 'Still'.

Kleist and the 'musicality of gesture'

Beckett's interest in Kleist's famous essay on puppetry and grace was first brought to public attention in Knowlson and Pilling's groundbreaking 1979 collaboration, prior to Knowlson focusing the matter further in his biography of 1996. When Beckett's interest was first reported in 1979 it was with an important caveat:

> If, on the little evidence available, there is no justification for speaking of actual influence, there is much common ground to be explored between Kleist's essay and Beckett's own ways of thinking about art, the theatre and life. (Knowlson and Pilling 1979, p. 277)

More than 30 years on there now appears to be a little more evidence for something that does resemble a complex type of 'influence'. Beckett's interest in puppetry, an interest that betrays a pivotal debt to Geulincx, was revived and intensified following what appears to be a discovery made by Beckett now datable to late 1969, and which resulted from Beckett's relationship with Barbara Bray. It is clear from their correspondence that Bray frequently sent Beckett works to read, and this is what appears to have happened with Kleist. In a letter dated 2 September 1969 (around 13 years into their voluminous correspondence) Beckett mentions what he calls 'grace in the Kleistian sense' (SB to BB, 2 September 1969, TCD MS 10948/1/432), and a month later he wrote 'Got the Kleist Marionetten theater [. . .] and other essays' (SB to BB, 3 October 1969, TCD MS 10948/1/440). Then on 13 October Beckett wrote that he had 'read Kleist's marvellous essay on Marionetten theatre with unforgettable anecdote of duel with bear' (SB to BB, 13 October 1969, TCD MS 10948/1/443). Other evidence indicates this period as Beckett's major phase of thinking about Kleist. Knowlson reveals that in late 1969 Beckett went looking for Kleist's memorial at Wannsee (which he did not find), and not long after the correspondence with Bray in Autumn 1969, Beckett mentioned Kleist on a number of occasions; during rehearsals for *Happy Days* in 1971, at the Schiller-Theater, for example, Beckett was trying to imbue Winnie with an air of something like what he had termed 'grace in the Kleistian sense':

> He was anxious to ensure that all of Winnie's movements should be as crisp, precise and economical as possible. He argued that precision and economy would produce the maximum of grace, quoting Kleist's essay on the Marrionette theatre to reinforce his argument. His aim was to achieve a musicality of gesture as striking as that of voice. (Knowlson 1996, p. 584)

In 1976 Beckett again referred Knowlson as well as Ronald Pickup to Kleist, when he cited the Marrionette essay to 'illustrate what he said about the relations between economy and the grace and harmony that he wanted to see in the movements of the protagonist of *Ghost Trio*' (p. 632).

Kleist's *Über das Marionettentheater* (1810) describes the marionettes of puppet-theatre as embodying a state of grace unattainable in a human world of self-consciousness. In a fictional dialogue between two men in a public park, narrated in the past tense by one of the interlocutors, Kleist uses a number of examples to argue that self-consciousness destroys the possibility of what he calls 'grace'. In one of these examples a 'young acquaintance of mine had lost his innocence before my very eyes' (Kleist 1978, p. 1211): An attractive youth of about 15, who had started to show 'faintly the first traces of vanity, a product of the favour shown him by women', noticed that he resembled a *Spinario* statue in one particular movement he made while putting his foot on a stool.

The youth's interlocutor had apparently just been noting to himself this same resemblance, and the coincidence flattered the youth's burgeoning vanity. Yet as he tried to replicate the movement in the very mirror in which he had originally noticed the similarity, to witness it again, the movements that had once manifested his spontaneous grace became grotesquely comic; his consciousness of the movement prevented him from actually performing that movement again, even as his awareness of it taunted him with its proximity. Consequently, over the following year the boy's attractiveness faded entirely, having owed its existence to a lack of awkward self-consciousness.

A similar story involves the 'fencing bear'. Kleist tells of a bear (a paradigm naturally lacking human self-consciousness) that could fence better than any human because it would never be fooled by its opponent's feints, responding only to genuine thrusts, which it could successfully parry. The encounter is visceral and salutary for the bear's human combatant:

> No human fencer could equal his perception in this respect. He stood upright, his paw raised ready for battle, his eye fixed on mine as if he could read my soul there, and when my thrusts were not meant seriously he did not move. (p. 1212)

According to Kleist, marionettes embody the state of grace that was in the boy before his narcissistic fall, and in the fighting bear that responds only to what is authentically intended. The selfless puppet affirms and enables the state of grace that humanity's self-consciousness prevents.

For Beckett, this conclusion is comparable to and compatible with Geulincx's 'guignol world', a world in which all is puppetry because all is dependent on God. Yet it is also different from Geulincx's thoughts along these lines, and Geulincx and Kleist taken together form something entirely new, something that might productively be termed a philosophical poetics of suffering. According to Geulincx, humanity lacks knowledge of how it is connected to the world around it, yet there is a connection, and it is the work of humanity's 'Pater ineffabilis' (*Op*, vol. 2, p. 188)[21] ['ineffable Father' (*Met*, 97)]. God (as Beckett transcribed from Geulincx's *Metaphysics*) is 'The Author of this union' (p. 94)[22] between humanity and the world, and 'neither we, nor our bodies, nor anything else, can move something without the cooperation of Him who is the author of motion' (p. 94).[23] Any physical movement that I experience is only thanks to God, who uses such movement 'as an instrument to engender various thoughts in our mind' (*Met*, p. 105).[24] These 'thoughts in our mind' are what distinguish Geulincx's puppetry from that of Kleist. Both Kleist and Geulincx's puppets are dependent on an external authority for anything to happen, but with an awareness of their being tied, Geulincx's puppets are subjected to further suffering – that of perceiving their own enslavement. No Kleistian puppet has to suffer such further ignominy. For Kleist, no puppet is capable of attaining this awareness of its own state; it is precisely a lack of such self-awareness – the 'innocence' which the vain youth loses – that brings about the 'grace' of Kleist's puppets as one of blissful ignorance. A Geulingian 'guignol world', therefore, is arguably a much crueler (though better-informed) place than that of the Kleistian puppet-world. Perhaps something like this distinction accounts for Beckett's description of Geulincx's puppet world as specifically 'guignol', a world that is not just playfully puppet-like, but cruel and autocratic; he may have had in mind the Parisian Théâtre du Grand-Guignol, a theatre once famous for its gothic depictions of murder, rape and suicide, its name even becoming shorthand for confrontational, violent performances.[25] Bringing Kleist into proximity with this imagining of puppetry would allow Beckett to conceive a new, unique world of simultaneous grace and horror.

'Still' presents just such a hybridized 'guignol world'. The estranged action in the short, tense piece is not only that of returning, echoing Occasionalist disconnection and the allusions this engenders in earlier works. It is also a newly graceful action, a movement of steady, puppet-like unselfconsciousness that simultaneously enacts 'grace in the Kleistian sense'. The nameless man of 'Still' is one of Beckett's exhausted protagonists. He is almost totally collapsed, not a little 'Corpsed' (*CDW*, p. 20), as Clov describes the world outside the window in *Endgame*, with the text's adjectives underscoring the state: His 'side by side' legs are '*broken* right angles' seen in a '*failing* light'. His 'trunk likewise *dead* plumb', his arms, like his legs, are '*broken* right angles at the elbows' (*TN*, p. 155, all my italics). From this crumpled and half-alive trembling pile a movement arises that is not fully resistance, yet neither is it fully resignation. As one part of his body comes together with another, the extremities with the shell of interiority – the fingers with the head – a circuit is made that visualizes a graceful climax of Beckett's late period works. It is a climax constructed in realist, visual prose, as an image that resembles the pose of Rodin's monument to poetic and philosophical reflection 'The Thinker', and that locates this part of Beckett's late period as a period of imagistic philosophical poetics.[26] Beckett does not, however, rest with this climactic stillness for long. The intensely visual 'Still' makes a sudden change in its final sentence, moving to a 'hence' that veers entirely away from consolations and possibilities of the visual and towards another sense entirely, that of the aural: 'Leave it so all quite still or try listening to the sounds all quite still head in hand listening for a sound' (p. 156). The achievements of philosophical, imagistic pause somewhere between resistance and resignation to the sufferings of a 'guignol world' are, as Krapp eventually realizes of his life's highlights, only momentary and transient. Just as for Geulincx life is a fleeting orbit around a still point, for Beckett in 1972 a finely calibrated stasis cannot be still for long before it must move to becoming something else.

'Chamber Telly' as 'Guignol World': *Ghost Trio* and *Nacht und Träume*[27]

Although Beckett had referred to Kleist while rehearsing *Happy Days* in 1971 in the context of Winnie's 'economy' of movement, it is his reference five years later when rehearsing *Ghost Trio* that more pointedly reveals the late period interests in puppetry, as recorded by Knowlson:

> Beckett applied Kleist's two examples to the figure in *Ghost Trio* as he moves to the window or the door, or looks up from the pallet to the mirror. From the two different kinds of movement in the play, one sustained, economical and flowing, the other abrupt and jerky, as F 'thinks he hears her', it is as if Beckett's figure is poised midway between two worlds. For his 'man in a room' is still, in spite of everything, a creature bound to the world of matter, not quite the still-life figure that at moments he appears to be. Nor is he totally free of self-consciousness, as his look in the mirror indicates, or wholly indifferent to the world of the non-self, as his responses to stimuli from outside or from within his own mind suggest. (Knowlson 1996, p. 633)

In another article on *Ghost Trio* Knowlson makes further parallels between the movements of F and Kleist's puppets, pointing out that the lack of footfalls heard when F walks reflects Kleist's ideas that puppets do not feel, or need to rebel against, the force of gravity. Kleist's argument is that 'puppets need the floor only to touch and enliven the swing of their limbs by momentarily retarding their action'.[28] Similarly, when the bodiless female voice V says of F that he will 'now think he hears her' (*CDW*, p. 410), Knowlson points out of the sudden movements in response, that in 'Beckett's German production, this raising of the hand is even more abrupt and puppet-like than in the BBC version' (Knowlson 1986, pp. 195–6).

An early manuscript version of *Ghost Trio* stipulates that F 'moves bowed through space with no visible propulsion'[29], a direction Ackerley describes as giving 'an incorporeal or immaterial quality to his actions' (Ackerley 2009, p. 144). Such movement is perhaps one reason that F might be considered one of the *Trio* of ghosts (along with V and the briefly appearing boy). This movement of 'no visible propulsion' is also, as well as being ephemeral, a form of Geulingian puppet-like movement. It is the gliding 'grace' of a marionette free of the floor. Consequently, it can be argued that the two types of movement in *Ghost Trio*, the jerky sudden surprise and the premeditated slow and steady repetition that more closely resembles the movement of 'Still', are both puppet-like movements. The protagonist of *Ghost Trio* is confined within the bounds of puppetry even while they might appear to rebel against them, as was also the case for the protagonist of *Act Without Words 1*. As Cohn describes it, there may be a 'cue to rebellion' (Cohn 2001, p. 338) in V's 'Ah!' when F declines her instruction, but as is implied by Knowlson, in whichever of the two types of action F pursues – ghostly steadiness 'with no visible propulsion' or jerky, seemingly spontaneous, rebellion – each is subject to its own kind of limitations. The 'guignol world' of *Ghost Trio*, then, is one in which rebellion too is a form of puppetry. Indeed, it was in order to illustrate just such a thesis of thoroughgoing constraint on rebellion that Geulincx construed the analogy of the slave on the ship that so appealed to Beckett. According to this image, the will of the other might be resisted, but resistance is futile because it is opposed to what is beyond opposition.

Whereas Beckett had considered using Schubert's music in what became *Ghost Trio*,[30] he went further with his final television piece, borrowing the title of a Lied. But this is not the only aspect of *Nacht und Träume* that makes real an idea Beckett had in mind earlier. As Cohn details, a number of the late pieces for television find newly viable forms for earlier matters. Just as '*Quad* successfully negotiated the geometries of the abandoned "J.M. Mime" of 1962, so *Nacht und Träume* successfully enfolds the dream of the abandoned *Mime du rêveur A* of 1954' (Cohn 2001, p. 374). The 1982 work eschews the comedy of the earlier protagonist (A) injecting himself with a 'seringue de sa fesse'[31] [syringe in his buttocks], and clumsily burning himself with a match that is used for seeing and sterilizing the needle. The types of Pavlovian narrative of education as serial punishment that inhere in A's dealings with the match would be utilized two years later in *Act Without Words 1*. *Nacht und Träume* does, however, return to the broader device of staging, here filming, a mime within a mime as a dream (the hypodiegetic dream of 1954's *Mime du rêveur A* remaining unwritten). The fleeting dream-existence in *Nacht und Träume* is this work's 'guignol world', forming as it does another turn in Beckett's Geulingian 'literary fantasia'.

Nacht und Träume brings in from off-screen an aspect of the multifarious off-stage/off-screen identities that in *Act Without Words 1* is the taunting faceless force offering temptations, in *Act Without Words 2* prompts the figures from their slumbering in sacks with a 'goad' (*CDW*, p. 210), and in *Ghost Trio* functions as the dislocated V. In *Nacht und Träume* such a mysterious and 'ineffable' figure manifests as synecdoche, as the hands offering comfort. The hands come into the frame when the protagonist (A) dreams of 'His dreamt self (B)' (p. 465). They place a Benedictine assurance on the brow of the dreamer and wipe his mouth after offering a cup. As A dreams of himself receiving these comforts he gives himself up to a guignol world where his rest, his momentary stasis and stillness, relies on this external authority of a disembodied pair of hands, on something akin to what *Murphy* called 'the friendship of a pair of hands' (*Mu*, p. 10). In one of the most striking puppet-like images in this piece, in Süddeutscher Rundfunk's production when L (the left hand) places itself on B's head and B wakes within the dream, L then moves gently back, fading off-screen, and as it takes itself away from B's head the synchronicity between the removing hand and A's rising head has all the looks of a hand pulling back the puppet-head of B with invisible strings. In the written text the movement is rendered only as 'B raises his head, L withdraws and disappears' (*CDW*, p. 465). Yet on screen, as Knowlson observed of *Geister Trio*, the puppet-like motion is much more pronounced. This invisible force with which L pulls back the head of A has a subtle streak of control that works against the images of benediction.

A remains himself in this dream even though he becomes B. That is, he dreams himself to be the same person he is, someone who is in need of such relief, and as such in his dream he is not truly free of the needs from which he suffers; his self-consciousness persists. In a revealing letter to Reinhart Müller-Freienfels (who had commissioned the play) Beckett responded to a question about whether the dreamer and his dreamt self could be played by two different actors:

> The dreamer's face is virtually invisible. Head resemblance alone is enough. So by all means 2 separate performers for the dreamer and his dreamt self. The more so as he may be supposed to dream himself somewhat other than he is. (SB to Müller-Freienfels, 5 August 1982)[32]

The dreamer's dreamt self could appear different, but not entirely distinct. He must be a version of himself in his moment of relief. Even though he is *stilled*, paused in one of Beckett's fleeting 'moments' for comfort, he is *still* himself needing this relief conveyed through the hands. As was the case with the off-screen authority in *Ghost Trio*, in *Nacht und Träume* this is a thoroughgoing authority; it does not offer substantial relief from the state of affairs in which it is needed, instead it gives only further dependence on temporary moments of relief.

Grayley Herren argues, as does Ulrika Maude, for the centrality of *Nacht und Träume*'s technological aspects in any critical assessment of it. Herren names these technological aspects the play's 'formal tensions', a move similar to Albright's, who describes Beckett's exploration of the limits of a particular mode of technology as his 'extraordinary doting on technique' (Albright 2003, p. 3). Herren writes that '*Nacht und Träume*'s formal tensions undermine its superficial harmonies, offering the manipulative powers of art as the only enduring consolation' (Herren 2000, p. 186). Herren points out that the dream in *Nacht und Träume* happens when called to happen by A. B is thereby, according to Herren, an artistic creation of A. Herren's conclusion is also similar to Albright's: the artistic act of making rather than anything resulting from this redeems the doomed attempt to make. Yet perhaps such a conclusion is a little too consolatory.

A 'guignol world' as a place of self-created temporary restfulness, of momentary stillness, such as is dreamt by A in *Nacht und Träume*, brings us back to *Murphy*. For Murphy also sought, by surrendering himself to, temporary relief in a trance-like version and vision of himself. For both Murphy and A, for the former explicitly so and for the latter implicitly, Geulincx's ethical Occasionalism is 'not enough' as a means of finding a freedom that is not also dependence and subservience. This is the truer 'manipulative' component of A's dreaming of B. B has a powerful hold over A such that A is a puppet of B; B is the product not of A's freedom, but rather of his enslavement. However, B in his turn is the puppet of the disembodied hands. *Nacht und Träume*, then, far from offering a play of consolation and transcendent religious relief, however temporary, implicates a series of dependence and subservience that produces a 'guignol world' not unlike that of the brutal series in *Comment c'est/How It Is*.

Geulincx might, therefore, be 'not enough' at the end of Beckett's oeuvre as at its beginning, but for one so focused on failure and incapacity, the possibilities that are enabled by a figure who is 'not enough' constituted, for Beckett, a deep wellspring from which to draw repeatedly.

Conclusion

It is fitting that the end of Beckett's 'literary fantasia' is reached with a discussion of explicitly musical works, *Ghost Trio* and *Nacht und Träume*. Beckett told Harvey that 'painting and music have so much better a chance' (Harvey 1970, p. 249) than his own or anyone else's writing in one of a number of places where he pointed to the importance of music for literature, and readers should be alert to the viability of vocabularies deriving from these different arts brought to bear on his texts. The 'fantasia' that has been traced in the current book must necessarily be seen with some hindsight, deriving as it does from a term presumably not intended by Beckett as a description of his extant works beyond the year in which he uttered the phrase – 1936 – whether or not he had ever meant it to apply to the rumoured monograph for Coffey. Yet it is more than an easy convenience that this musical term should be co-opted into a discussion of Beckett's oeuvre. The term 'fantasia', connotative of fantasy and unrestrained mutability, so immediately alien to Beckett's stark, minimal and tightly controlled texts, nonetheless allows a critical tracking and tracing of changes, incorporations and Beckett's progressive vision that brings Geulincx as a single line of influence and confluence among many clearly into view. In turn, this line brings broader patterns, trajectories of continuation and discontinuation across Beckett's works into view, giving a particular historical rootedness to the sense that these works can be read as a serial development, as the 'series' he pointed to.

There was never any reason to expect, in a body of work so altered as Beckett's between 1936 and 1982, that Geulincx would be a fixed and stable point of reference. The foregoing readings stay close to the different and diverse identifiable moments at which Geulincx breaks to the surface of Beckett's often strict and unyielding prose, revealing also latent, though sometimes explicit, presences in works well beyond what is traditionally thought of as 'the most Geulincxian of the works', *Murphy*. Yet throughout these multifarious, reasserted recurrences Geulincx in Beckett's works retains something of a residue of freedom memorialized, conveying a sense of limited freedom that is simultaneously etched into the memory while it is also dead and buried. Thus it is what I have called, with reference to the pockets and their contents belonging to the narrator of *La Fin/The End*, en-graved.

Geulincx provides a way of reading across the shifting 'series' that maps the contours of a determinedly changeable aesthetic, while never requiring such a route through the Beckett Country to become a definitive, neat, single pathway. While the 'moments' at which Geulincx's presence is asserted predominantly relate to differing conceptions of constrained freedom, the foregoing analyses also point to those moments at which the residual, remembered presences complicate or confound a neat reading with which one might, with hindsight, fix Beckett as working through and then beyond the struggles he determinedly set himself as a young man. In a body of work so concerned with memory, obligation and frustrated or entropic attempts at kinds of emancipation, the memorialized presence of one who promised such a strange and complex formulation of freedom is deferred to at the same time as it is critiqued even in Beckett's very late years. Geulincx's presence remains beyond Beckett's great realization that 'all I am is feeling'[1] to become one of few philosophical figures of feeling in the middle to later period works. In Geulingian parlance, therefore, he is a figure of both affection and *obligatione*.

There is also little surprise in the fact that Beckett was so drawn to the imagery of the slave on the ship. Not only is the galley-man an analogy serving both metaphysics and ethics that encapsulates the complexities of a strand of seventeenth-century Occasionalist philosophy in a neatly balanced image to accommodate the neatly balanced axiom, he also functions as an image of the creative act itself as one of momentary relief, futile yet determined. As Geulincx wrote and Beckett transcribed, 'Every analogy is lame' (*Et*, p. 323) (even though 'lame' is itself arguably metaphorical). Nevertheless, Beckett also used an analogy to describe the artistic will to 'go on' that mirrors the constrained freedom of the slave on board the ship:

> 'What do you do,' Beckett once asked, 'when "I can't" meets "I must"'; and he compared himself to a man 'on his knees, head against the wall – more like a cliff – with someone saying "go on" – Well, the wall will have to move a little, that's all.' (Cited in Graver and Federman (eds) 1979, p. 29)

For Geulincx 'I can't' also meets 'I must'. While the ethical axiom counsels abstention, his pragmatic realization was also that one must act in the world even if one cannot. When the then struggling to become known writer encountered the little-known philosopher in 1936 the kinship and admiration Beckett felt is palpable in his correspondence. His moving away from thoroughgoing enthusiasm and indebtedness over the following decades was itself only a matter of going so far within limited bounds, within self-imposed constraints. The difficulties and necessities of this manoeuvring produce Beckett's 'literary fantasia' as itself a philosophical and ethical manoeuvring that is characterized by both incapacity and obligation that speaks of both 'I can't' as well as 'I must'.

Geulincx is, of course, far from being the only philosopher whom Beckett variously employed and deployed in ways that go beyond how that philosopher might have been willing to sanction. To return to the thinker whom Beckett sets up in collaboration and contrast with Geulincx, the pre-Socratic atomist Democritus is his figure of 'the laughing philosopher', for example, as he also was for Horace.[2] Directed at pretensions to immortality, Democritus's mythological–poetic laugh is a response to the realization that the body and soul are made of an infinite number of atoms that move eternally in a void, a void as real as the atoms therein, and all things thereby constituted will eventually completely disintegrate (as Arsene also describes). Atoms themselves are eternal, yet the objects they constitute are not. The Democritean laugh is a laugh of indifference towards manifest atomic impermanence, and by extension it is directed towards any attachment in the world whatsoever. For attachments, happy or unhappy, are fleeting and illusory. For Beckett it served as one of the ways by which he might bring comedy and tragedy together. Thus the mirthless last laugh of *Watt*:

> It is the laugh of laughs, the *risus purus*, the laugh laughing at the laugh, the beholding, the saluting of the highest joke, in a word the laugh that laughs – silence please – at that which is unhappy.

It is the 'dianoetic laugh, down the snout' (*W*, p. 40) that corresponds to a third and final stage of 'successive excoriations of the understanding' (p. 39) that so many other of Beckett's characters either attempt or achieve, in various different ways. In 'Yellow', for example, Belacqua braces himself for his operation and makes panicked recourse to Democritus. He cannot settle on the question 'Was it to be laughter or tears?' (*MPTK*, p. 155) and a little phrase-bomb comes to him in his near dark:

> *Now among our wise men, I doubt not but many would be found, who would laugh at Heraclitus weeping, none which would weep at Democritus laughing.* This was a godsend and no error. Not the phrase as a judgement, but its terms, the extremes of wisdom that it tendered to Belacqua. (pp. 154–5)

The phrase is revolved for observation similarly to how with 'a phrase in Hardy's *Tess*, won by dint of cogging in the Synod' (the phrase that is '*When grief ceases to be speculative, sleep sees her opportunity*'), Belacqua had 'manipulated that sentence for years now, emending its terms, as joy for grief, to answer his occasions' (p. 151). Much as Belacqua variously consoles himself with Donne, Democritus and Hardy, similarly Beckett with Geulincx. That is, with a commitment evident from his early years onwards to 'extremes of wisdom'; extremes that are not of transcendental mysticism or rationalism, or even the two come together, but instead as manifested in the structuring possibilities of syntax, of philosophical language and imagistic residues in poetic performance.

Beckett's literary laughing philosopher certainly diverges from the Democritus bequeathed to scientific history. Opinions of Democritus's atomism and conceptions of nothingness have come a long way since fellow Abderites judged him insane, and his work in the meantime has come to be seen by a number of scientists as the initiation of a project that is only now coming to fruition in contemporary particle physics. As Erwin Schrödinger wrote:

> Matter is constituted of particles, separated by comparatively large distances; it is embedded in empty space. This notion goes back to Leucippus and Democritus, who lived in Abdera in the fifth century B.C. This conception of particles and empty space [. . .] is retained today [. . .] and not only that, there is complete historical continuity. (Schrödinger 1996, p. 117)

Writing on Democritus, Paul Cartledge disputes this continuity, citing the splitting of the atom in 1932 (around the time Beckett was making his extensive notes on Democritus) as rather 'the crucial *dis*continuity' (Cartledge 1998, p. 3): Democritus theorized atoms as whole and unbreakable, as the smallest constituents, whereas manifestly they can be split. Ancient atomism also does not endear itself to some modern physicists by extending its theory to encompass notions of soul. This latter move, Schrödinger writes, 'was sad, because it was bound to repel the finest and deepest thinkers' of later periods, condemning Democritus's theory 'to become a "sleeping beauty" for so many centuries' (Schrödinger 1996, p. 76).

Geulincx addresses Democritus explicitly in *Ethics* a number of times, referring to his atomist void as a 'bottomless well' (*Et*, p. 20) that is categorically 'not even consistent with Reason, let alone incumbent on us under Holy Scripture' (p. 90). Yet there is also a historical line of continuity between the two philosophers, a link made by Descartes with the introduction of atomism into modern science. Schrödinger again writes lucidly on the subject, pointing to the determinism deriving from a particular reading of Democritean atomism as something that Descartes would seek to address:

> [Democritus] admitted
>
> (a) that the behaviour of *all* the atoms inside a living body was determined by the physical laws of Nature [. . .].
>
> [I]f you admit (*a*), the motion of your body is predetermined and you fail to account for your sensation that you may move it at will, whatever you may think about the mind. (Schrödinger 1996, p. 80)

While Beckett's 'literary fantasia' of philosophical, ethical form and influence is, I have argued, very much in opposition to a 'fach' system of 'right or wrong', it is nevertheless important to point out that it does also follow certain contours in more widely accepted philosophical and scientific history. Beckett's 'series' is very much his own, and derives from his 'extremes of wisdom' as textual structure, but it also finds its ways along routes more widely travelled, without drawing overt attention to such lineages.

A study that traces a single line of influence through Beckett's complex, interleaved oeuvre cannot hope to give an exhaustive account of the fullness of that oeuvre. But as Beckett himself wrote in his very first published work, 'Literary criticism is not book-keeping' (*Dis*, p. 19). What such a study can achieve, however, is a proper appraisal of this single line as it persists through the oeuvre. Taking Beckett at his word when it comes to assessments or descriptions of his own work can be a fraught process, but the foregoing analysis of Beckett's fascinations with and recourses to Geulincx seeks to provide a way in which philosophy in Beckett might be tracked and traced that simultaneously pays due attention to all the evidence available, to that which is textual, published, as well as that from the greyer canon of contextual correspondence and draft versions. Geulincx was an idiosyncratic figure of philosophy when he was alive, and he was an idiosyncratic interest of Beckett's. Yet he has come to hold a vital position in philosophical studies of Beckett, and if our full assessment of their relationship is to move beyond the all-too-overtly philosophical as well as the all-too-easy reliance on throwaway remarks and asides by Beckett, then the philosophical and the archival might be brought somewhat closer together through the main true object of both approaches – Beckett's texts themselves; that is, through attentive close reading.

Thanks to Beckett's interest, Geulincx's importance to philosophical and literary histories is even now extending across borders and languages. The *Ethics* of 2006, as well as *Metaphysics* (1999), have been of invaluable use to this study. A French translation of *Ethica* (by Hélène Bah-Ostrowiecki) was published by Brepols in 2010, and Beckett's notes to *Ethica*, along with those to *Metaphysica Vera* and to *Quaestiones Quodlibeticae* are also being translated with a collection of essays on Beckett's interests in Geulincx to be published by Les Solitaires Intempestifs in 2012. One wonders what Geulincx himself would make of the twenty-first century's sideways revival of his philosophy, and this being owed predominantly to the singular literature of Samuel Beckett. There seems something of a friendship across centuries between the two thinkers, an ethical and obligated relationship to which Beckett (as the only one of the two who could) repeatedly returned.

Sustaining a full-length study of Geulincx's importance for Beckett's work is not the same as claiming that the full length of Beckett's work is sustained by Geulincx's importance. Nevertheless, such a study does allow surprising trajectories to come into view, and sheds new light on the familiar routes. Geulincx's importance to Beckett's oeuvre can hopefully now be seen in a fuller light, and in turn future philosophical studies of Beckett – as well as of other modern writers – might find some use in such a reading. For Geulincx, as for Beckett, letting go is the most difficult but most necessary act. A study that explores Geulincx's significance for Beckett's work might perhaps be forgiven for holding Geulincx fairly close, but it must also admit that he needs to be let go. Beckett only ever claimed that Geulincx was a point 'of departure' for a study of his work, not that the philosopher promised a point of neat or complete closure or arrival. This study is one among many that hopes to bring some scholarly insight to Beckett's works, and with *humilitas* it must also offer itself for consideration in consultation with others.

Notes

Prelims

[1] The 'Philosophy Notes' are undated. See Frost and Maxwell (2006, pp. 67–89) for an attempt to date the bulk of the work to 1932 as well as for detailed descriptions of the notes themselves.
[2] Cited in Feldman (2006, p. 7).
[3] Malraux (2009, p. 243). See Malraux (1968, p. 232) for the French original.
[4] Cited in Frost and Maxwell (2006, p. 145).
[5] See Pilling (2006a, p. 58).

Introduction

[1] Cited in Frost and Maxwell (2006, p. 144).
[2] See Mintz (1959). Samuel Mintz's article laid much of the groundwork for future study of Beckett's relationship with Geulincx in an argument focused on Murphy's adopted farce of astrology. Murphy is, according to Mintz, 'committed to a method of determination outside the scope of theism' (Mintz 1959, p. 160), and is thereby, as David Hesla called him in 1971 in a description C. J. Ackerley cited in 2004, 'an Occasionalist without at the same time being a Deist' (Ackerley 2004a, p. 122).
[3] See Kenner (1961, pp. 83–96). Hugh Kenner wrote of Geulincx that what 'qualifies him for repeated mention in the Beckett canon, is not simply the ceremonious resignation of his prose, but the curious doctrine it serves. It is the doctrine of a "bodytight" mental world' (Kenner 1961, p. 83). Kenner points to the 'strange detachment' (p. 84) Beckett's protagonists live with between their bodies and their minds, all of them also well aware that these parts are somehow bound together. Kenner goes on to argue that themes of congruence and disconnection in Beckett's work more broadly owe a debt to Geulincx. Kenner's arguments are addressed in detail in Chapter 3.
[4] See Mintz (1959); Kenner (1961, pp. 83–96); Hesla (1971, pp. 30–41); Pilling (1979, pp. 114–16); Dobrez (1986, pp. 12–74); Wood (1993); Ackerley (2004); Weller (2005, pp. 74–93, 2010); Uhlmann (2004, 2006a, 2006b, pp. 65–113); Casanova (2006, pp. 59–74); Feldman (2006, 2009a).
[5] The second of the three works by Geulincx from which Beckett took notes (*Metaphysica Vera*) was translated into English as *Metaphysics* in 1999.

6 In 2012 a new and authorised French translation of Beckett's Geulincx transcriptions will be published, following French translation of *Ethica* in 2010. See Geulincx (2010) and Doutey (ed.) (2012).
7 They are, of course, not to be entirely blamed for this. As is detailed in Chapter 1, written occurrences of his name vary greatly even within single editions. *The Dictionary of Seventeenth and Eighteenth-Century Dutch Philosophers* notes spellings of 'Arnold (or Arnout) Geulincx: Geulinx, Geulings, Geulincs, Geulingius, Geulingh' (van Bunge et al. (eds) 2003, p. 322). H. J. de Vleeschauwer also offers 'an older form of the name, Aernout' (de Vleeschauwer 1957, p. 13). Land clarifies the pronunciation of the name in a paper outlining his 14 years of research that led to the collected edition of 1891–3, published just prior to that edition, where he helpfully points out 'the *eu* is pronounced as *oe*' (Land 1891, p. 224).
8 Bair offers little textual evidence for this claim and underestimates how long *Murphy*'s composition took.

Chapter 1

1 Brian Cooney and de Vleeschauwer are among a minority of critics who consider Geulincx's Occasionalism not to be the nucleus of his thought, despite this being the epithet posterity has bestowed. See Cooney (1978) and de Vleeschauwer (1957, pp. 14–23).
2 Among whom the philosopher Abū al-Ghazālī (1058–1111) is well known as a precedent for seventeenth-century Occasionalist thought (even though it is more demonstrable that Malebranche was familiar with this period of philosophical history than Geulincx was). Al-Ghazālī was a Sunni and an important member of the Asherite school of early Muslim philosophy. His most famous works (among his more than 70) include *The Incoherence of the Philosophers* and his autobiography *The Deliverance from Error*. See also Fakhry (1958).
3 This effort to suppress Geulincx came from his previously loyal admirer, Ruardas Andala (1665–1727). As a supporter of Geulincx's work at the height of its popularity towards the end of the seventeenth century, Andala had championed it precisely as an antidote to the perceived atheism of Spinoza. However, Andala came to believe himself duped and he accused Geulincx of 'having fallen into the "sin" of Spinozism' (Nadler 1999a, p. 165). There followed what de Vleeschauwer describes as 'an unbroken stream of polemical writings [in which Andala] fought against the long dead Geulinx [sic] so bitterly, that one would say it was a luring and personal foe against whom he was writing' (de Vleeschauwer 1957, p. 25). Andala was an influential figure, and in turn others also came to regard Geulincx as one of the 'Spinozizing pseudo-philosophers' (Lange 1727, cited by van Ruler 2006, p. 93). For a survey of the sustained attacks against Geulincx's posthumously published work, their shortcomings as well as effectiveness, see de Vleeshauwer (1957).
4 See Nussbaum (2001).
5 See Cottingham (1998).

6. On these confluences see, for example, Uhlmann (2006a, p. 99, *Et*, p. xxviii), Garrett (1996, pp. 269–72) and Aalderink (2006). For discussion of specific textual congruencies between Geulincx and Spinoza see van Ruler (2006, pp. 94–9), where evidence for the hypothesis of Geulincx's direct influence on Spinoza is weighed against that for a broader theoretical confluence and context. Refusing to settle on easy comparisons, van Ruler describes how 'it is hard to prove anything with respect to possible connections between Geulincx and Spinoza' (van Ruler 2006, p. 98), and concludes that 'the only thing that can be established with any certainty is that Spinoza had formulated most of his ideas before Geulincx had published his' (p. 99).

7. Many of Geulincx's other *Quaestiones* are somewhat less grand. As Land details, they include 'whether riches, or the poverty usual in his state, is most profitable to a scholar; whether women should be admitted to philosophical discourses; whether it becomes well-behaved youths always to dress in the fashion; whether it is advisable to set good liquor before friends who come to pay you a visit' (Land 1891, p. 225). *Quaestiones Quodlibeticae* has never been published in an English translation. All translations from *Quaestiones Quodlibeticae* in this book are by Dr Anna Castriota. They were originally produced for Matthew Feldman as an appendix to his unpublished PhD thesis, *Sourcing Aporetics: An Empirical Study on Philosophical Influences in the Development of Samuel Beckett's Writing* (Oxford Brookes University, 2004). I am grateful to Castriota and Feldman for permission to cite them here.

8. It cannot be verified that the marriage to Susanna was a main cause of Geulincx being removed from office, as the meeting in which the decision was made to eject him was conducted in camera. However, a number of commentators have pointed to the possibility of the familial marriage as a cause of his sudden fall from grace. See Land (1891, pp. 227–8) for an investigation of this and a summary of further commentators' views. Land describes Susanna as Geulincx's cousin, while van Bunge et al. call her his niece (see van Bunge et al. (eds) 2003, p. 324).

9. Land speculates, following Jean Noël Paquot, that Geulincx may have had property confiscated to pay debts. See Land (1891, p. 228) and Paquot (1768, pp. 69–73).

10. A letter of unknown authorship but most likely by Heidanus and two colleagues (Johannes Coccejus (1603–69) and Johannes Hoornbeek (1617–66)) survives, which recommends Geulincx for the position at Leyden. See A. Eekhof, 'De Wijgeer Arnoldus Geulincx te Leuven en te Leiden', *Nederlandish Archief voor Kerkgeschiedenis*, new series, no. 15 (1919), pp. 1–24 (the letter is on pp. 18–20).

11. There is no mention of their children in accounts of money (which remained unpaid) left to Susanna upon her husband's death, so Land infers that they too succumbed to the disease.

12. Where the terms 'body' or 'bodies' are of course taken to mean both inanimate objects and living 'bodies'.

13. See, for example, Bardout (2002, pp. 140–8) for discussion of La Forge and Cordemoy's Cartesian inheritance as deriving principally from physics.

14. Cf., *Op*, vol. 2, p. 147.

[15] Cf., *Op*, vol. 2, p. 148.
[16] Cf. TCD MS 10971/6/14v and TCD MS 10971/6/35 (*Ethica*, where is it transcribed 'Quod nescis quomodo fiat, non facis').
[17] For discussion of how such a paradigm of volitional agency has precedents in medieval Aristotelians, see Nadler (1999b, pp. 270–1).
[18] Geulincx writes, for instance, 'I call that body mine [. . .] by whose occasion diverse thoughts arise in my mind that do not depend on me' (*Met*, p. 41). Cf. TCD MS 10971/6/2v and *Op*, vol. 2, p. 154.
[19] Cf. TCD MS 10971/6/3r, and *Op*, vol. 2, p. 155.
[20] Ackerley and Gontarski point out that Beckett was even unknowingly also demonstrating just how much it was the shape of an idea that matters over and above its place in a history of ideas by misremembering the author of the phrase as St Augustine, when it is from Robert Greene's *The Repentance of Robert Greene*. In *Repentance* Greene does, however, give the source of the 'golden sentence' (Greene 1592, p. 9) as St Augustine. The phrase also appears in Beckett's 'Whoroscope' Notebook of the 1930s, where it is rendered as 'Never despair (1 thief saved)/nor presume (only 1 saved)' (cited in Ackerley and Gontarski 2006, p. 593).
[21] See the letter to Sighle Kennedy, 14 June 1967.
[22] Cf. *Op*, vol. 3, p. 30.
[23] Ackerley describes Beckett's annotation of these notes by claiming that 'Beckett added in annoyance: "What anthropologism!"' (Ackerley 2005a, p. 97). This assessment of the interpolation, while quite possibly accurate, does not tell the whole story. Beckett's addition merely modifies Windelband's own description of Occasionalism's inheritance of a Cartesian dualist ontology, illustrated via the synchronized clocks: 'This *anthropological* rationale of *Occasionalism* fits from the beginning into a more general metaphysical course of thought' (Windelband 1901, p. 416, italics are Windelband's).
[24] This major controversy, which lasted around 3 years and risked miring Leibniz's prestigious reputation in accusations of plagiarism, followed the work of 'an unknown private scholar, Berthold' (de Vleeschauwer 1957, p. 45), who discovered that Leibniz's famous simile of the synchronized clocks as an illustration of pre-established harmony bore a suspicious resemblance to Geulincx's lesser-known and earlier use of precisely this same image. For more on this, see de Lattre (1970, pp. 553–66) and de Vleeschauwer (1957, pp. 45–56).
[25] Cf. Windelband 1901, p. 417, n. 2.
[26] TCD MS 10971/6/1r.
[27] TCD MS 10971/6/2r-6v.
[28] TCD MS 10971/6/7r-36r.
[29] 162 x 200 mm.
[30] 203 x 329 mm.
[31] 203 x 329 mm.
[32] See *Et*, pp. 306–9, and Frost and Maxwell (2006, pp. 141–7).
[33] There is an overlap of two sides of material which survives as typescript at the end of the second fair copy and as handwritten notes at the beginning of the manuscript.

34 Cited in Frost and Maxwell (2006, p. 145).
35 Beckett also moved paragraphs that originally appear at the end of sections to the beginnings. Uhlmann describes Beckett's paragraph alterations clearly, and I quote him here: 'In Geulincx, and in Beckett's first fair copy, the Argument to a given heading (which summarizes what is discussed under that heading) is given at the end of the Annotations to that Number. In the second fair copy Beckett moves all of these Arguments to the top of each section, under the relevant headings. This, no doubt, allowed for easier reference' (*Et*, p. 308).
36 Cf. *Et*, p. 322. This quotation is from the first fair copy of Beckett's notes, although the editors of *Ethics* assert that they are using the second fair copy as the basis for their transcription of Beckett's notes. The minor anomaly is perhaps intentional; in the second fair copy Beckett abbreviated his interjection as 'G's fictitious apostrophee, virtuous but hasty' (TCD MS 10971/6/21r).
37 See *L1*, p. 109.
38 See Pilling (2006a, pp. 50–5).
39 We can be sure that Beckett did indeed consult *Opera*, as this is the only edition in which *Quaestiones Quodlibeticae* has been published.
40 See Pilling (1995) for further details of Beckett's uses of and expertise in Latin after his time at TCD. John Pilling divides Beckett's uses of Latin into three areas: 'i) familiar utilitarian phrases; proverbs of no known specific origin; maxims and apophthegms (what *Dream of Fair to Middling Women* calls "the tag and the ready made"); ii) actual quotations from known and identifiable sources; deliberate misquotations from these sources; quotations and/or misquotations from memory, or from other sources; iii) interesting individual instances of learned vocabulary, or what Dr. Johnson in his *Idler* paper on them (no. 70) called "hard words" ' (Pilling 1995, p. 7). Pilling also provides citations for occurrences in Beckett's prose and his notebooks of further reading in Latin (Horace, Spinoza, Bacon, Kempis and extracts from Burton's *Anatomy of Melancholy*).
41 Cited in Frost and Maxwell (2006, p. 144).
42 See Knowlson (1996, pp. 47–51).
43 A decision made ignominiously official in a telegram sent to TCD from Germany in January 1932. See Knowlson (1996, p. 145).
44 The bulk of Coffey's own collected correspondence, held at the University of Delaware, begins in 1974, and the few surviving earlier letters have no bearing on the issue. These earlier letters, acquired for Delaware's 'Coffey papers' collection as a supplement to the main collection, do date from the 1930s, yet they are mostly new year greeting postcards and none make any reference to a monograph series, or to Geulincx.
45 Nixon in private correspondence, January 2009.
46 When Beckett confessed to MacGreevy that he 'had tried it in vain in English' (SB to TM, 19 August 1936, cited in Knowlson (1996, p. 219)) after Coffey's enthusing about Spinoza, Coffey lent Beckett French editions of Spinoza's works and critical commentary. Beckett tantalizingly said of this further reading 'He lent me Brunchwiff's Spinoza et ses Contemporains, the Ethica in the Classiques Garnier with Latin en regard, of which I have had time only for enough to give me a glimpse of Spinoza as a solution & a salvation (impossible in English

translation)' (SB to TM, 19 September 1936: *L1*, pp. 370–1) [the correct spelling is Brunschvicg]. This cliff-hanger (though he may be alluding to Coffey's thoughts on Spinoza rather than describing his own) came to an unenlightening conclusion in a further letter from Beckett to Ussher in 1938 where Beckett writes 'I cannot see anyone throwing much light on Spinoza except Spinoza' (SB to AU, 6 April 1938, cited in Knowlson (1996, p. 746 n. 127)). A number of scholars have, however, read Spinoza's influence on Beckett as substantial. See, for example, O'Hara (1981), Murphy (1994, pp. 222–39) and Dowd (2007, pp. 77–82).

[47] www.oxfordmusiconline.com. Last accessed 1 May 2011.

[48] For details of specific musical fantasias that Beckett saw performed see *L1*, for example, p. 142 ('Flight of the Bumble Bee' by Nikolai Andreyevich Rimsky-Korsakov), and p. 173 (Liszt's 'Après une lecture du Dante, fantasia quasi sonata').

[49] Beckett also used the word 'fantasia' in the seventh of the *Textes pour rien*, where it appears in the context of memory and near the word 'occasion'. It is translated later as 'riot'. Beckett writes 'j'appelle ça délices, je parle de délices, au lieu de profiter de l'occasion, elle ne reviendra pas de sitôt, si j'ai bonne mémoire, mais elle reviendra, c'est ma consolation, avec sa fantasia d'instants' (Beckett 1955, p. 176). In English this becomes 'I call that revelling, now's my chance and I talk of revelling, it won't come back in a hurry if I remember right, but come back it must with its riot of instants' (*TN*, p. 29).

[50] Beckett appears to have forgotten that he mentioned these difficulties of locating Geulincx at the National Library to MacGreevy a week earlier.

[51] Malraux (2009, p. 243). See Malraux (1968, p. 232) for the French original.

[52] See, for example, Ackerley and Gontarski (2006, p. 50) for a summary of Berkeleyan resonances in other of Beckett's works.

[53] *Endgame*'s Hamm, for example, is blind, his eyes having 'gone all white' (*CDW*, p. 94), as is A in *Rough for Theatre 1*. Both protagonists rely instead on variously wheeled contraptions and a bullied collaborator. In what might be read as a later visceral critique of the visionary capacities of a sightless seer, the narrator of *The Unnamable* is unable to determine if their eye sockets are weeping or perhaps leaking 'liquefied brain' (*U*, p. 3).

[54] See Ackerley and Gontarski (2006, pp. 251–2) for more on Becket utilizing these ideas from Heraclitus.

[55] Telephus is also mentioned at the beginning of *Proust*, where Beckett writes that 'In Proust each spear may be a spear of Telephus', his illustration of the 'Proustian equation' imagined as 'that double-headed monster of damnation and salvation – Time' (*Pr*, p. 11).

[56] Cited in Frost and Maxwell (2006, p. 145).

[57] Duthuit (who was Henri Matisse's son-in-law) edited the English-language French publication *transition* after 1947 (taking over from Eugene Jolas), and corresponded in detail with Beckett. According to Knowlson, 'over the period from 1948 to 1952, [Duthuit] seems to have taken on Tom MacGreevy's role as Beckett's main confidant' (Knowlson 1996, p. 371). Their collaborative

Notes

58 See TCD MS 10971/6/2r, and below.
59 SB to GD, 9 March 1949. Cited in Gontarski and Uhlmann (eds) (2006, p. 19). Translated from 'se livre de temps en temps à une petite séance d'autologie, avec un bruit goulu de succion' (p. 16).
60 The *OED* cites first use of the word in 1633 by Phineas Fletcher: 'He that would learn Theologie must first study autologie. The way to God is by our selves'.
61 See also Uhlmann (1999, p. 54 and 2006a, p. 78). Franzen had not understood how the image of someone crawling within a boat's limited bounds could convey 'grosse Freiheit für jemanden' ['great freedom for someone'].
62 Hutchinson, a member of the Bloomsbury group, published a book of short stories and essays in 1927 entitled *Fugitive Pieces*. See Pilling (2006a, p. 235).
63 'Par quel bout le prendre' ['where to start'].
64 Colloquial French use of 'guignol' is as an insult, despite the fact that Guignol himself is witty and tends to triumph over adverse circumstances. The puppet was designed as a peasant figure intended to represent provincial men from the Daupiné region, likely by the puppet-master Laurent Mourguet (1769–1844). The name was later used by the Théâtre du Grand-Guignol, founded in 1897, a company that specialized in depicting gothic murder, rape and suicide.
65 Cited in Tucker (2011, p. 184).
66 Cited in Kennedy (1971, p. 302).
67 I would like to express my gratitude to Mark Nixon and Dirk Van Hulle for their permission to cite this marginalia from *A New Theory of Vision, and Other Writings*, deriving as it does from their forthcoming publication on Beckett's Paris library (Cambridge University Press). Beckett had been reading other works by Berkeley in 1933, and it is therefore arguable that 'Against Geulincx' is a response to the Geulincx of the 'Philosophy Notes'. In 1933 the Irish critic and biographer Joseph Hone (1882–1959) gave Beckett a copy of Berkeley's *Commonplace Book*, 'which is full of profound things, and at the same time of a foul (& false) intellectual canaillerie, enough to put you against reading anything more' (SB to TM, 23 April 1933: *L1*, p. 154).

Chapter 2

1 Cited in Beckett (1999a, p. xiii). See also Nixon (2011, pp. 100–10) on Beckett's 'notesnatching'.
2 Beckett in interview with Knowlson, 27 October 1989. Cited in Knowlson (1996, p. 105).
3 Knowlson viewed the manuscript for financial valuation and verification purposes.
4 See Knowlson (1996, p. 203).
5 See SB to Sergei Eisenstein (2 March 1936: *L1*, p. 317).
6 See Ackerley (2004, pp. 116–25). In a letter to MacGreevy a few days after Jung's lecture (the same letter in which he reported having written about 20,000

words of *Murphy*) Beckett described the presentation in which Jung had shown a tripartite diagram of the mind, and how in response to questions following the lecture (transcribed along with the lecture itself in a published record of the series) Jung had discussed the case of the girl who had 'never been born entirely' (Jung 1982, p. 107), a case that also finds its way into *Watt*'s addenda.

[7] See Ackerley (2004, pp. 208–9) and *Mu*, p. 167.

[8] See Uhlmann (2006a, pp. 78–85).

[9] See *Et* (pp. 332, 340), corresponding to TCD MS 10971/6/15v (first fair copy), TCD MS 10971/6/22 and TCD MS 10971/6/26 (second fair copy).

[10] The question of the extent to which Murphy is responsible for his own death is not a clear one and a number of critics have adduced various solutions. Rubin Rabinovitz proposes Cooper as perpetrator (See Rabinovitz 1984, pp. 113–18), while Ackerley proposes (with due qualifications) Ticklepenny. Others assume Murphy himself. There is one clear-cut case of suicide in the novel: the Old Boy's throat is cut by his own cut-throat razor for no better reason than, according to Ackerley and Gontarski, to cut his throat follows from the nature of his object (see Ackerley and Gontarski 2006, p. 546). When it comes to the opinions of characters within the novel, 'a classical case of misadventure' (*Mu*, p. 164) is the coroner's vague (and vaguely literary) diagnosis, which fittingly un-resolves the issue. Beckett wrote in a letter of 1951 to Mania Péron that Murphy 'pas de suicide', and that his intentions in this regard do not in the end even matter because he had already committed 'suicide mental' (SB to Mania Péron, 29 April 1951: *L2*, p. 246).

[11] For an entirely different perspective on the context in which chairs function in relation to 'Beckett's Seated Figures', see Brater (2009).

[12] See Weller (2005, pp. 88–90).

[13] Cited in Nixon (2011, p. 73).

[14] Spinoza (1992, p. 218) (*Ethica* V, proposition no. 35).

[15] *Ethica* V, proposition no. 36.

[16] In the first fair copy of his transcriptions Beckett wrote this italicized phrase as 'Humility no virtue for the ancients' (TCD MS 10971/6/7r). Both are Beckett's own interjections.

[17] Beckett's reference to Geulincx's axiom in *Murphy* has a precedent in an entry in the 'Whoroscope' notebook, which reads '21. Murphy: I am not of the big world, I am of the little world: ubi nihil valeo, ibi nihil velo (I quote from memory) & inversely' (UoR MS 3000, cited in Feldman 2006, p. 7).

[18] Cited in Feldman (2006, p. 64).

[19] Skinner was involved in a number of psychological theories and projects. He invented 'operant conditioning', and received many awards (including the National Medal of Service, awarded by Lyndon Johnson). He had a curious preference for pigeons as his experimental creature of choice, and during the Second World War concocted 'Project Pigeon', a plan for a pigeon-guided missile where the bird, trained to recognize a picture of the target, would peck at a directional screen in the nose cone of a missile, in a comic but destructive 'mind' and machine binary.

[20] See Uhlmann (2006a, pp. 75–7).

21 Knowlson points out regarding Mr. Endon that this figure 'owes as much to Beckett's readings about the unconscious, as it did to the patient whom he saw in the mental hospital where Geoffrey Thompson was working' (Knowlson 1996, p. 218). The real life precedent is revealed in the note that was the basis for Knowlson's published assertion, in which Knowlson quotes Beckett saying Bethlem was indeed 'where I saw Mr. Endon' (James and Elizabeth Knowlson collection, UoR).

22 Publishers were not forthcoming, and Beckett stated he would spend his life 'regretting the monkeys' (cited in Ackerley and Gontarski 2006, p. 380) after reminding Reavey a number of times to try to get this picture into the novel. Once the novel had found a publisher he asked 'what about apes' (SB to GR, 13 January 1938: *L1*, p. 586) then lamented further that 'I suppose also my apes have faded out as a possibility. I am disappointed' (SB to GR, 17 January 1938: *L1*, p. 587). The image has been preserved, however, and appears on the cover of *Demented Particulars*.

23 Described by Ackerley as a reference to Geulincx's *Ethics*, specifically to the post-Cartesian problem addressed therein of the interaction between mind and body, rather than to mediation between good or bad moral qualities. See Ackerley (2004, p. 120).

24 Beckett uses this term 'vicarious autology' again only two paragraphs later in an instance of repetition unlike other uses of terms derived from Geulincx in *Murphy* and thereby, it is tempting to postulate, perhaps making a 'mistake'.

25 Cited in Tucker (2010, p. 201). Cf. *Op*, vol. 2, p. 147. The Greek subtitles for each of Geulincx's three chapters are all handwritten by Beckett onto the typescript, as is to be expected.

26 Cf. TCD MS 10971/6/2r.

27 Cf. TCD MS 10971/6/2r.

28 Cf. TCD MS 10971/6/2v.

29 I am grateful to Mark Nixon for help with quotations from TCD MS 10948/1.

30 Ackerley argues in brief new introduction to a 2010 reprint of *Demented Particulars* that such changes are why authors should avoid 'correcting' their earlier works.

31 Beckett in his turn appears to have not been overly enamoured with Thomas. In a 1958 letter to Bray he wrote: 'I listened to Dylan Thomas reading his fat poems and being witty on poetry, poets and himself and didn't like any of it, the pulpit voice and hyper-articulation and sibilation, but I'm lousy public' (SB to BB, 29 November 1958, TCD MS 10948/1/13).

32 Geulincx wonders, for example, how 'when I want to walk, my feet are flung forward' (*Et*, p. 33). Geulincx's concern with the movement of limbs is discussed in further detail in Chapter 6.

Chapter 3

1 See, respectively Smith (2006), Benjamin (1997), Doherty (1971, pp. 34–48) and (for example) Hoefer (1959).

2 For a useful summary of these up to 1984, see Büttner (1984, pp. 7–26).

[3] There is no reliable citation for this quote, despite its frequent critical deployment. In a letter to Reavey after the war, however, Beckett did write of publication troubles: 'I knew H.H. was hatching a dead egg, or rather that Watt was under a dead hen' (SB to GR, 18 November 1947: *L2*, p. 64). The 'H.H.' presumably refers to the publisher Hamish Hamilton, who 'sat on *Watt* for several months' (Pilling 2006a, p. 102) before rejecting it.

[4] This and certain other quotations Harvey attributes to Beckett (such as that which pertains to the 'syntax of weakness') are frequently misquoted. Typically such misquotation has Beckett stating *Watt* was 'only a game', whereas Harvey quotes just two words from Beckett ('a game'), adding the 'only' himself. The difference is perhaps both minor and major; *Watt* is many things as well as 'a game'. The originator of the error may be Bair, who bases her reading of *Watt* as autobiographical psychological self-therapy partly on this misattribution. See, for example, Bair (1978, p. 346) and Ackerley (2005a, p. 12).

[5] Beckett also spoke of *Watt* as part of this 'series' a year later: 'I am now retyping, for rejection by the publishers, Malone Meurt, the last I hope of the series Murphy, Watt, Mercier & Camier, Molloy, not to mention the 4 Nouvelles & Eleuthéria' (SB to GR, 8 July 1948: *L2*, p. 80).

[6] The Ur-*Watt*'s single typescript, as Ackerley details, does not 'constitute or correspond with any one period of creation' (Ackerley 2005a, p. 22). It does not neatly collate only material from the early notebooks, to which the later notebooks only add. However, despite some overlap of material the typescript can be seen to roughly correspond to a stage of composition following production of the first four notebooks and prior to completion of the final two (see Ackerley 2005a, pp. 239–43).

[7] Mary Bryden describes Deleuze's system, according to which Langue I 'is what Deleuze calls "cette langue atomique" [this atomic language] (Deleuze 1992, p. 66). It is a language of enumeration, in which combinatory relations replace syntactical ones. This language is associated with the novels, culminating in *Watt*, where words proliferate in circles of permutation' (Bryden 2002, p. 85, translation by Bryden).

[8] See particularly Ackerley (2005a).

[9] See Ackerley (2005b). The Paleozoic Era (roughly 542–251 million years ago) is the earliest of three geologic eras of the Phanerozoic Eon. The Silurian is the third of the six geological periods into which the Paleozoic Era further divides (roughly 444–416 million years ago), the Cambrian is the first (roughly 542–488 million years ago) and the Carboniferous is the fifth (roughly 359–299 million years ago). 'Carboniferous' means 'coal-bearing', and derives from the many coal beds that were laid during this period as rainforests collapsed due to climate change.

[10] It is too far because it 'reminds us of the rocks at Greystones' (*Watt* Typescript, p. 149). Greystones was a fishing village in County Wicklow that served as a seaside holiday resort for Beckett's family in his youth where, according to Knowlson, 'The Beckett and Roe children used to play on the stony beach with its large grey and pink pebbles' (Knowlson 1996, p. 28). This autobiographical injection is, then, a further example of Watt's composition process as partly characterized by refinement from the explicit, or more overtly connotative, to the implied, hidden and abstracted.

11. In a different scene, Ackerley reveals that Watt's 'mind' is changed to 'understanding' in what became 'reason offered to the understanding' (*W*, p. 55) at the compositional stage currently missing from the archives, the inferred final typescript. See Ackerley (2005a, p. 250).
12. Cited in Ackerley (2005a, p. 24).
13. Cited in Tucker (2010, p. 203).
14. Ibid. Presumably the spelling is intended to be Baile's, perhaps an allusion to W. B. Yeats's 1904 play *On Baile's Strand*. Or perhaps just to Baile's Strand, the seashore around Dundalk, County Louth. It may even be a joke at the expense of the Irish coast, opting in preference for the sunnier Baiae on the bay of Naples.
15. Cited in Pilling (1997, p. 180). The *OED* defines an autoscope as 'An instrument invented by [Ernst] Coccius for the self-examination of the eye'. It is perhaps therefore the kind of instrument that Quin's more autoerotic explorations lack.
16. Cited in Pilling (1992, p. 20).
17. Ackerley detects the presence of Samuel Johnson in the passages on Watt's walking. While also describing the walk as 'an Occasionalist dyspraxia, a lack of synchronization', Watt's 'tardigrade' might also be seen to derive from Johnson's *Dictionary* entry for '*tardigradous*', or 'slow-moving'. See Ackerley (2005a, pp. 51–2).
18. While Kenner's reference to what was, Kenner claimed in 1961, 'the type of all up-to-date technology' (Kenner 1961, p. 87) might now seem quaint, his fundamental point remains a strong one underlined by his insight, still pertinent, that Beckett was 'profoundly right in finding the seventeenth-century Occasionalists aesthetically relevant to an age that has no difficulty in diagnosing their speculative shortcomings' (p. 85).
19. Cf. *Op*, vol. 3, p. 37.
20. See also Ackerley (2005a, p. 134).
21. Ackerley adds that Ps. 121.8 plays an important role in these conceptions of transiting ('The Lord shall preserve thy going out and thy coming from this time forth, and even for evermore'), as well as 'the Occasionalist ethos of Geulincx', which he derives from the description in *Metaphysics* of 'Motion thus has two parts, *from being* and *to being*' (Ackerley 2005a, p. 80).
22. Cf. TCD MS 10971/6/6r.
23. Cited in Nixon (2011, pp. 177–8).
24. My thanks to Shane Weller for suggestions regarding this translation.
25. For example, Lawrence Graver reads that most famous of Beckett's names as self-reflexively compound:

> Closest in sound is godet, the name of a popular cognac, but also the French word for 'a wooden bowl' or 'mug', which in different usages refers to the bowl of a pipe (smoked by Pozzo who carelessly refers to Godot as Godet) and a small glass of wine (which washes down Pozzo's chicken). [. . .] Inevitably, as Colin Duckworth has concluded, the receptacle called a godet might in the broad sense hold any meaning put into it. Graver (1989, pp. 44–5).

26. See, for example, Ackerley (2005a, p. 66), which mentions both Schopenhauer and Leopardi. Leopardi's '*e fango è il mondo*' ['the world is mud'] was an epigraph

for *Proust*, though it does not appear in the English Calder edition. Ackerley quotes Schopenhauer on *ennui*: 'the absence of satisfaction is suffering, the empty longing for a new wish, languor'. Even more concisely in *On The Suffering of the World*, Schopenhauer states 'Want and boredom are indeed the twin poles of human life' (Schopenhauer 1970, p. 45), boundaries that Malone perhaps alludes to with his 'Dish and pot, dish and pot, these are the poles' (*MD*, p. 9).

27. It is implied in the novel that a fall from a ladder in a farmyard was the cause of Mr Hackett's hunch. According to Ackerley, when Mr Hackett sits on the bench, inviting Mr and Mrs Nixon to sit with him, his 'pose is that of Punch' (Ackerley 2005a, p. 30). Perhaps, then, the introductory character Mr Hackett might be seen as ushering a reader gently in to a somewhat 'guignol world'.

28. Beckett cut the section from the final draft where the ineffable is intervened upon by the sorts of hysterical howls, the 'long loud bursts', which similarly intrude into the fractured three-way narrative of *Play*. In this editing, the passage is subject to the kinds of changes that can be seen in a number of developments from Ur-*Watt* to final novel, where the messy stuff of physicality, of 'crying and laughing', of Quinn's arse, of 'the waste' of the endless boggy marshes, is refined out of the novel's rationalist serializing, but leaving a ghostly 'shadow' of Beckett's own prior 'purpose', even if that purpose appears multifarious and exploratory, difficult to pin down, itself somewhat 'ineffable'.

29. Cf. TCD MS 10971/7/5r.

30. Cited in Knowlson (1996, p. 342).

Chapter 4

1. Beckett in undated interview with Lawrence Harvey. Cited in Knowlson (1996, p. 358).

2. In Faber & Faber's (2009) *The Expelled/The Calmative/The End & First Love* Christopher Ricks opts for translating the fragmented title *Suite* as 'What Follows'. With its complete title (*Suite et Fin*) it is perhaps closer to *Continuation and Conclusion*, a doubled, oxymoronic or self-negating title similar to the audibly multi-faceted *Comment c'est*. See *E* (p. vii).

3. Beckett wrote to de Beauvoir at *Les Temps modernes* expressing his disappointment and frustration at *Suite et Fin* being severed in half. De Beauvoir refused to publish the second part of the novella in what Beckett called 'Sartre's canard' (SB to GR, 27 May 1946, cited in Knowlson (1996, p. 358)), due to a misconceived appraisal of Beckett as having sought rather slyly to publish in two issues, pushing his luck as a relatively unknown author. According to Knowlson, the piece contained 'in the second half, too many references to itches in the privates and the arse and far too much pissing and farting to be compatible with the tone or, as Beckett put it later, "la bonne tenue" of the review' (Knowlson 1996, p. 359). On the controversy, see Overbeck and Fehsenfeld (2006) and Van Hulle (2011).

4. See, for example, Calder's *No's Knife: Collected Shorter Prose 1945–1966* (1967, reprinted in 1984 as *Collected Shorter Prose 1945–1980*), Grove's *Stories and Texts for Nothing* (1967) and Calder's *Four Novellas* (1977), among other places. Its

more recent publication has been by Grove (as *The Complete Short Prose* in 1995), Penguin (2000) and in 2009 by Faber & Faber, which reprints Calder's *Collected Shorter Prose* version of 1984.

5. See Chapter 5 for discussion of this term 'vaguening'.
6. This may be 'insufficient'.
7. This may be 'imagined'.
8. I would like to express my gratitude to John Pilling and Mark Nixon for their help with this transcription from the 'Suite' notebook.
9. Cited in Knowlson (1996, p. 393).
10. Beckett wrote to Pamela Mitchell on the same day, thanking her for sending a copy of *Merlin*, telling Mitchell he'd written 'a stinker' to Trocchi and that he was 'Fed up with them' (SB to Pamela Mitchell, 27 August 1954, UoR MS MIT/037, cited in Knowlson (1996, p. 397)).
11. Cited in Beplate (2011, p. 106).
12. See also Seaver's account published in 2006, which re-quotes much of the material from earlier.
13. Cited in Ackerley (2005a, p. 245).
14. See Ackerley (2005a, p. 245) and Coetzee's PhD thesis *The English Fiction of Samuel Beckett: An Essay in Stylistic Analysis* (University of Texas at Austin, 1969).
15. Casanova's 2006 monograph is a translation of *Beckett l'abstracteur: Anatomie d'une révolution littéraire* (1997). Casanova was presumably finalizing the French book as Knowlson's 1996 biography was published, and appears not to have consulted *Damned to Fame*. Unfortunately, then, by the time of the 2006 English translation some of the book's points are less sharp, while others appear quite wide of the mark.
16. Thus partly derives some of the importance of the comma for Beckett: in nearly but not quite stopping.

Chapter 5

1. Cited in Gontarski (1977, p. 36). See also Poutney (1988, pp. 133–56).
2. Cited in Uhlmann (1999, p. 54). Cf. Uhlmann (2006a, p. 78). See also *L2* (pp. 458–9).
3. See *Et* (p. 182).
4. *Op*, vol. 1, p. 177, cited and translated by van Bunge et al. (eds) (2003, p. 325).
5. Cited in Harmon (ed.) (1998, p. 24).
6. It appears on p. 146 of the 1958 Grove edition Uhlmann uses.
7. See Pilling (2004, p. 235) and Ackerley (2005a, p. 132) (where Ackerley also relates the 'Galileo's cradle' of *Watt* to Geulincx's baby-cradle in the context of *Dream*'s 'Cartesian earthball').
8. Nixon points out, for example, that 'Beckett sailed to Hamburg from the port of Cobh on board the S.S. Washington on 29 September 1936' (Nixon 2011, p. 6).
9. Although this passage originates in Lucretius, Beckett transcribed it indirectly, from Volume 2 of Schopenhauer's *The World as Will and Representation* into the 'Whoroscope' notebook. He wrote: 'Suave mari magno ("It is sweet, when on

the mighty sea the winds raise the waves, to contemplate from dry land the terrible [?] of others")' (UoR MS 3000). The passage, then, reveals a similar fusion of sources to that of the ship image in *Molloy*, which brings Dante and Homer together.

[10] See Pilling (2006a, pp. 126–7).
[11] See de Vleeschauwer (1957, p. 62).
[12] See Gontarski (1985).
[13] Windelband points out that different editions of *Ethics* present the scenario differently: 'the first edition of the *Ethics* (1665), in fact, introduced more the *deus ex machina*, while the annotations added in the second edition (1675) presented throughout the profounder view' (Windelband 1901, p. 415).
[14] On the nineteenth-century controversy surrounding the discovery of the analogy in Geulincx's work and the impact this had on the perceived originality of Leibniz's analogy see de Lattre (1970, pp. 553–66) and de Vleeschauwer (1957, pp. 45–56).
[15] Ackerley's reference to Geulincx's 'Temple of Wisdom' is a reference to *Ethics*' preface, titled 'To the Curators of the University of Leiden'. See *Et* (pp. 3–5).
[16] Cited in Uhlmann (2006a, p. 86).
[17] My italics.

Chapter 6

[1] Cited in Graver and Federman (eds) (1979, p. 244).
[2] Cited in Caselli (2005, p. 151).
[3] I follow the convention in relation to this novel outlined by Beckett to Kenner of referring to a 'narrator/narrated', rather than to a narrator. See Kenner (1973, p. 94), where Kenner applies the terms to *Molloy*.
[4] See, for example, Knowlson (1996, pp. 462–3) for discussion of refracted autobiographical recollections in this novel, which include visiting a friend in hospital, praying as a young boy with his mother and even shutting himself away from his many callers while writing the novel.
[5] When Beckett returned to Ireland in December 1935 from London he might well have felt as though he were going to die, as he was forced to spend a week in bed with pleurisy before embarking on the Geulincx research the following January. He was 30 years old, and described helping his brother Frank in 1936 with calculations such as 'a pressing tot or square' for the family quantity surveying business.
[6] Luce also served as a referee for Beckett's 1937 application to Cape Town for a lectureship in Italian (see Knowlson 1996, p. 754, n. 5).
[7] It was about such views that Malebranche had his extensive argument with Antoine Arnauld (1612–94). Schmaltz describes this exchange: 'The exchange between Malebranche and Arnauld on the issue of the nature of ideas, which was one of the major intellectual events of the early modern period, appears at times to be a battle for the soul of Descartes' (Schmaltz 2000, p. 61).
[8] The wax, held to the fire, was for Descartes a paragon of physical impressionability.

[9] Verhoeven (1973, p. 78). Translated and cited by van Bunge et al. (eds) (2003, p. 329).

[10] Berkeley quoted in Luce (1934, p. 90). It is a 'summary statement', as Luce describes it, which resembles Beckett's own perceptive annotation in his edition of Berkeley's *Theory of Vision*.

[11] 'fantoccini' – 'puppet' or 'doll'; 'secco' – 'dry'.

[12] Beckett's reference to Aliosha is to one of the brothers in Dostoevsky's *The Karamazov Brothers*.

[13] Cited in Harmon (ed.) (1998, p. 12).

[14] Cited in Gontarski (1993, p. 31).

[15] *Act Without Words 1* has been presented as a mime using puppets. In 1964 Bruno and Guido Bettiol made a 10-minute film of the mime using puppets, and in 1983 Margaret Jordan filmed a 17-minute animated version.

[16] Beckett used the term with Bray to describe his work in the second notebook in which he was composing the beginning of *Pim*, as *Comment c'est* was then called. On 11 March 1959, Beckett wrote 'I'm struggling along with the new moan, trying to find the rhythm and syntax of extreme weakness, penury perhaps I should say' (SB to BB, 11 March 1959, TCD MS 10948/1/22.). See also Harvey (1970, p. 249).

[17] Cf. TCD MS 10971/6/2v (*Metaphysica Vera*), TCD MS 10971/6/14v and TCD MS 10971/6/35 (*Ethica*).

[18] The word also appears at the beginning of *Ulysses*' 'Oxen of the Sun' chapter, where it is spelled 'Deshil' and is one of three incantatory words along with 'Holles' and 'Eamus'. My thanks to Chris Ackerley for reminding me of this.

[19] 'The bastard, he doesn't exist' paraphrases a quotation from Hamm in *Endgame*, but Beckett reportedly also replied to a question from Edna O'Brien (who was writing an article for the *Sunday Times Magazine* in 1986) with the same sentence: ' "God – do you have any thoughts you would like to air, about God?" "No . . . no . . . none . . . Wait, [vigorously] I do – the bastard, he doesn't exist" ' (O'Brien 1986, p. 53).

[20] www.oxfordmusiconline.com. Last accessed 1 May 2011.

[21] Cf. TCD MS 10971/6/5r.

[22] Cf. TCD MS 10971/6/5r.

[23] Cf. TCD MS 10971/6/5r.

[24] Cf. TCD MS 10971/6/5v.

[25] Théâtre du Grand-Guignol was founded in 1897, and had its heydays under various directors in the first three decades of the twentieth century prior to its being taken over in 1930 by Jack Jouvin. After the Second World War the theatre declined until it eventually closed in 1962. 'Nous n'aurions pas pu concurrencer Buchenwald' [We could not compete with Buchenwald] was the assessment of Charles Nonon, the theatre's final director, on why the post-war audience had less appetite for fictional visceral horror (cited in Pierron 1995, p. xxxiv). There were, however, also accusations of wartime collaboration levelled at the theatre. For a history of *Le Grand-Guignol*, see Hand and Wilson (2002).

[26] 'The Thinker' was originally intended by Rodin to represent Dante contemplating his epic poem while sitting beside the gate to Hell. Rodin's pose, then, of

'broken right angles', the head in the hands, is an image of literary as well as of philosophical thinking.

[27] While Beckett had said 'Possible title for TV piece: TRYST' (SB to BB, 16 January 1976, TCD MS 10948/1/597), and had given the piece this title in its manuscript (UoR MS 1519/1), 'Chamber Telly' was another 'Idea for a perhaps better title' he also sent to Bray (SB to BB, 24 January 1976, TCD MS 10948/1/599).

[28] Kleist quoted in Knowlson (1986, p. 197).

[29] UoR MS 1519/1. Cited in Ackerley (2009, p. 144).

[30] See letter to Bray of 22 January 1976, where Beckett writes he had been thinking of using a 'Schubert quartet I hope', but had not decided which (TCD MS 10948/1/498).

[31] UoR MS 1227/7/16/1 fol.2. Cited in Gontarski (1985, p. 196).

[32] Cited in Maude (2009, p. 129).

Conclusion

[1] Cited in Graver and Federman (eds) (1979, p. 240).

[2] Horace wrote that 'Democritus had the character of a laughing philosopher, one who turned things habitually into ridicule' (Horace 1860, p. 553).

Bibliography

Works by Beckett

— (1946) 'Suite'. *Les Temps modernes* 10 (July): 107–19.
— (1951) *Malone Meurt*. Paris: Éditions de Minuit.
— (1954) 'The End'. *Merlin* 2 (3): 144–59.
— (1955) *Nouvelles et Textes pour rien*. Paris: Éditions de Minuit.
— (1958) *The Unnamable*. New York: Grove Press.
— (1960) 'The End'. *Evergreen Review* 15 (November–December): 22–41.
— (1961) *Comment c'est*. Paris: Éditions de Minuit.
— (1967a) *No's Knife: Collected Shorter Prose 1945–1966*. London: Calder and Boyars.
— (1967b) *Stories and Texts for Nothing*. New York: Grove Press.
— (1970) *Mercier et Camier*. Paris: Éditions de Minuit.
— (1977) *Four Novellas*. London: Calder.
— (1983) *Disjecta*. London: Calder.
— (1984) *Collected Shorter Prose 1945–1980*. London: Calder.
— (1990) *Complete Dramatic Works*. London: Faber & Faber.
— (1993) *Dream of Fair to Middling Women*. New York: Arcade Publishing.
— (1995) *The Complete Short Prose 1929–1989*. New York: Grove Press.
— (1999a) *Beckett's 'Dream' notebook*. John Pilling (ed.). Reading: Beckett International Foundation.
— (1999b) *Proust and Three Dialogues with Georges Duthuit*. London: Calder.
— (2000) *First Love and Other Novellas*. London: Penguin.
— (2009a) *Company, Ill Seen Ill Said, Worstward Ho, Stirrings Still*. London: Faber & Faber.
— (2009b) *The Expelled, The Calmative, The End with First Love*. London: Faber & Faber.
— (2009c) *How It Is*. London: Faber & Faber.
— (2009d) *The Letters of Samuel Beckett, Volume 1*. Martha Fehsenfeld and Lois More Overbeck (eds). Cambridge: Cambridge University Press.
— (2009e) *Molloy*. London: Faber & Faber.
— (2009f) *Murphy*. London: Faber & Faber.
— (2009g) *Selected Poems 1930–1989*. London: Faber & Faber.
— (2009h) *Watt*. London: Faber & Faber.
— (2010a) *Malone Dies*. London: Faber & Faber.
— (2010b) *More Pricks Than Kicks*. London: Faber & Faber.
— (2010c) *Texts for Nothing and other Short Prose*. London: Faber & Faber.
— (2010d) *The Unnamable*. London: Faber & Faber.

— (2011) *The Letters of Samuel Beckett, Volume 2*. George Craig, Martha Dow Fehsenfeld, Dan Gunn and Lois More Overbeck (eds). Cambridge: Cambridge University Press.

Works by Geulincx

Bontekoe, Cornelis (1688) *Metaphysica et liber singularis de motu, nec non ejusdem oeconomia animalis, opera posthuma: quibus accedit Arnoldi Geulincx physica vera opus posthumum*. Lugduni Batavorum: J. de Vivié & F. Haaring.
Geulincx, Arnold (1667) *Van de Hooft-deuchden: De eerste Tucht-verhandeling*. Leiden: Philips de Croy.
— (1675) *Gnothi Seauton Sive Arnoldi Geulincs Ethica*. Leiden: A. Severini.
— (1709) *Gnothi Seauton Sive Ethica*. Amsterdam: Janssonio-Waesbergius.
— (1891–3) *Arnoldi Geulincx Opera Philosophica*, Volumes I–III. Jan Pieter Nicolaas Land (ed.). Hagae Comitum: Apud Nijhoff.
— (1999) *Metaphysics*. Martin Wilson (trans.). Wisbech: Christoffel Press.
— (2006) *Ethics: with Samuel Beckett's Notes*. Han van Ruler and Anthony Uhlmann (eds). Martin Wilson (trans.). Leiden and Boston: Brill.
— (2010) *Éthique*. Hélène Bah-Ostrowiecki (trans.). Turnhout: Brepols.

Unpublished Material

Beckett, Samuel *Collected Shorter Prose 1945–1980*, corrected galley proofs. Series I, BV4, Carlton Lake Collection, Harry Humanities Research Center, The University of Texas at Austin.
— *German Diaries*. Beckett International Foundation Archives, University of Reading.
— *Ghost Trio*. MS 1519/1, Beckett International Foundation Archives, University of Reading.
— Letters to Barbara Bray. MS 10948, Trinity College Dublin.
— Letters to Georges Duthuit. Duthuit Archives, Fondation des Héritiers Matisse, Paris.
— Letters to Mary Hutchinson. Mary Hutchinson Papers, Series II, Subseries B, Box 2, Folder 4, Harry Ransom Humanities Research Center, The University of Texas at Austin.
— Letters to Mania Péron. Series II, Box 17, Folder 18, Carlton Lake Collection, Harry Ransom Humanities Research Center, The University of Texas at Austin.
— Letters to George Reavey. Box 45, Folder 6, George Reavey Collection, Harry Ransom Humanities Research Center, The University of Texas at Austin.
— Letters to Richard Seaver. Richard Seaver Collection, Harry Ransom Humanities Research Center, The University of Texas at Austin.
— Mime du rêveur A. MS 1227/7/16/1, Beckett International Foundation Archives, University of Reading.

— Notes to Arnold Geulincx. MS 10971/6, Trinity College Dublin.
— 'Philosophy Notes'. MS 10967, Trinity College Dublin.
— 'Suite' notebook, 1946, The Calvin Israel – Samuel Beckett Collection, MS 91-9 and 91-5, John J. Burns Library, Boston College.
— *Watt* Notebooks, Box 6: folders 5–7, Samuel Beckett Collection, Harry Ransom Humanities Research Center, The University of Texas at Austin.
— *Watt* Typescript, Box 7: folders 5–6, Samuel Beckett Collection, Harry Ransom Humanities Research Center, The University of Texas at Austin.
— '*Whoroscope*' notebook. MS 3000, Beckett International Foundation Archives, University of Reading.
Brian Coffey Papers. Special Collections Department, University of Delaware.
'Collection Merlin'. McMaster University Samuel Beckett collection.
James and Elizabeth Knowlson Collection. Beckett International Foundation Archives, University of Reading.

Online Resource

Grove Music Online. www.oxfordmusiconline.com.

Critical and General Works

Aalderink, Mark (2006) 'Spinoza and Geulincx on the Human Condition, Passions, and Love'. *Studia Spinozana* 15: 67–86.
Abbott, H. Porter (1996) *Beckett Writing Beckett: The Author in the Autograph*. Ithaca: Cornell University Press.
Ackerley, C. J. (1998) *Demented Particulars: The Annotated Murphy*. Tallahassee, FL: Journal of Beckett Studies Books.
— (2000) 'Samuel Beckett and Thomas à Kempis: The Roots of Quietism'. *Samuel Beckett Today/Aujourd'hui* 9: 81–92.
— (2004a) *Demented Particulars: The Annotated Murphy* (2nd edn). Tallahassee, FL: Journal of Beckett Studies Books. Reprinted 2010 Edinburgh University Press.
— (2004b) '"Perfection is Not of This World": Samuel Beckett and Mysticism'. *Mystics Quarterly* 30 (1–2): 28–55.
— (2005a) *Obscure Locks, Simple Keys: The Annotated Watt*. Tallahassee, FL: Journal of Beckett Studies Books.
— (2005b) 'Samuel Beckett and the Geology of the Imagination: Toward an Excavation of *Watt*'. *Beckett The European*, Dirk Van Hulle (ed.), pp. 150–63. Tallahassee, FL: Journal of Beckett Studies Books.
— (2008) '"I Think I am": Review of Arnold Geulincx: *Ethics*'. Leiden and Boston: Brill, 2006. *Journal of Beckett Studies* 17: 199–210.
— (2009) '"Ever Know What Happened?": Shades and Echoes in Samuel Beckett's Television Plays'. *Journal of Beckett Studies* 18: 136–64.
Ackerley, C. J. and S. E. Gontarski (2006) *The Faber Companion to Samuel Beckett: A Reader's Guide to his Works, Life, and Thought*. London: Faber & Faber.

Adorno, Theodor (1982) 'Trying to Understand Endgame'. *New German Critique*, 26 (Spring–Summer): 119–50.
Albright, Daniel (2003) *Beckett and Aesthetics*. Cambridge: Cambridge University Press.
Alexander, Archibald B. D. (1922) *A Short History of Philosophy* (3rd edn). Glasgow: Jackson and Co.
Al-Ghazālī, Abū (1997) *The Incoherence of the Philosophers*. Michael E. Marmura (trans.). Provo, UT: Brigham Young University Press.
— (2001) *Deliverance from Error and Mystical Union with the Almighty*. Muhammad Abūlaylah (trans.). Washington DC: Council for Research in Values and Philosophy.
Atik, Anne (2001) *How It Was: A Memoir of Samuel Beckett*. London: Faber & Faber.
Auster, Paul (2003) *Collected Prose*. London: Faber & Faber.
Badiou, Alain (2003) *On Beckett*. Manchester: Clinamen Press.
Baillet, Adrien (1691) *La Vie Des Monsieur Descartes*. Paris: Daniel Horthemels.
Bair, Deirdre (1978) *Samuel Beckett: A Biography*. London: Jonathan Cape.
Balzac, Honoré de (2007) *The Unknown Masterpiece and Other Works*. Maryland: Wildside Press.
Bardout, Jean-Christophe (2002) 'Occasionalism: La Forge, Cordemoy, Geulincx'. In *A Companion to Early Modern Philosophy*, Steven Nadler (ed.), pp. 140–51. Oxford: Blackwell Publishing.
Beer, Ann (1985) '"Watt," Knott and Beckett's bilingualism'. *Journal of Beckett Studies* 10: 37–75.
Begam, Richard (1996) *Samuel Beckett and the End of Modernity*. Stanford: Stanford University Press.
Benjamin, Shoshana (1997) 'What's Watt'. *Poetics Today* 18 (3) (Autumn): 375–96.
Beplate, Justin (2011) 'Samuel Beckett, Olympia Press and the Merlin Juveniles'. In *Publishing Samuel Beckett*, Mark Nixon (ed.), pp. 97–109. London: The British Library.
Berkeley, George (1926 [1910]) *A New Theory of Vision, and Other Writings*. London: Dent.
— (1931) *Berkeley's 'Commonplace Book'*. G. A. Johnston (ed.). London: Faber & Faber.
Bloom, Harold (1997) *The Anxiety of Influence: A Theory of Poetry* (2nd edn). Oxford: Oxford University Press.
Boldrini, Lucia (2001) *Joyce, Dante, and the Poetics of Literary Relations*. Cambridge: Cambridge University Press.
Borges, Jorge Luis (1970) 'Kafka and His Precursors'. In *Labyrinths*, pp. 234–6. London: Penguin.
Boxall, Peter (2009) *Since Beckett: Contemporary Writing in the Wake of Modernism*. London: Continuum.
Brater, Enoch (1987) *Beyond Minimalism: Beckett's Late Style in the Theatre*. New York: Oxford University Press.
— (2004) 'Intertextuality'. In *Palgrave Advances in Samuel Beckett Studies*, Lois Oppenheim (ed.), pp. 30–44. Houndmills: Palgrave Macmillan.
— (2009) 'The Seated Figure on Beckett's Stage'. In *The Tragic Comedy of Samuel Beckett: 'Beckett in Rome'* 17–19 April 2008, Daniela Guardamagna and Rossana Sebellin (eds), pp. 259–76, Rome: Laterza.

Bryden, Mary (1998) *Beckett and the Idea of God*. Basingstoke: Macmillan.
— (2002) 'Deleuze Reading Beckett'. In *Beckett and Philosophy*, Richard J. Lane (ed.), pp. 80–92. Basingstoke: Palgrave Macmillan.
Bryden, Mary, Julian Garforth and Peter Mills (1998) *Beckett at Reading: Catalogue of the Beckett Manuscript Collection at the University of Reading*. Reading: Whiteknights Press and the Beckett International Foundation.
Burnet, John (1914) *Greek Philosophy, Part 1: Thales to Plato*. London: Macmillan.
Burton, Robert (2001) *The Anatomy of Melancholy*. New York: New York Review Books.
Büttner, Gottfried (1984) *Samuel Beckett's Novel Watt*. Philadelphia: University of Pennsylvania Press.
Cartledge, Paul (1998) *Democritus*. London: Phoenix.
Casanova, Pascale (2006) *Samuel Beckett: Anatomy of a Literary Revolution*. London: Verso.
Caselli, Daniela (2005) *Beckett's Dantes: Intertextuality in the Fiction and Criticism*. Manchester: Manchester University Press.
Clément, Bruno (2006) 'What the Philosophers do with Samuel Beckett'. In *Beckett after Beckett*, S. E. Gontarski and Anthony Uhlmann (eds), Anthony Uhlmann (trans.), pp. 116–37. Gainsville, FL: University Press of Florida.
Coetzee, J. M. (1969) 'The English Fiction of Samuel Beckett: An Essay in Stylistic Analysis', unpublished PhD thesis, University of Texas at Austin.
Coffey, Brian (1991) 'Memory's Murphy Maker: Some Notes on Samuel Beckett'. *Eonta: Arts Quarterly* 1 (1): 3–8.
Cohn, Ruby (1960) 'A Note on Beckett, Dante, and Geulincx'. *Comparative Literature* 12 (1) (Winter): 93–4.
— (1962) *Samuel Beckett: The Comic Gamut*. New Brunswick, NJ: Rutgers University Press.
— (2001) *A Beckett Canon*. Ann Arbor: University of Michigan Press.
Cole, John R. (1992) *The Olympian Dreams and Youthful Rebellion of René Descartes*. Urbana and Chicago: University of Illinois Press.
Connor, Steven (1988) *Samuel Beckett: Repetition, Theory, and Text*. Oxford: Basil Blackwell.
— (2008) 'Beckett and Bion'. *Journal of Beckett Studies* 17: 9–34.
Cooney, Brian (1978) 'Arnold Geulincx: A Cartesian Idealist'. *Journal of the History of Philosophy* XVI(2): 167–80.
Cottingham, John (1998) *Philosophy and the Good Life: Reason and the Passions in Greek, Cartesian and Psychoanalyitic Ethics*. Cambridge: Cambridge University Press.
Dante Alighieri (2003) *The Divine Comedy, Volume 1: Inferno*. Mark Musa (trans.). London: Penguin.
— (1985) *The Divine Comedy, Volume 2: Purgatory*. Mark Musa (trans.). London: Penguin.
— (2007) *The Divine Comedy, Volume 3: Paradiso*. Robin Kirkpatrick (trans.). London: Penguin.
Davies, Paul (1994) 'Three Novels and Four Nouvelles: giving up the ghost be born at last'. In *The Cambridge Companion to Beckett*, John Pilling (ed.), pp. 43–66. Cambridge: Cambridge University Press.

De Cordemoy, Géraud (1968) *Œuvres philosophiques, avec une étude bio-bibliographique*. Paris: Presses Universitaires de France.

De la Forge, Louis (2010) *Treatise on the Human Mind (1664)*. Dordrecht: Kluwer Academic Publishers.

De Lattre, Alain (1970) *Arnold Geulincx: Présentation, Choix de Textes et Traduction*. Paris: Seghers.

De Vleeschauwer, H. J. (1957) *Three Centuries of Geulincx Research: A Bibliographic Survey*. Pretoria: Communications of the University of South Africa.

Deleuze, Gilles (1992) 'L'Epuisé'. In *Quad et autres pièces pour la télévision*, Samuel Beckett, pp. 55–106. Paris: Éditions de Minuit.

— (1995) *Negotiations, 1972–1990*. Martin Joughin (trans.). New York: Columbia University Press.

Descartes, René (1984a) *Principles of Philosophy*. Valentine Rodger Miller and Reese P. Miller (trans.). Dordrecht: Kluwer Academic Publishers.

— (1984b) *The Philosophical Writings of Descartes, Volume 2*. John Cottingham, Robert Stoothoff and Dugald Murdoch (trans.). Cambridge: Cambridge University Press.

— (1985) *The Philosophical Writings of Descartes, Volume 1*. John Cottingham, Robert Stoothoff and Dugald Murdoch (trans.). Cambridge: Cambridge University Press.

— (1991) *The Philosophical Writings of Descartes, Volume 3*. John Cottingham, Robert Stoothoff, Dugald Murdoch and Anthony Kenny (trans.). Cambridge: Cambridge University Press.

Dobrez, L. A. C. (1986) *The Existential and its Exits: Literary and Philosophical Perspectives on the Works of Beckett, Ionesco, Genet and Pinter*. London: Athlone Press.

Doherty, Francis (1971) *Samuel Beckett*. London: Hutchinson.

Doutey, Nicolas (ed.) (2012) *Notes de Beckett sur Geulincx* (Coll. "Expériences philosophiques"). Besançon: Les Solitaires Intempestifs.

Dowd, Garin (2007) *Abstract Machines: Samuel Beckett and Philosophy after Deleuze and Guattari*. New York: Rodopi.

— (2008) 'Prolegomena to a Critique of Excavatory Reason: Reply to Matthew Feldman'. *Samuel Beckett Today/Aujourd'hui* 20: 375–88.

Eekhof, A. (1919) 'De Wijgeer Arnoldus Geulincx te Leuven en te Leiden'. *Nederlandish Archief voor Kerkgeschiedenis*, new series, 15: 1–24.

Eliot, T. S. (1997) 'Tradition and the Individual Talent'. In *Revolutions of the Word: Intellectual Contexts for the Study of Modern Literature*, Patricia Waugh (ed.), pp. 208–11. New York: Arnold.

Fakhry, M. (1958) *Islamic Occasionalism*. London: George Allan & Unwin.

Feldman, Matthew (2004) 'Sourcing Aporetics: An Empirical Study on Philosophical Influences in the Development of Samuel Beckett's Writing', unpublished PhD thesis, Oxford Brookes University.

— (2006) *Beckett's Books: A Cultural History of Samuel Beckett's 'interwar notes'*. New York: Continuum.

— (2009a) 'A "suitable engine of destruction"? Samuel Beckett and Arnold Geulincx's Ethics'. In *Beckett and Ethics*, Russell Smith (ed.), pp. 38–56. New York: Continuum.

— (2009b) '"But what was this pursuit of meaning, in this indifference to meaning?"': Beckett, Husserl and "Meaning Creation"'. In *Beckett and Phenomenology*, Ulrika Maude and Matthew Feldman (eds), pp. 13–38. London: Continuum.

Fletcher, John (1964) *The Novels of Samuel Beckett*. London: Chatto and Windus.

Freud, Sigmund (2001) 'Some Dreams of Descartes'. In *The Complete Works, Volume XXI: 'The Future Of An Illusion', 'Civilisation And Its Discontents' and Other Works*, pp. 199–204. London: Vintage.

Frost, Everett and Jane Maxwell (2006) 'Catalogues of Beckett's Reading Notes and Other Manuscripts at Trinity College Dublin'. *Samuel Beckett Today/Aujourd'hui* 16, 13–199.

Gabbey, Alan and Robert E. Hall (1998) 'The Melon and the Dictionary: Reflections on Descartes's Dreams'. *Journal of the History of Ideas* 59 (4)(October): 651–68.

Garnier, Pierre (1885) *Onanisme seul et à deux, sous toutes ses formes et leurs consequences*. Paris: Libraire Garnier Frères.

Garrett, Don (1996) 'Spinoza's Ethical Theory'. In *The Cambridge Companion to Spinoza*, Don Garrett (ed.), pp. 267–314. Cambridge: Cambridge University Press.

Gontarski, S. E. (1977) *Beckett's Happy Days: A Manuscript Study*. Columbus: The Ohio State University Libraries Publications.

— (1985) *The Intent of Undoing in Samuel Beckett's Dramatic Texts*. Bloomington: Indiana University Press.

— (1993) '"Birth Astride of a Grave": Samuel Beckett's Act Without Words 1'. In *The Beckett Studies Reader*, S. E. Gontarski (ed.), pp. 29–34. Gainsville, FL: University Press of Florida.

Gontarski, S. E. and Anthony Uhlmann (eds) (2006) *Beckett After Beckett*. Gainsville, FL: University Press of Florida.

Graver, Lawrence (1989) *Beckett: Waiting for Godot*. Cambridge: Cambridge University Press.

Graver, Lawrence and Raymond Federman (eds) (1979) *Samuel Beckett: The Critical Heritage*. London: Routledge & Kegan Paul.

Greene, Robert (1592) *The Repentance of Robert Greene*. London: Cutbert Burbie.

Hamilton, Alice and Kenneth Hamilton (1976) *Condemned To Life: The World of Samuel Beckett*. Grand Rapids, MI: Eerdmans.

Hand, Richard J. and Michael Wilson (2002) *The Grand-Guignol: The French Theatre of Horror*. Exeter: Exeter University Press.

Harmon, Maurice (ed.) (1998) *No Author Better Served: the Correspondence of Samuel Beckett and Alan Schneider*. Cambridge, MA: Harvard University Press.

Harvey, Lawrence (1970) *Samuel Beckett: Poet and Critic*. Princeton, NJ: Princeton University Press.

Hassan, Ihab (1967) *The Literature of Silence: Henry Miller and Samuel Beckett*. New York: Alfred A. Knopf.

Henning, Sylvie Debevic (1983) 'The Guffaw of the Abderite: Murphy and the Democritean Universe'. *Journal of Beckett Studies* 10: 5–20.

Herren, Grayley (2000) 'Splitting Images: Beckett's Nacht und Träume'. *Modern Drama* 43 (2): 182–91.

— (2002) 'Nacht und Träume as Beckett's Agony in the Garden'. *Journal of Beckett Studies* 11 (1): 54–70.

Hesla, David (1971) *The Shape of Chaos: An Interpretation of the Art of Samuel Beckett*. Minneapolis: University of Minnesota Press.
Hill, Leslie (1990) *Beckett's Fiction: In Different Words*. Cambridge: Cambridge University Press.
Hoefer, Jacqueline (1959) 'Watt'. *Perspective* XI (Autumn): 166–82.
Horace (1860) *The Works of Horace, with English Notes, Revised and Edited by Reginald H. Chase*. Cambridge: John Bartlett.
Hutchinson, Mary (1927) *Fugitive Pieces*. London: Hogarth Press.
Jager, Bernd (1968) 'The Three Dreams of Descartes: A Phemomenological Exploration'. *Review of Existential Psychology and Psychiatry* 8: 195–213.
Johnson, Samuel (1810) *A Dictionary of the English Language* (10th edn). London.
Joyce, James (1992a) *A Portrait of the Artist as a Young Man*. Oxford: Oxford University Press.
— (1992b) *Finnegans Wake*. London: Penguin.
— (1993) *Ulysses*. Oxford: Oxford University Press.
Juliet, Charles. (1995) *Conversations with Samuel Beckett and Bram van Velde*. Janey Tucker (trans.). Leiden: Academic Press Leiden.
Jung, Carl G. (1982) *Analytical Psychology: Its Theory and Practice (The Tavistock Lectures)*. London and New York: Routledge & Kegan Paul.
Keevak, Michael (1992) 'Descartes's Dreams and Their Address for Philosophy'. *Journal of the History of Ideas* 53 (3) (July–September): 373–96.
Kemp Smith, Norman (1963) *New Studies in the Philosophy of Descartes: Descartes as Pioneer*. New York: Russell & Russell.
Kempis, Thomas à. (1940) *Of The Imitation Of Christ*. London: Oxford University Press.
Kennedy, Sighle (1971) *Murphy's Bed: A Study of Real Sources and Sur-Real Associations in Samuel Beckett's First Novel*. Lewisburg, PA: Bucknell University Press.
Kenner, Hugh (1961) *Samuel Beckett: A Critical Study*. New York: Grove Press.
— (1973) *A Reader's Guide to Samuel Beckett*. London: Thames & Hudson.
Kleist, Heinrich von (1978) 'On the Marionette Theatre'. Idris Parry (trans.). In *The Times Literary Supplement*, 20 October, 1211.
Knowlson, James (1972) *Light and Darkness in the Theatre of Samuel Beckett*. London: Turret Books.
— (1983) 'Beckett's "Bits of Pipe"'. In *Samuel Beckett: Humanistic Perspectives*, Morris Beja, S. E. Gontarski and Pierre Astier (eds), pp. 16–25. Ohio: Ohio State University Press.
— (1986) 'Ghost Trio / Geister Trio'. In *Beckett at 80 / Beckett In Context*, Enoch Brater (ed.), pp. 193–207. Oxford: Oxford University Press.
— (1996) *Damned to Fame: The Life of Samuel Beckett*. London: Bloomsbury.
Knowlson, James (ed.) (2006) *Beckett Remembering, Remembering Beckett*. London: Bloomsbury.
Knowlson, James and John Pilling (1979) *Frescoes of the Skull: The Later Prose and Drama of Samuel Beckett*. London: Calder.
Lake, Carlton (ed.) (1984) *No Symbols Where None Intended: A Catalogue of Books, Manuscripts, and Other Materials Relating to Samuel Beckett in the Collections of the Humanities Research Center*. Austin: Harry Ransom Humanities Research Center.

Land, Jan Pieter Nicolaas (1891) 'Arnold Geulincx and His Works'. *Mind* 16 (62), (April): 223–42.
Lange, Joachim (1726) *Nova anatome, seu idea analytica systematis metaphysici Wolfiani*. Frankfurt and Leipzig: Knochianus.
Le Juez, Brigitte (2008) *Beckett before Beckett*. London: Souvenir Press.
Locatelli, Carla (1990) *Unwording the World: Samuel Beckett's Prose Works after the Nobel Prize*. Philadelphia: University of Pennsylvania Press.
Luce, A. A. (1934) *Berkeley and Malebranche: A Study in the Origins of Berkeley's Thought*. Oxford: Oxford University Press.
Lucretius, Titus (1821) *De Rerum Natura / Von der Natur der Dinge*. Leipzig: Bei G. J. Göschen.
— (2007) *On The Nature of Things*. Alicia Stallings (trans.). London: Penguin.
Mahaffy, J. P. (1901) *Descartes*. Edinburgh and London: William Blackwood.
Malebranche, Nicolas (1997) *The Search After Truth: With Elucidations of The Search After Truth*. Thomas M. Lennon and Paul J. Olscamp (trans.). Cambridge: Cambridge University Press.
Malraux, André (1968) *La Condition Humaine*. London: University of London Press.
— (2009) *Man's Fate*. Philip Gourevitch (trans.). London: Penguin.
Maritain, Jacques (1944) *The Dream of Descartes, together with some Other Essays*. New York: Kennikat Press.
Maude, Ulrika (2009) *Beckett, Technology and the Body*. Cambridge: Cambridge University Press.
Mays, J. C. C. (2010) 'Brian Coffey's Review of Beckett's Murphy: "Take Warning While You Praise"'. In *Other Edens: The Life and Work of Brian Coffey*, Benjamin Keatinge and Aengus Woods (eds), pp. 83–100. Dublin: Irish Academic Press.
Mintz, Samuel (1959) 'Beckett's Murphy: A Cartesian Novel'. *Perspective* XI (Autumn): 156–65.
Montgomery, Niall (1954) 'No Symbols where None Intended'. *New World Writing: Fifth Mentor Selection*, April, 324–7.
Mooney, Michael E. (1978) 'Molloy, part 1: Beckett's "Discourse on method"'. *Journal of Beckett Studies* 3, 40–55.
Mooney, Sinéad (2011) *A Tongue Not Mine: Beckett and Translation*. Oxford: Oxford University Press.
Morot-Sir, Eduard (1976) 'Samuel Beckett and Cartesian Emblems'. In *Samuel Beckett and the Art of Rhetoric*, Eduard Morot-Sir (ed.), pp. 25–104. Chapel Hill: University of North Carolina Press.
Murphy, P. J. (1994) 'Beckett and the Philosophers'. In *The Cambridge Companion to Beckett*, John Pilling (ed.), pp. 222–39. Cambridge: Cambridge University Press.
Nadler, Steven. (1999a) *Spinoza: A Life*. Cambridge: Cambridge University Press.
— (1999b) 'Knowledge, Volitional Agency and Causation in Malebranche and Geulincx'. *British Journal for the History of Philosophy* 7 (2): 263–74.
— (2010) *Occasionalism: Causation Among the Cartesians*. Oxford: Oxford University Press.
Nixon, Mark (2011) *Samuel Beckett's German Diaries, 1936–1937*. London: Continuum.
Nussbaum, Martha (2001) *Upheavals of Thought: The Intelligence of Emotions*. Cambridge: Cambridge University Press.

O'Brien, Edna (1986) 'Samuel Beckett at 80'. In *The Sunday Times Magazine*, 6 (April): 50–3.
O'Brien, Eoin (1986) *The Beckett Country: Samuel Beckett's Ireland*. Dublin: Black Cat Press.
O'Hara, James Donald (1981) 'Where There's a Will There's a Way Out: Beckett and Schopenhauer'. *College Literature* 8 (3): 249–70.
— (1997) *Samuel Beckett's Hidden Drives: Structural Uses of Depth Psychology*. Gainesville: University Press of Florida.
Overbeck, Lois More and Martha Dow Fehsenfeld. (2006) 'In Defence of the Integral Text'. *Samuel Beckett Today/Aujourd'hui* 16, 347–71.
Ovid (2004) *Metamorphoses*. London: Penguin.
Paquot, Jean Noël (1768) *Memoires pour Servir à L'histoire Litteraire des Dix-sept Provinces des Pays-Bas de la Principauté de Liège et de Quelques Contrées Voisines*. Louvain: De l'Imprimerie académique Louvain.
Perloff, Marjorie (1996) *Wittgenstein's Ladder. Poetic Language and the Strangeness of the Ordinary*. Chicago: University of Chicago Press.
Pierron, Agnès (1995) *Le Grand Guignol: le Théâtre des Peurs de la Belle Époque*. Paris: R. Laffont.
Pilling, John (1978) 'The Significance of Beckett's "Still"'. *Essays in Criticism* XXVIII (2): 143–57.
— (1979) *Samuel Beckett*. London: Routledge & Kegan Paul.
— (1992) 'From a (W)horoscope to Murphy'. In *The Ideal Core of the Onion: Reading Beckett Archives*, John Pilling and Mary Bryden (eds), pp. 1–20. Reading: Beckett International Foundation.
— (1995) 'Losing One's Classics: Beckett's Small Latin, and Less Greek'. *Journal of Beckett Studies* 4 (2): 5–13.
— (1997) *Beckett Before Godot*. Cambridge: Cambridge University Press.
— (2004) *A Companion to Dream of Fair to Middling Women*. Tallahassee, FL: Journal of Beckett Studies Books.
— (2005) 'Dates and Difficulties in Beckett's *Whoroscope* Notebook'. In *Beckett The European*, Dirk Van Hulle (ed.), pp. 39–48. Tallahassee, FL: Journal of Beckett Studies Books.
— (2006a) *A Samuel Beckett Chronology*. Basingstoke: Palgrave Macmillan.
— (2006b) '"For Interpolation": Beckett and English Literature'. *Samuel Beckett Today/Aujourd'hui* 16: 203–35.
— (2011) *Samuel Beckett's 'More Pricks than Kicks': In a Straight of Two Wills*. London: Continuum.
Poulet, Georges (1956) *Studies in Human Time*. Baltimore: Johns Hopkins Press.
Poutney, Rosemary (1988) *Theatre of Shadows: Samuel Beckett's Drama 1956–76*. Gerards Cross: Colin Smythe Ltd.
Price, David Walter (1999) *History Made, History Imagined: Contemporary Literature, Poiesis, and the Past*. Urbana: University of Illinois Press.
Rabinovitz, Rubin (1972) '*Watt* from Descartes to Schopenhauer'. In *Modern Irish Literature: Essays in Honour of William York Tindall*, Raymond J. Porter and James D. Brophy (eds), pp. 261–87. New York: Iona College Press.
— (1984) *The Development of Samuel Beckett's Fiction*. Urbana: University of Illinois Press.

Rabinovitz, Rubin and Michéle Alna Barale (1988) *A KWIC Concordance to Samuel Beckett's trilogy: Molloy, Malone Dies, and The Unnamable.* New York: Garland.
— (1990) *A KWIC Concordance to Samuel Beckett's Murphy* New York: Garland.
Rimbaud, Arthur (2009) *Collected Poems.* Martin Sorrell (trans.). Oxford: Oxford University Press.
Robinson, Michael (1979) 'From Purgatory to Inferno: Beckett and Dante Revisited'. *Journal of Beckett Studies* 5: 69–82.
Rousset, Bernard (1999) *Geulincx: Entre Descartes et Spinoza.* Paris: Vrin.
Saberhagen, Fred (1988) *Berserker Man.* London: Victor Gallancz.
Schmaltz, Tad M. (2000) 'Malebranche on Ideas and the Vision in God'. In *The Cambridge Companion to Malebranche*, Steven Nadler (ed.), pp. 59–86. Cambridge: Cambridge University Press.
Schopenhauer, Arthur (1966a) *The World As Will and Representation, Volume 1.* E. F. J. Payne (trans.). New York: Dover.
— (1966b) *The World As Will and Representation, Volume 2.* E. F. J. Payne (trans.). New York: Dover.
— (1970) *Essays and Aphorisms.* R. J. Hollingdale (trans.). London: Penguin Classics.
Schouls, Peter A. (1989) *Descartes and the Enlightenment.* Edinburgh: Edinburgh University Press.
Schrödinger, Erwin (1996) *'Nature and the Greeks' and 'Science and Humanism'.* Cambridge: Cambridge University Press.
Seaver, Richard (1976) 'Introduction'. In *I can't go on, I'll go on: A Selection from Samuel Beckett's Work*, Richard Seaver (ed.), pp. ix–xlv. New York: Grove Press.
— (2006) 'Richard Seaver on Translating Beckett'. In *Beckett Remembering, Remembering Beckett.* James Knowlson (ed.). London: Bloomsbury.
Sebba, Gregor (1987) *The Dream of Descartes.* Carbondale: Southern Illinois University Press.
Smith, Frederik N. (2002) *Beckett's Eighteenth Century.* New York: St Martin's Press.
— (2006) 'Watt, Watson and Sherlock Holmes: Watt as Detective Fiction'. *Samuel Beckett Today/Aujourd'hui* 16: 299–317.
Smith, Norman Kemp (1963) *New Studies in the Philosophy of Descartes.* New York: Russell & Russell Inc.
Spinoza, Baruch (1992) *Ethics, Treatise on the Emendation of the Intellect and Selected Letters.* Seymour Feldman (ed.). Samuel Shirley (trans.). Cambridge, IN: Hackett.
Taylor, Neil and Bryan Loughery (1989) 'Murphy's Surrender to Symmetry'. *Journal of Beckett Studies* 11 & 12: 79–90.
Thomas, Dylan (1938) 'Recent Novels'. In *The New English Weekly*, 17 March: 454–5.
Tonning, Erik (2007) *Samuel Beckett's Abstract Drama: Works for Stage and Screen 1962–1985.* Bern: Peter Lang.
Tucker, David (2009) '*Murphy*, Geulincx and an Occasional(ist) game of Chess'. In *The Tragic Comedy of Samuel Beckett: 'Beckett in Rome' 17–19 April 2008*, Daniela Guardamagna and Rossana Sebellin (eds), pp. 190–209, Rome: Laterza.
— (2010) 'Towards an Analysis of Geulincx and the Ur-*Watt*'. *Samuel Beckett Today/Aujourd'hui* 22: 197–208.
— (2011) 'Beckett's Guignol Worlds: Arnold Geulincx and Heinrich von Kleist'. *Sofia Philosophical Review* (Special Issue: Samuel Beckett/Philosophy), 169–92.

Uhlmann, Anthony (1999) *Beckett and Poststructuralism*. Cambridge: Cambridge University Press.
— (2004) '"A Fragment of a Vitagraph": Hiding and Revealing in Beckett, Geulincx, and Descartes'. *Samuel Beckett Today/Aujourd'hui* 14: 341–56.
— (2006a) *Samuel Beckett and the Philosophical Image*. Cambridge: University of Cambridge Press.
— (2006b) 'Samuel Beckett and the Occluded Image'. In *Beckett After Beckett*, S. E. Gontarski and Anthony Uhlmann (eds), pp. 79–97. Gainsville, FL: University Press of Florida.
Van Bunge, Wiep, Henri Krop, Bart Leeuwenburgh, Han van Ruler, Paul Schuurman and Michiel Wielema (eds) (2003) *The Dictionary of Seventeenth and Eighteenth-Century Dutch Philosophers (Volume 1)*. Bristol: Thoemmes Press.
Van Hulle, Dirk (2008) *Manuscript Genetics, Joyce's Know-How, Beckett's Nohow*. Gainsville, FL: University Press of Florida.
— (2011) 'Publishing "The End": Beckett and *Les Temps modernes*'. In *Publishing Samuel Beckett*, Mark Nixon (ed.), pp. 73–95. London: The British Library.
Van Ruler, Han (2003) 'The Shipwreck of Belief and Eternal Bliss: Philosophy and Religion in Later Dutch Cartesianism'. In *The Early Enlightenment in the Dutch Republic, 1650–1750: selected papers of a conference, held at the Herzog August Bibliothek, Wolfenbüttel 22–23 March 2001*, pp. 109–36. Leiden: Brill.
— (2006) 'Geulincx and Spinoza: Books, Backgrounds and Biographies'. *Studia Spinozana* 15: 89–106.
Verhoeven, Cornelis (1973) *Het Axioma van Geulincx*. Bilthoven: Ambokoeken.
Vico, Giambattista (1988) *The New Science of Giambattista Vico*. Thomas Goddard Bergin and Max Harold Fisch (trans.). Ithaca, NY: Cornell University Press.
Weller, Shane (2005) *A Taste for the Negative: Beckett and Nihilism*. London: Legenda.
— (2008), 'Not Rightly Human: Beckett and Animality'. *Samuel Beckett Today/Aujourd'hui* 19: 211–21.
— (2009) '"Some Experience of the Schizoid Voice": Samuel Beckett and the Language of Derangement'. *Forum for Modern Language Studies* 45 (1) (January): 32–50.
— (2010) 'Unwords'. In *Beckett and Nothing: Trying to Understand Beckett*, Daniela Caselli (ed.), pp. 107–24. Manchester: Manchester University Press.
Windelband, Wilhelm (1901) *A History of Philosophy* (2nd edn), James Tufts (trans.). London: Macmillan.
Wood, Rupert (1993) 'Murphy, Beckett; Geulincx, God'. *Journal of Beckett Studies* 2 (2): 27–51.
— (1994) 'An endgame of aesthetics: Beckett as Essayist'. In *The Cambridge Companion to Beckett*, John Pilling (ed.), pp. 1–16. Cambridge: Cambridge University Press.
Yeats, W. B. (1997) *Selected Plays*. London: Penguin Classics.
Žižek, Slavoj (2004) 'Is it Possible Not to Love Spinoza?' In *Organs Without Bodies. On Deleuze and Consequences*, pp. 33–41. New York: Routledge.

Index

Aalderlink, Mark 185
Achilles 35
Ackerley, C. J. viii, xvi, 1–2, 18, 43, 45, 47–8, 52, 54–5, 66–7, 71, 73, 75–6, 78, 87, 92–3, 113, 129, 139–41, 163–4, 166, 173, 183, 186, 188–98
Addyman, David viii
Adorno, Theodor 132, 147
Aix 9
Al-Ghazālī, Abū 184
Albright, Daniel 155, 175
Alexander, Archibald xiii
Andala, Ruardas 122, 184
Antwerp 8, 122
Arikha, Avigdor 98
Aristotle 19
Arnauld, Antoine 196
Augustine of Hippo (St. Augustine) 9, 17–19, 186
Auster, Paul 102

Bacon, Francis 77, 187
Bah-Ostrowiecki, Hélène 181
Bailey, Iain viii
Baillet, Adrien 82
Bair, Deirdre xiii, 2, 57, 97, 184, 192
Balzac, Honoré de xiv
   Le Chef d'oeuvre inconnu 34–5
Bardout, Jean-Christophe 12, 185
Barrès, Maurice 32
BBC 173
Beachy Head 128
The Beckett Digital Manuscript Project 113
Beckett, Frank 36, 48, 196

Beckett International Foundation, University of Reading viii, xi, 113
Beckett, Samuel (works),
   Act Without Words 1 5, 162–5, 167, 169, 173–4, 197
   Act Without Words 2, 174
   'All Strange Away' 167
   'Assumption' 63
   The Calmative x, 194
   Cascando 100
   Collected Shorter Prose (Calder) 115, 194–5
   Comment c'est xv, 5, 38, 83, 129, 148–50, 152, 154–62, 169, 176, 194, 197
   Company x, 10–11, 46, 82, 148
   Compagnie 148
   Complete Dramatic Works x, 8, 17, 34, 43, 74, 99, 128, 138, 164–5, 172–5, 188
   Complete Short Prose (Grove) x, 63, 195
   Dante...Bruno.Vico..Joyce 39, 86, 181
   'Denis Devlin' 88–9
   'Les Deux Besoins' xiv, 88–9
   Le dépeupleur 148
   Disjecta x, xvi, 39, 43, 59, 79, 86, 88–9, 105, 109, 181
   Dream of Fair to Middling Women x, 29, 45–6, 57, 62, 77–8, 82–3, 103, 108–9, 128–9, 145, 148, 150, 153, 187, 195
   'Dream' Notebook 55, 76, 120, 189
   Eleuthéria 192
   The End x, xiv, 4, 95–106, 110–14, 116–17, 126, 132, 136, 146–7, 153–4, 177, 194

Endgame 105, 132, 172, 188, 197
The Expelled x, 194
Film 34, 40, 51, 99
La Fin xiv, 4, 95–8, 100, 103, 106, 115–17, 126, 146–7, 153–4, 177
Fin de Partie 132
First Love x, 95, 194
Fizzles 165
Foirades 165
Four Novellas 194
From an Abandoned Work 71, 108, 148, 169
Geister Trio 175
Ghost Trio xvi, 162, 170, 173–5, 177
'Gnome' 4
Happy Days 118, 138, 170, 173
How It Is x, xv, 5, 38, 83, 117, 129, 148–62, 169, 176
Ill Seen, Ill Said x
J. M. Mime 174
Krapp's Last Tape 3, 172
L'Expulsé 112, 114
L'Innommable xv, 5, 38, 114, 117–18, 126, 131–2, 144, 150–1
The Letters of Samuel Beckett, Volume 1 x, xiii–xiv, 7, 12, 29–30, 32–4, 36, 44–5, 47–8, 66–7, 100, 162, 187–9, 191
The Letters of Samuel Beckett, Volume 2 x, 37, 72, 95, 112, 190, 192, 195
The Lost Ones 148
'Love and Lethe' 161
Malone Dies x, xv, 5, 46, 95, 117–18, 126, 129–32, 150, 194
Malone meurt xv, 5, 46, 95, 113, 117–18, 126, 131–2, 192
Mercier and Camier xiv, 94–7, 104–5, 118, 192
Mercier et Camier xiv, 94–6, 192
Mime du rêveur A 174
Molloy x, xiv–xv, 1, 5, 11, 37–8, 53, 82, 95, 98, 105, 108, 117–20, 122, 125, 127–8, 130–1, 134, 137–9, 151, 154, 159–60, 167, 192, 196
More Pricks Than Kicks x, 62, 116, 120, 145, 148, 161, 168, 179

Murphy x, xiii–xvi, 1–4, 13, 18, 20, 25, 27–30, 33, 36–9, 42–71, 74–5, 77–8, 83, 85–7, 91, 95, 103, 106, 116, 118, 130, 133, 136, 140, 144, 146–7, 149, 153–5, 161–2, 167, 174–7, 183–4, 189–92
Nacht und Träume xvi, 162, 173–7
No's Knife: Collected Shorter Prose 1945–1966 114, 194
Not I 138
Nouvelles et Textes pour rien 98, 110, 113
Ohio Impromptu 8, 74, 121
Play 138, 194
Premier amour 95, 113
Proust x, 145, 188, 194
Quad 7, 174
Review of Jack B. Yeats 105
Rockaby 51, 99
Rough for Theatre 1 188
Selected Poems 1930–1989 x, 4, 82
'Sounds' 166
'Still' xvi, 5, 162, 164–9, 172–3
'Still 3' 166
Stirrings Still x
Stories and Texts for Nothing 113–15, 194
Suite xiv, 4, 97–8, 106, 108, 110, 113, 115, 126, 146–7, 194
'Text' 120
Texts for Nothing x, 123, 134, 144
Textes pour rien 114, 144, 188
Three Dialogues with Georges Duthuit x, 135–6, 189
Unnamable, The x, 5, 18, 38, 65, 81–2, 95, 99, 117–19, 122–37, 140–4, 146–51, 162, 188
Waiting for Godot 7, 17, 43, 82, 85, 128, 136
Watt x, xiv, 4, 7, 10, 16–17, 40, 65, 70–97, 99, 102–3, 105, 112, 132–3, 135, 140, 146–7, 156, 158, 164, 167–8, 179, 190, 192–3, 195
Way, The 83
What Where 117, 138
'Whoroscope' 30, 81, 82
Worstward Ho x

Index

'Yellow' 116, 179
unpublished material,
  German Diaries 53, 86–7
  'Philosophy Notes' xiii, 1, 9, 17, 22–4, 26, 32, 55, 57, 65, 71, 73, 105, 137–8, 153–4, 183, 189
  Sasha Murphy manuscript 47, 50, 60, 68
  'Suite' notebook xiv, 98, 106–10, 112, 114, 195
  transcriptions from Geulincx xii, 8, 13–14, 20, 24–8, 55, 60, 73, 84, 141, 167, 186–7, 189–91, 193–4, 197 *see also* Geulincx, Arnold (*Ethics*)
  Ur-*Watt* 73–80, 84–5, 92–3, 99, 107, 112–13, 116, 144, 147, 192, 194
  'Whoroscope' notebook xiii, 43, 52, 56, 73, 76–7, 80, 186, 190, 195–6
Beer, Ann 113
Beethoven, Ludwig van 168–9
Benjamin, Shoshana 191
Beplate, Justin 195
Bérard, Victor 120
Berkeley, George xiv, xvi, 34, 89, 99, 145, 153, 160, 188, 197
  A New Theory of Vision, and Other Writings 40–1, 153, 189
  Principles of Human Knowledge 40–1
Bethlem Royal Hospital 48
Bettiol, Bruno 197
Bettiol, Guido 197
Bion, Wilfred 78
Bloom, Harold 132, 147–8, 152
Bontekoe, Cornelius 25–6
Boxall, Peter viii
Boyle, Kay 148
Brater, Enoch 190
Bray, Barbara xi, xvi, 67, 166, 170, 191, 197–8
British Library 26, 28
British Museum 25–6
Bruno, Giordarno 86, 92
Bryden, Mary 192
Burnet, John xiii
Burns Library, Boston College viii

Burton, Robert 187
Büttner, Gottfried 191

Calder, John 67, 114–15, 194–5
Campbell, Julie viii
Cape Town, University of 196
Carducci, Giosuè 32
Cartledge, Paul 180
Casanova, Pascale 2–4, 116, 183, 195
Caselli, Daniela viii, 148, 152, 156, 196
Castriota, Anna 185
Clément, Bruno 123, 130
Clerselier, Claude 13
Cobh 150, 195
Coccejus, Johannes 185
Coccius, Ernst 193
Coetzee, J. M. 113, 195
Coffey, Brian xiii, 29–31, 33, 68–9, 177, 187
Cohn, Ruby 45–6, 71, 85, 106–8, 118, 151, 158, 164, 173–4
Cole, John 82
Colerick, William 152
Connor, Steven 78
Cooldrinagh 168
Cooney, Brian 184
Cordemoy, Géraud 6, 13, 185
Cottingham, John 6–7, 184
Crangle, Sara viii
Cunard, Nancy 81

D'Alembert, Jean le Rond 37
Dante xv, 56, 124–6, 147–9, 152, 158, 196–7
  Inferno 38, 119–20, 125, 155–6
  Purgatorio 2
Davies, Paul 138–9
De Beauvoir, Simone 98, 106, 110, 115, 194
De Lattre, Alain 186, 196
De Vleeschauwer, H. J. 10, 17, 134, 184–6, 196
Déchevaux-Dumesnil, Suzanne 78
Delaware, University of 187
Deleuze, Gilles 73, 141, 192
Democritus xv–xvi, 3, 35, 39–40, 90, 127–8, 133, 179–80

Descartes, René 3, 9, 12–13, 15–16, 22, 30, 81–3, 92, 129, 135, 140, 153–4, 157, 163, 180, 196
Devlin, Denis 88–9
Diakoulakis, Christoforos viii
Dobrez, L. A. C. 183
Doherty, Francis 191
Le Dôme, Montparnasse 111
Donne, John 179
Dostoevsky, Fyodor 197
Doutey, Nicolas 184
Dowd, Garin 30, 70, 188
Drabkin, William 168
Driver, Tom 146
Dublin 20, 26–8, 38, 83, 152
Dun Laoghaire 150
Dundalk 193
Duthuit, Georges xi, xv, 37, 40, 65, 91, 133, 135, 188–9

Les Éditions de Minuit 98, 112, 115
Eekhof, A. 185
Eisenstein, Sergei 48, 189
Eliot, T. S. 7, 38
Éluard, Paul xiii, 30
Esquire 114
Evergreen Review 98, 114

Faber & Faber 114, 194–5
Fakhry, M. 184
Faust 66
Federman, Raymond 16, 178, 196
Fehsenfeld, Martha 29, 194
Feldman, Matthew viii, 43–4, 72, 91–2, 105, 116, 120, 140, 163, 183, 185–6, 190
Ficino, Marsilio 139
Fifield, Peter viii
Fletcher, Phineas 189
Foxrock 26
Franzen, Erich xi, xv, 37–8, 40, 119–20, 127, 189
Freud, Sigmund 66
Frost, Everett 25–8, 183, 186–8

Galway 48
Gardamagna, Daniela viii

Garrett, Don 185
Garver, Elizabeth viii
Geulincx, Arnold (works),
    Ethica xiv, 1–2, 10, 12, 14, 17, 19, 21–8, 36–8, 54, 65, 83, 109, 115, 138, 141, 181, 184, 186, 197
    Ethics x, xii, xiv, 1–2, 6–7, 10, 14–21, 23, 26, 37, 38, 50–1, 54–5, 60, 63–5, 69, 74, 77–8, 81, 84, 90–1, 93, 97–8, 100–5, 107–8, 110–11, 114, 116, 119–22, 128, 134–43, 156–60, 165, 167, 178, 180–1, 185–7, 190–1, 195–6
    Metaphysica Vera 12–13, 14, 16–17, 20, 24, 26, 36–7, 65, 83, 141, 160, 167, 181, 183, 197
    Metaphysics x, 13–14, 16–18, 20, 49, 65–6, 75, 85, 93, 141, 158, 160, 166, 167, 171, 181, 183, 186, 193
    Opera Philosophica x, 2, 8, 24–8, 57, 65, 166, 171, 184–7, 191, 193, 195
    Physica Vera 26, 83
    Quaestiones quodlibeticae 8, 24, 36, 181, 185, 187
Gontarski, S. E. xvi, 2, 18, 118, 137, 164–6, 186, 188–91, 195–8
Graver, Lawrence 16, 178, 193, 196
Greene, Robert 186
Greystones 192
Grove Music 31
Grove Press 67, 111, 113–15, 122

Hamburg 195
Hamilton, Alice 127–8
Hamilton, Kenneth 127–8
Hamish Hamilton 192
Hand, Richard J. 197
Hardy, Thomas,
    Tess of the d'Urbervilles 179
Harmon, Maurice 195, 197
Harry Ransom Humanities Research Center viii, xi, 38, 47, 73, 113–14
Harvey, Lawrence xvi, 40, 72, 166, 177, 192, 194, 197

Hassan, Ihab 164
Hegel, Georg Wilhelm Friedrich 32
Heidanus, Abraham 10, 185
Heidegger, Martin 163
Heraclitus xiv, 34–5, 188
Herren, Grayley 175
Hesla, David 44, 183
Hobson, Harold 17
Hochheim, Eckhart von 12
Hoefer, Jacqueline 191
Homer 15, 120, 148, 196
Hone, Joseph 189
Hoornbeek, Johannes 185
Horace 142, 179, 187
Hume, David 6
Husserl, Edmund 76
Hutchinson, Mary xi, xv–xvi, 38, 40, 56, 162, 189
Hyde Park 58
Hyland, Justine viii

Icarus 125
Isle of Wight 128

Jakobson, Roman 101
Jansen, Cornelius 9
Janus 34–5, 100–1, 119
John (of Ruysbroeck) 12
John the Baptist 95
Johnson, Lyndon 190
Johnson, Samuel 187, 193
Jolas, Eugene 188
Jordan, Margaret 197
Jouvin, Jack 197
Joyce, James xvi, 39, 43, 46, 74, 148
  Finnegans Wake [*Work in Progress*] 32, 59
  A Portrait of the Artist as a Young Man 125, 161
  Ulysses 197
Juliet, Charles 11–12
Jung, Carl 48, 189–90
Juno 66

Kant, Immanuel 71–2, 77, 134, 163
Kaun, Axel 43, 79
Kemp-Smith, Norman 82

Kennedy, Sighle xi, xvi, 38–40, 69, 128, 144, 186, 189
Kenner, Hugh 80–1, 83, 102, 183, 193, 196
Kiuchi, Kumiko viii
Kleist, Heinrich von xvi, 5, 169–70
  Über das Marionettentheater 170–3, 197
Knowlson, James viii, 28, 39, 43–4, 47, 59, 73–4, 106, 152, 169–70, 173–5, 187–9, 191–2, 194–6
Köhler, Wolfgang 163–4
Kontou, Tatiana ix

La Forge, Louis de 6, 9, 13, 154, 185
Lake, Carlton 73, 83
Land, Jan Pieter Nicolaas 2, 6, 8–10, 24–6, 28, 65, 184–5
Land's End 128
Lange, Joachim 184
Lawlor, Seán viii
Leibniz, Gottfried 23, 81, 137, 186, 196
Leopardi, Giacomo 32, 90, 193
Leuven, University of 8–9
Leyden, National University of Holland 9–10, 185
Liszt, Franz 188
London 25–8, 48, 83, 196
Loughery, Bryan 67
Luce, A. A. 153–4, 160, 196–7
Lucretius 130, 195

MacGreevy, Thomas xi, xiii–xiv, 1, 7, 12, 24–5, 29–32, 34, 36, 40, 43–5, 47–8, 66, 100, 162, 187–9
Mahaffy, J. P. 81
Malebranche, Nicolas xv, 6, 9, 15, 55, 152–5, 160, 184, 196
Malraux, Andre xiii, 57, 66
  La Condition Humaine 33, 57, 65, 133, 183, 188
Matisse, Henri 188
Maude, Ulrika 175, 198
Mauroc, Daniel 112
Mauthner, Fritz 92
Maxwell, Jane 25–8, 183, 186–8
Mays, J. C. C. 68
Merlin 98, 106, 110–13, 115, 195

Milán, Louis de 31
Mintz, Samuel 46, 183
Mitchell, Pamela 195
Mondrian, Piet 79
Montgomery, Niall xv, 37, 40, 144
Morin, Emilie viii
Morot-Sir, Edouard 149
Moscow State School of
  Cinematography 48
Mourguet, Laurent 189
Müller-Freinfels, Reinhart 175
Murfet, A. T. M. 28
Murphy, P. J. 3, 71–2, 188

Nadler, Steven 15, 184, 186
Narcissus 62, 66
National Library, Ireland xiii, 2, 29, 33, 38, 188
Newman, Philip viii
Newton, Isaac 55, 62
Nicholas (of Autrecourt) 6
Nineveh 15
Nixon, Mark viii, 30, 33, 43, 45, 86–7, 187, 189–91, 193, 195
Nonon, Charles 197
Nussbaum, Martha 6–7, 184

O'Brien, Edna 197
O'Hara, J. D. 3, 66, 144–6, 188
Old Testament 7
Overbeck, Lois 29, 194
Ovid 66

Paquot, Jean Noël 185
Paris 73, 111, 172
Penguin 195
Péron, Alfred 73
Péron, Mania 73, 190
Pestell, Alex viii
Picador 67
Pickup, Ronald 170
Pierron, Agnès 197
Pillars of Hercules 38, 120, 124–5
Pilling, John viii, 43–4, 76, 79, 94, 120, 129, 152, 166, 168–9, 183, 187, 189, 192–3, 195–6
Plato 32, 50, 55, 87

Plempius, Vopiscus Fortunatus 9
Plotinus 139
Portora Royal School 28
Pound, Ezra 39
Poutney, Rosemary 118, 195
Price, David Walter 33
Protagoras 105
Proust, Marcel xvi, 32, 39, 66
  À la recherche du temps perdu 18
Pythagoras 55, 139

Rabinovitz, Rubin 190
Ragg, T. M. 95
Read, Herbert Edward 95
Reading, University of viii
Reavey, George xi, xiii, 3, 29, 31, 33, 40, 67, 72, 95, 110, 191–2, 194
Ricks, Christopher 194
Rimbaud, Arthur 34, 100
  'Les Poètes de septans' 34
Rimsky-Korsakov, Nikolai Andreyevich 188
Robinson, Michael 155
Rodin, Auguste 172, 197
Rosset, Barney viii, 114
Rousset, Bernard 140
Routledge 67, 95
Rudmose-Brown, Thomas 29

Saberhagen, Fred 52–3
St. James' Church, Antwerp 8
St. John of the Cross 12
Salisbury, Laura viii
Sartre, Jean-Paul 76, 98, 194
Schiller-Theater 170
Schneider, Alan 122, 162
Schopenhauer, Arthur 31–2, 90, 132, 145–6, 193, 195
Schrödinger, Erwin 180
Schubert, Franz 174, 198
Seale, Rev. Ernest G. Seale 28
Seaver, Richard xi, 98, 110–15, 195
Sebellin, Rossana viii
Shakespeare, William 149
  Hamlet 149
Shmaltz, Tad 153, 196
Skinner, B. F. 60, 190

Index

Smith, Frederik N. 191
Socrates 77
Les Solitaires Intempestifs 181
Southern, Terry 114
Spinoza, Baruch 3, 6–7, 53–5, 71, 77, 154, 184–5, 187–8
  Ethics 30, 54, 190
Stieve, Friedrich 86
Strickers, Susanna 9–10, 185
Süddeutscher Rundfunk 174
Sunday Times Magazine 197
Sussex, University of viii
Sutherland, Keston viii

Tavistock Clinic 78
Taylor, Neil 67
Telephus 34–5, 100, 188
Les Temps modernes 98, 106, 112–13, 194
Tenerife 163
Théâtre du Grand-Guignol 172, 189, 197
Thomas à Kempis 44–5, 47, 104, 187
Thomas, Dylan 68–9, 191
Thompson, Geoffrey 48, 191
Tonning, Erik viii
Transition 46, 188
Trinity College, Dublin xi, xiii–xiv, 1–2, 7, 24–5, 28–9, 33, 36, 38, 47–8, 57, 67, 153, 155, 187
Trocchi, Alexander xi, 110, 112, 114, 195

Uhlmann, Anthony 6, 18, 27, 37, 50–1, 61, 69, 71, 104, 106, 118–19, 122, 127, 138–41, 183, 185, 187, 189–90, 195–6

Ulysses 37–8, 119–20, 125–6, 152
Ussher, Arland xi, xiv, 20, 36, 40, 45

Van Bunge, Wiep 8, 184–5, 195, 197
Van Hulle, Dirk viii, 189, 194
Van Ruler, Han 6, 10, 19, 27, 122, 184–5
Van Velde, Bram 37, 113, 136
Van Velde, Geer 113
Verhoeven, Cornelis 160, 197
Vico, Giambattista 32–3, 46, 73
Virgil 56, 78

Wannsee 170
Weller, Shane viii, 35, 39, 52, 72, 119, 128, 133, 163, 183, 190, 193
Wicklow (county) 11, 192
Wilson, Martin 18, 27, 55
Wilson, Michael 197
Windelband, Wilhelm xiii, 1, 22–3, 65, 76, 137–8, 186, 196
Winstanley, Adam viii
Witsius, Herman 122
Wittgenstein, Lugwig 92
Wood, Rupert 56, 103, 142, 183
Woodworth, Robert 163
World War Two 44, 73, 78, 87, 94, 106, 190, 197

Yeats, Jack B. 105
Yeats, W. B.,
  On Baile's Strand 193

Zeno 105
Žižek, Slavoj 6–7